AN ADMINISTRATIVE HISTORY OF
PT'S
IN WORLD WAR II

OFFICE OF NAVAL HISTORY

15 February 1946

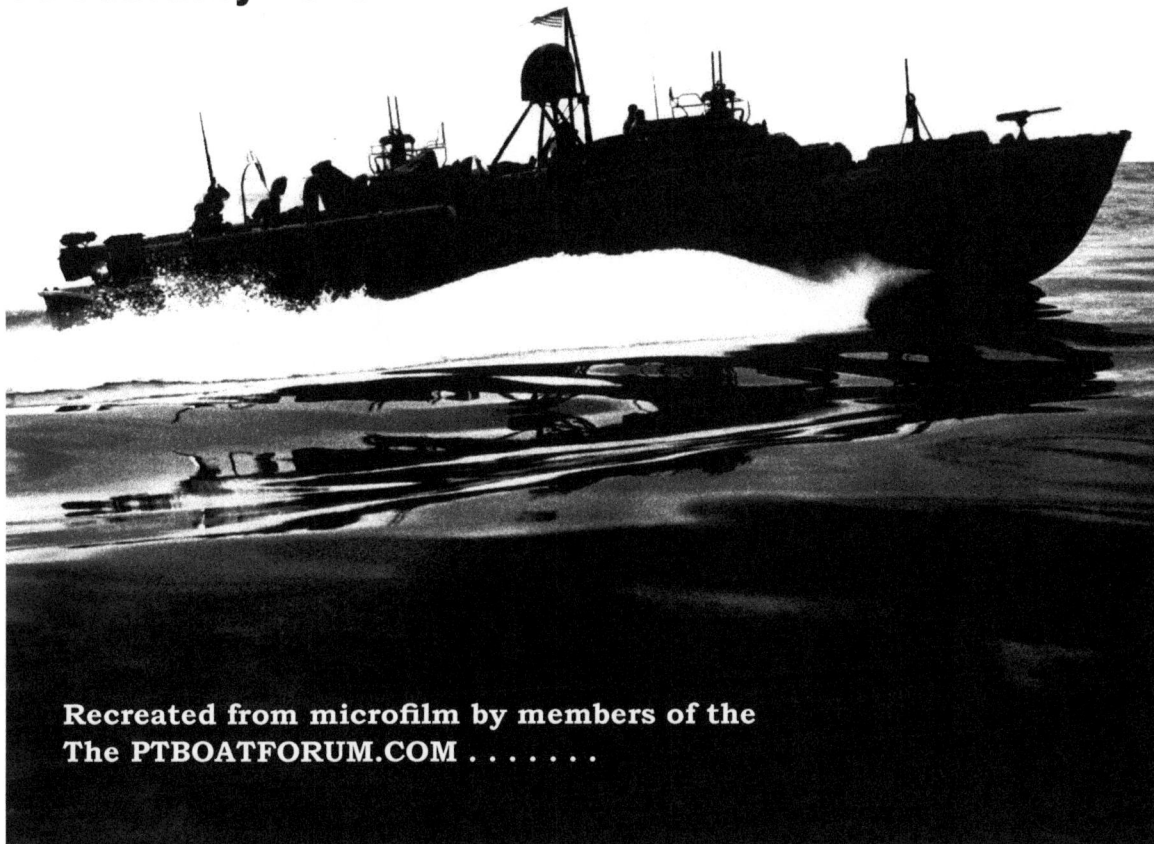

AN ADMINISTRATIVE HISTORY OF PT's IN WORLD WAR II
(Recreated October 25, 2010 by the members of the PT Boat Forum message board)

3

Document Recreated, October 26, 2010
(From a microfilmed copy of the original Navy document.)

This post World War II Navy document from 1946, has been recreated from microfilm copy by a group of PT boat message board members from the PT Boat Forum website (www.ptboatforum.com). All textural content has been retyped, charts redrawn, and where possible, photographic content has been replaced with a better copy of the same image or a very similar image. The format of the document has also been changed from the original 1946 typewriter style document (356 pages) to a more finish published book appearance. A detailed table of contents has been added, as well as assigning figure numbers to all photographs and charts with their page location listed at the end of the table of contents and as a final change the Appendices section has been page numbered. Although these changes have been added, the actual document content has not been changed except for obvious typographic errors. Because of the Lexicon and military writing style from the nineteen forty's era; the content, spelling and acronym used can't be verified.

This recreation has been made as a historical note, making it more available for those with the desire to learn more about the World War II Motor Torpedo Boat service and its boats.

The following individuals contributed to the recreation of this document (all names are listed in alphabetical order):

Frank Andruss Sr.
Jeff Davidson
Will Day
Jerry Gilmartin
Gary Paulsen
Al Ross
Ted Walther
Mary Ann Washichek
Richard Washichek

What we want to know
is, "How come PT's?".

Captain A. D. Turnbull
Special Assistant to the Director,
Office of Naval History

This administrative history of PT boats in World War II
was originally prepared for the U.S. Navy by:
Lt. Frank A. Tredinnick, Jr., USNR, and
Lt. Comdr. Harrison L. Bennett, USNR.

AN ADMINISTRATIVE HISTORY OF PT's IN WORLD WAR II
(Recreated October 25, 2010 by the members of the PT Boat Forum message board)

5

TABLE OF CONTENTS

AN ADMINISTRATIVE HISTORY OF PT's IN WORLD WAR II
(Recreated October 25, 2010 by the members of the PT Boat Forum message board)

7

CHAPTER FIVE - CONTINUED

CHAPTER SIX

CHAPTER SEVEN

CHAPTER SEVEN CONTINUED

CHAPTER EIGHT

AN ADMINISTRATIVE HISTORY OF PT's IN WORLD WAR II
(Recreated October 25, 2010 by the members of the PT Boat Forum message board)

9

CHAPTER EIGHT - CONTINUED

Photographs and Charts Continued

AN ADMINISTRATIVE HISTORY OF PT's IN WORLD WAR II
(Recreated October 25, 2010 by the members of the PT Boat Forum message board)

11

INTRODUCTION

Looking back at the evolution of PT boats and the integral administrative work, any comprehensive survey shows missteps, false tacks, and incongruities; but considering this evolution from the limbo in which the modern pioneers of this craft worked, a history points out that at the time the missteps were actually progress, for the negated accepted theories, the false tacks were earnest gropings for the right answer, and the incongruities were logical. The program was undertaken blindly, but the fact that illumination came – slowly and often erratically to be sure – is an ipso facto proof of the success of the administrative organization of PT's.

But because a plan, a machine or an idea works is no reason to presuppose that there is no better method, system or theory. The PT administrative system was a product of fortuitous exigencies, the organization worked, but often spottily and at times with but a modicum of efficiency. The main stumbling block with PT's was the novelty of the type. Springing full-blown from Secretary Charles Edison's mind, the PT progress had to be tackled warily and deliberately.

Without a doubt the Navy had been backward in the matter of Motor Torpedo Boats, for as is shown in the section dealing with the history of the type, our Navy was strangely quiescent, while Britain and the Continental powers were making far reaching strides in motor torpedo boat design and tactics. But it was this start from scratch that makes the evolution of the PT program significant.

In writing this history it would be possible to offer the premise that the job was done, and done well, and that the purpose of this volume is but to record the manner in which the job was done. But this volume tries to go further by including criticism of the methods and means employed to do the job, by endeavoring to show some of the difficulties that confronted the administrators of the PT program and by offering alternate suggestions which would be helpful in the event that it was again necessary to set up a similar program.

For a purely historical narrative, objectivity would be necessary only as a means of determining the correct application of emphasis upon the various phases of the program, and of obtaining a strictly disinterested technique of writing. But in a critical narrative, although the writer must still maintain his objectivity, he must also look beyond what happened and consider what might have happened, and then determine which of the two courses was the better for the program and for the Navy as a whole.

The difficulty that arises in applying this critical technique to the PT program is the fact that essentially the whole program was well conceived, and the additional, and more important, fact that these conceptions were prosecuted with a large degree of success. In effect, in writing the history of a project as successful as the PT program, it would be entirely possible to write the kind of history first proposed – the straight narrative – and then to sum the writings up by saying that the correct thing was done, the right effort was applied at the right time, and the program was successful. And such a history would be completely justifiable in view of the subject considered, if the history were written without the benefit of hindsight.

In an effort to get away, from this type of history, it has been necessary to make hindsight paramount and to take a hypercritical view-point of the decision made and the methods employed in the PT program. Because examination of different phases of the program may have brought to light only minor faults and yet at the same time it has been necessary to make some comment, a number of criticisms in this volume may appear hyperbolic of superfluous. The criticisms are offered only in the constructive sense, and in no way detract from the overall character of the job done.

By this method of examination, the history offers an alternative and better method whenever possible, in an effort to smooth the road for the next traveler. There are points in question, however, which are beyond the scope of this volume. These matters generally have their root in overall naval policy, and while it is possible to suggest a different stand by the Navy on these matters, such as a commentary would be a tertiary, or at the best a secondary, function of a history of this type.

This does not mean that the PT aspect of these problems does not apply to the results obtained in the program, but rather that the PT aspect in itself was a small part of the whole program. This can be aptly illustrated by allusion to the reluctant bride role played by the Navy in regard to PT's in the twenty years following the Armistice in 1918.

This was part and parcel the national policy, not merely the Navy's policy, in regard to the building of combatant ships. Following World War I, this country had drawn within itself, nationalism was dominant, and the nation rested smugly within its hard shell of isolationist thinking.

This was definitely not a time for offensive plans for the Navy, and so it is small wonder that the General Board was hesitant even to experiment with offensive craft, in the shape of PT's. When the decision to experiment did come, it came only with the qualifications that PT's would be of use only in the later stages of a war, and even then, their function could be absorbed by converted yachts.

Thus the initiation of a PT program was hampered by the overall isolationist sentiment throughout the country, and by the consequent reluctance of the Navy to construct any large number of purely offensive craft. This is but one example, and yet it suffices to show that some of the problems which

AN ADMINISTRATIVE HISTORY OF PT's IN WORLD WAR II
(*Recreated October 25, 2010 by the members of the PT Boat Forum message board*)

13

confronted the men in the PT program had roots in ground much deeper than that covered in this work.

For a historian, much of the developmental work in PT's seem to have been marked by the failure to keep records. Much was done in off the record conferences; new ideas had their inception in chance, informal conversations; and weighty decisions were made during unrecorded telephone calls. This has made conversations and interviews with men who were in positions of authority during the PT program one of the larger sources of material.

An effort has been made to draw conclusions as they presented themselves, and in cases where the weight of the evidence makes conclusion by inference inevitable, no attempt has been made in dictating conclusions.

Pages are numbered consecutively, and footnotes are numbered by the chapter. Both the Elco and the Higgins companies have contributed valuable material to this work. Lieutenant Commander R. J. Dressling, USN, was a helpful source of information for the chapters on the Commissioning Details and Commander T. G. Warfield has provided other wise unobtainable facts for the chapters on Motor Torpedo Boat Squadrons Training Center. Charts are by Lieutenant G.S. Persons of the Office of Naval History.

14

AN ADMINISTRATIVE HISTORY OF PT's IN WORLD WAR II
(Recreated October 25, 2010 by the members of the PT Boat Forum message board)

CHAPTER ONE

DEVELOPMENT OF THE MTB TO 1939

At dawn on April 23, 1891 insurgents aboard the 3500 ton Chilean battleship "Blanco Encalada", brusquely awakened by a loud explosion, found their ship slowly sinking from torpedo hit. [1] The fatal torpedo was fired by a Chilean government gunboat, which, at the same time it sank the rebel ship, set in motion the evolution which produced one of the most powerful weapons of opportunity of World War II – the modern motor torpedo boat.

Although the boat sank the "Blanco Encalada" was a gunboat jury-rigged for torpedoes, it proved that Whitehead's weapon could be effectively used by small surface craft. The more powerful nations of the world were not blind to the significance of this feat, but it took the stinging defeat of the Russian Navy at Port Arthur on February 8, 1904 by Japanese surface torpedo craft followed by the torpedo administered coup de grace at Tsushima on May 27 and 28, 1905 to awake the world to the extent of the lethal potentialities of the torpedo. In no sense of the word were the Japanese vessels counterparts or prototypes of MTB's, but Port Arthur and Tsushima did force naval boards of strategy to search for the most efficacious method of delivering torpedoes to the firing point. The parallel development of the internal combustion engine made the development of MTB's inevitable.

EUROPEAN DEVELOPMENT

Before Motor Torpedo Boats could be built, it was necessary to adapt the internal combustion engine to marine uses, and by 1905, gasoline engines were installed in small craft. Development was rapid, and one such experiment by the Admiralty produced a boat capable of 20 knots with a cruising radius of 200 miles. In Italy, an engineer named Napier, concluded a series of experiments on the design of a high speed marine engine. Yarrow, the British boat builder, snapped up the rights to the engine, and used it in a small boat which he launched in 1905. [2] It was actually an experimental model for its overall length was 15', but it made 25 knots and carried two torpedoes. At the time Yarrow was experimenting with this boat, a compatriot builder, John T. Thornycroft, built a larger craft for torpedo work. His boat was 40' overall, carried a single torpedo in a rack and had a flank speed of 18 knots, and a displacement of 4-1/2 tons. Launching of the torpedo was a precarious business, however, for

---

1. Encyclopedia Britannica
2. Sketch given by W. Kaemmeror before a meeting of the Verein Deutscher Ingeniesure in 1906.

AN ADMINISTRATIVE HISTORY OF PT's IN WORLD WAR II
(Recreated October 25, 2010 by the members of the PT Boat Forum message board)

15

it greatly endangered the stability of the boat. These two designs of Thornycroft and Yarrow may rightly be termed the precursor of all motor torpedo boats.

The experiments of these two companies started work on motor boats of all types all over the world. America made its entry in the race, but paradoxically enough, on the behalf of another power: Lewis Nixon designed, built and sold to Russia ten motor torpedo boats in 1908. These boats were ambitious mechanically in that they were powered by two six cylinder benzine-fueled engines.[3] This power plant drove two shafts which were reversed by compressed air. Nixon was anxious to prove the seaworthiness of his design, and one of these boats (which resembled monitors at a quick glance) went from New York to Sevastopol under its own power in a moderate sea with no damage to the boat.[4]

The building race was on, and motor torpedo boats of every variety spewed from yards all over the world, and every builder had but one idea in mind – more speed, and more speed was to be obtained by more powerful engines. In focusing their attention on their new types the internal combustion engine, naval boat builders found little time to work on hull improvement or to utilize the extant V and step type hulls. As a result there was no direct proportions between the increase in horsepower and the increase in speed of MTB's. The design tendency was toward a long overall with a narrow beam, and the larger craft embodying this principle were particularly disappointing. The French naval architects were the first to recognize this deficiency and to take steps to remedy it. Borrowing their ideas from the growing cult of speed boat enthusiasts, the French Navy began extensive experiments with V bottom and stepped hulls. Simultaneously the automotive industry began to produce marine engines with a more favorable horsepower-weight ratio. Finally new screw designs were drawn and put into production to permit more efficient operations at high speed, for screws perfectly adapted for steam power had proved dismal misfits on the speedy shafts of the gasoline powered boats.[5]

The internal combustion engine fitted in perfectly with torpedo boat principles. Torpedo boats of steam design had been built with three principles in mind: high speed, economy, and low target area. To obtain all three of these characteristics with steam engine power had proved difficult, and the gasoline engine appeared a panacea to those eager naval architects worrying about more powerful torpedo boats. The transition from steam to internal combustion presented no major external characteristic qualifications changes, but rather simplified the job of the designers and builders.

Within two years the Yarrow and Thornycroft specimens hit the water, the French were showing the way with an MTB constructed of thin steel, which

---

3. Scientific American, December 30, 1905.
4. Cassier, January, 1908.
5. Nautical Gazette as quoted in Naval Institute Proceedings, September, 1907.

16

AN ADMINISTRATIVE HISTORY OF PT's IN WORLD WAR II
(Recreated October 25, 2010 by the members of the PT Boat Forum message board)

displaced a comparatively heavy eight tons. Instead of a torpedo rack which had been a feature on the early models, the Gallic version mounted a single torpedo tube built into the bow. It was powered by one reversible Cazes type engine. Its shakedown and tests produced such unexpectedly pleasing results that the French Admiralty waxed enthusiastic, and urged further experiments with this type of vessel.[6]

EARLY UNITED STATES DEVELOPMENT

The United States navy could no longer ignore the strides in boat building which the continental powers had made. In 1908 the Assistant Secretary of the Navy recommended the building of a number of small MTB's which would be laid up on shore as a defense measure against an unexpected outbreak of hostilities. The recommendation stage was as far this proposition progressed, however, and the plan was never carried out. In 1909 Congress took the first concrete action in the United States development of MTB's by appropriating $445,00 for the development of a sub-surface torpedo boat. This craft was definitely in a class by itself. From its compartmented unsinkable surface hull hung a submarine hull, equipped with a torpedo tube for firing fish underwater. If the torpedo failed to reach its mark, or if the mechanism fouled, the boat had an additional feature of a semi-suicidal nature: the compartments of the surface hull were stuffed with about a half a ton of gun cotton with a contact operated electrical detonator attached. After closing the target, the crew was supposed to set the ship on a collision course, lock the rudder, open the throttles, and go over the side in a life ring. The operational efficiency of such a craft seems highly doubtful. Be that as it may, this 46 foot six and a half ton monstrosity never got beyond the experimental stage, but its designers learned the hopelessness of a compromise between MTB's and submarines.[7]

TACTICAL USE

Of significance in the early days of MTB's is the notice which the French took in the tactical value of the boats. As early as 1908 the French Admiralty recognized the potentialities of small torpedo boats, despite the fact that they had been unable to equip their craft with internal combustion engines. Exercises were conducted with the fleet and flotillas of torpedo boats, and the results observed and conclusions drawn have been found to be employable today. The outstanding tactical decisions were:

1. The best time for attack is at the end of evening twilight or at the beginning of morning twilight when thee is no moon.

2. Attacks should be made from ahead of the line of ship with units of five or six boats going in on both bows at intervals of a minute or so

---

6. Ibid.

7. This highly original craft was designed by Clarence L. Burger, C.E., of New York City, with calculations by Toms, Lemoine and Crane.

AN ADMINISTRATIVE HISTORY OF PT's IN WORLD WAR II
(Recreated October 25, 2010 by the members of the PT Boat Forum message board)

17

in order that one side be left unwatched while concentrating attention on the first attacking boats. At least five boats should be used on each attacking wave so the attacks will be successful in spite of casualties.

3. Continuous attacks should be made in order to harass the enemy until he has sustained some losses.

4. The boats should make no noise, smoke or wake while getting into firing position undetected. The enemy, by the same token, will travel slowly in order not to be seen by the telltale wake and smoke of fast steaming.

While these exercises were conducted with steam driven torpedo boats, the results were such that they have been largely applicable to our present day torpedo boats while operating against the enemy in both the Pacific and in the Mediterranean.[8]

By 1910 the United States Navy's sentiments were that "the use of the torpedo during a fleet action can no longer be neglected." Rapid improvements during the first decade of this century had made it unfashionable to disregard the possible developments of this weapon. Even in 1910, with the torpedo itself just coming into its own, there was high feeling that a fast torpedo craft would soon accompany the main fleet as both offensive and defensive satellites. The focus of attention was sharpened on torpedo boat maneuvers in offensive action. Previously, maneuvers had been routine or conventional, and while remaining at this static level, possessed little or no tactical value. Initiative and elasticity became the watchwords together with simplicity, and these three elements were stressed again and again when conducting the torpedo attacks on fleet maneuvers.[9]

Flexibility of formation and readiness for changes of plans were recognized as of prim importance in the use of torpedo boats. Detailed tactics had been worked out on how to make the most successful attacks with torpedo boats, but for the most part these additions to doctrine were simply enlargements on the findings set forth by the French after their torpedo boat exercises of 1908.

WORLD WAR I DEVELOPMENT

Upon the recommendations of the Chief of the Bureau of Ordnance, Rear Admiral Joseph Strauss, the Navy Department decided to purchase in 1915 a high powered motor boat in order to conduct experiments to ascertain the value of this type of craft. The boat was to be at least 40 feet overall and thoroughly seaworthy. Equipment was to comprise 18 inch torpedo tubes and a one pounder rapid fire gun. The estimated cost was $30,000 and delivery was expected in early 1916. This was the first of this type requested by the Navy

---

8. Vice Admiral de Jonquiares conducted these exercises in 1908 to determine the effectiveness of torpedo boats as an individual arm of the Navy.

9. Naval Institue Proceedings, September, 1910.

18

AN ADMINISTRATIVE HISTORY OF PT's IN WORLD WAR II
(Recreated October 25, 2010 by the members of the PT Boat Forum message board)

Department, and was in accordance with the British policy of using small, fast motor boats for anti-submarine work. [10]

This recommendation resulted in the Navy's acceptance of plans for a 50 foot torpedo boat to be built by the Greens Basin and Construction Company. The boat was designed for a maximum speed of 43 miles per hour. It was slated to carry quick firing guns and a single 16 inch torpedo tube. Power was to be provided by two six cylinder Harbeck engines of 300 hp each. The progressive step with this design was the addition of armament in the form of machine guns. Now for the first time, a torpedo boat would be powerful enough to resist, and in some cases to destroy, enemy vessels of comparable displacement without the use of torpedoes. [11]

Because of the restrictions of security, little publicity was given at the time to the fine work accomplished by the Italian torpedo boats, (MAS – Motobarche Anti-Sommergibili) as well as the British counterparts (CMB' – Costal Motor Boat) during World War I. [12] Both the CMB's and MASS were successful in riding over minefields and jumping nets, no mean accomplishment, to attack enemy bases or to close enemy shipping to torpedo firing range. The Italians were notably successful in the Adriatic, where the MAS took part in a number of daring attacks on shipping in Austrian held harbors, culminating with the famous exploit of Rizzo's – the sinking of the Austrian battleship "St. Stephen". [13] The high point in CMB combat operation in the post-war period in 1919 after the Russian Revolution, when the boats in an attack on Kronstadt sunk a Russian Communist cruiser, the "Oleg", and damaged or disabled two other capital ships and two destroyers. The CMB's were extremely fortunate and lost only two boats in this operation. [14]

The CMB's, despite their variegated capabilities, proved exceptionally vulnerable to aircraft, and in on ill-starred action on August 10, 1918, 8 low flying German planes attacked 6 CMB's on patrol. The boats were jumped in the daylight hours, and with their light armament could put up little return fire. When the Germans finally withdrew, all six of the boats were out of commission. The Aircraft had proved itself just the weapon to combat fast motor boats, and this is a tactical truth that has lost none of its forcefulness through the years. The Japanese used float planes to combat MTB's with not much success in World War II.

The CMB's were a much more competent boat architecturally speaking than the Italian version. The CMB's were skimming or planning boats. Their construction embodies two planes with a single step. Convex sections were used instead of the usual flat ones, and a downward re-verse curve near

10. Shipping illustrated, November 13, 1915.
11. Shipping Illustrated February 19, 1916.
12. Rudder, June, 1917.
13. The Italian Fleet and the European War, Comdr. Wilanesi's notes edited by Alfieri and Lacroix, published by the Admiralty at Milan, Italy, 1919.
14. Naval Institute Proceedings, June 1922.

AN ADMINISTRATIVE HISTORY OF PT's IN WORLD WAR II
(Recreated October 25, 2010 by the members of the PT Boat Forum message board)

19

were used instead of the usual flat ones, and a downward re-verse curve near the chine was supposed to reduce adhesion and defect spray. Although the boats remained wet travelers despite this unusual feature, they did gain with this type of design, for the convex sections eliminated the need for careful balance of weight between the fore and aft planes. This was a great advantage during torpedo firing when sudden and marked changes of weight altered stability radically on flat planned boats. The Italian boats incorporated none of these beneficial features in their design, and had it not been for the intrepidity and daring-do of the crews who manned these early craft, the MAS would no doubt have been written off as too slow and materially deficient. [15]

Actually three young lieutenants in the Harwich Force of the Royal Navy were responsible for the development of the CMB. They conceived the plan of crossing the German mine fields in small, shallow draft boats to attack enemy North Sea bases. They took their plan to Commodore Tyrwhitt, then commander of the Harwich Force, who in turn passed it on to the First Sea Lord, Admiral Sir Henry Jackson. The First Sea Lord ordered a single boat from Thornycroft which the Admiralty tested extensively in 1915. Specifications called for a 40 foot overall length, wooden construction, and a speed of 33.5 knots – a fast, powerful boat, but still light enough (four and a half tons) to be lifted by a cruiser's davits. The last specification designated the boat as an integral addition to a larger ship's armament, rather than as a new weapon. [16]

The tests proved successful on the experimental boat, and a dozen more were ordered. Thornycroft, meanwhile, had designed a 55 foot boat, capable of operating as an independent unit, and soon the company was producing both types of boat in number. Some of the boats were sent to Harwich, thereby making the lieutenants' dream an actuality, while others were based at Dunkirk. Their tasks were legion, but primarily some were used strictly as torpedo boats, others were fitted with depth charges and dropping gear and were used for anti-submarine work (The Italian MAS was originally and primarily an anti-submarine boat), while still others took aboard new equipment for laying mines off the enemy coast. By November of 1918, Great Britain had commissioned 66 CMB's, and of these, 13 had been stricken, but only five of these 13 were lost in action. Had the war lasted longer, the English had a design for a 70' boat which could have been put into action with little delay by the fall of 1919. [17]

Despite the fact that continental powers were active in the development and use of motor torpedo boats and motor anti-submarine boats throughout World War I, the United States evinced little interest in the type. The lack of interest may be attributed largely to the geographical position of this country. Boats of

---

15. Naval Institute Proceedings, July 1940. Much of the information in this section from this page on has been taken from this issue of the Proceedings which featured an excellent article by Gordin Adamson and Douglas Van Patten: "Motor Torpedo Boats: a Technical Study".
16. Naval Institute Proceedings, July 1922.
17. Naval Institute Proceedings, July 1940.

the MTB type were primarily designed for use in strikes against enemy shipping and fleet units within 100 miles of a home base, and fleet power of the Central Powers in 1917-18 was such that any naval attack upon the continental U.S. seemed highly improbable. Japan was on the winning side in the first World War, and equipping the Philippines, Panama or Hawaii with MTB's seemed at the time to be completely unnecessary and diplomatically hazardous.

Nevertheless, in 1917 the Navy went as far as to test a 40 foot boat capable of 40 knots. The rough action of this boat in a seaway, and its tendency towards heavy pounding in anything more than a moderate sea led the Navy to write it off the books as unseaworthy. The next year another boat, designed by Shearer, was taken under consideration, but as this 27 foot version could develop only nine knots, the General Board felt that any money that might be invested in experiments on this boat could be better used on improvements in extant types. [18]

One of the more interesting developments during the first war was the production of the Sea Sled designed by W. Albert Hickman, a Nova Scotian, in 1911. The boat was not produced soon enough to be used in actual combat work, and had it been used its success as a torpedo boat is conjectural, but the design principle involved is worthy of consideration here. Hickman in explaining the design for the hull of a new boat said that he had, in effect, taken a V hull, split it along the keel, and then put it together the other way round." The chines were thereby the lowest par of the hull, while the keel was the highest. By this arrangement, the integral sections assumed the appearance of a "W". The concavity between the sections was deep at the bow, and grew shallower towards the stern. The Navy finally found a use for the boat as a plane carrier. It was used with a Caproni triplane, by carrying the aircraft to the desired launching point, and then running full speed into the wind until the plane was airborne. [19]

POST WAR DEVELOPMENT

The first big step in making the United States a torpedo-boat conscious nation came in 1920, when SecNav approved a recommendation of BuC&R and the General Board of purchase two Thornycroft's Royal Navy CMB's. One was to be of the 40 foot type and the other of the 55 foot class. It was not until 1922 that the navy began to run tests on these two boats, and found that they could make 32 and 35 knots respectively. No further experimental use was made of the 40 foot boat after the tests were concluded, and it was used for torpedo recovery work until 1928 when it was converted to a crash-boat. In 1934 it was condemned. Experiments were conducted with the 55 foot boat until 1930, when it was relegated to the scrap pile. [20]

---

18. General Board Files, 1918.
19. Naval Institute Proceedings, July 1940.
20. General Board Letter GB No. 420-14 (Serial No. 1740) of April 9, 1937.

AN ADMINISTRATIVE HISTORY OF PT's IN WORLD WAR II
(Recreated October 25, 2010 by the members of the PT Boat Forum message board)

21

The American government was not the only buyer of Thornycrofts after the last war, for boats of both the 40 foot and 55 foot types made their appearance in sheltered coves and inlets on the east coast of this country. These boats were definitely under private sponsorship. Their operations at the time were highly interesting to the Department of Internal Revenue, and the boats were instrumental in helping a goodly number of Americans evade the provisions of the Eighteenth Amendment. Several of the these former rum-runners are reported to be laid up in yards in the east coast at present, although the have been so altered that they would no longer be recognizable as CMB's. [21]

The year after the 45 foot Thornycroft had been scrapped, the Navy became interested in another foreign design. This time BuC&R looked smilingly on a design by J.F. Bogaerts of Brussels for a 28 ton boat, The General Board scuttled this project by refusing to allow expenditure of funds for analysis of the Belgian's design. This was the only step the Navy made during the year towards a further study of fast motor boats, but in 1936, the well known designer, J. Starling Burgess, began to make public his designs for an aluminum hull for a high speed destroyer, In conjunction with these experiments, he produced a 33 foot model which not only exemplified all his design characteristics, but proved that they were worth while by ripping off a fast 38 knots during trial runs. No action was taken by the Navy on this hull. [22]

Meanwhile development of MTB's abroad had proceeded with no slacking of the pace. The French, British and Germans were the leaders in the European fields, but the Germans did the only experimenting with other than gasoline engines. They attempted several combinations of hulls and diesels and achieved a modicum of success on the larger hulls which could assume the weight of this type engine much more readily than the smaller boats. The three countries had produced a number of designs ranging from 5 to 50 tons and had achieved speeds up to 46 knots. Gradually the step-plans type of boat was abandoned, and V-bottoms and hard chines entered the field.

Although the planning hull was not utilized at the immediate beginning of the MTB program, the type had been invented and patented before the advent of the gasoline engine. As early as 1870, an English clergyman offered the Royal Navy plans of a skimming type hull for use on its warships, but the weight horsepower ratio of steam plants made its employment unfeasible. Thornycroft himself patented a planning type hull in 1877, but despite these precocious developments, designers of the first MTB's shied away from any hull with skimming characteristics. [23]

When the hull was recognized for what it was worth, around 1905, it became a feature on all MTB's and consequently most of the boats in action in

---

21. This information through the courtesy of Lt. (jg) Ralph A. Richardson of the Radio Experimental Laboratory at Anacostia
22. General Board File 414-20 1935.
23. Naval Institute Proceedings, July 1940.

World War I were of this type. Planning boats were successful in smooth to light seas, but as the weather became heavier, the tendency of the boats to pound became greater. Even the most carefully balanced boats were rendered inefficient in a blow of any strength. Experiments have continued with the planning boats to the present day, but because of the need for versatility in all weather, the V bottomed, hard chined boat came into preponderance. [24]

THE SCOTT-PAINE DESIGN

After a long period of latency in design and development, the MTB program took a new lease on life in 1934, when Hubert Scott-Paine completed plans on a new 60 foot boat, which he offered to the Admiralty. This boat's hull design was based on hulls, which had been in use with the RAF. The Admiralty was favorably impressed and ordered two of the Scott-Paine boats, and later augmented this order by four. The first boat was completed and tested in 1936, and before the end of the year the other five boats slid down the British Power Boat Company's ways. This was beginning of a brilliant and stormy career for designer Scott-Paine, who was destined to be the greatest single influence in MTB design in World War II.

The boats were organized into a flotilla, and were ordered to Malta for experimental duty. In 1937 the boat made the trip to Malta under their own power in heavy weather, and proved extremely successful. High winds and heavy seas during the trip forced many larger ships to take cover, but the MTB's were able to make the trip with little trouble. The shallow draft of the boats (they draw but two feet eleven inches in quiet water) enabled them to ride up and down the waves instead of plowing through the heavy seas. [25]

NEW UNITED STATES INTEREST

In January of 1937, SecNav, in a letter to the General Board, requested that the General Board make a complete study of MTB's and submit a report with opinions on the prospective values of MTB's to the United States Navy. This report was to contain further recommendations, if necessary, concerning the extent to which development of this type craft should be undertaken by the Navy Department. If the Board considered active development desirable, it was to make further recommendations as to the characteristics which should be set up as standard for attainment in the initial development progress. [26]

In its report, the Board recognized the advancement made by European Navies with MTB's and noted the effectiveness of the boats for defense of local areas. The Board sated that because of the anomalous strategic position of the United States compared to the European powers, the use of MTB's would

---

24. From a conversation with Mr. Sidney Peters, naval architect for patrol craft with the Bureau of Ships.
25. Naval Institute Proceedings, July 1940.
26. SecNav's letter Op-23c-KM S82-3/L5-2 (361216) of 5 January 1937 with all endorsements.

AN ADMINISTRATIVE HISTORY OF PT's IN WORLD WAR II
(Recreated October 25, 2010 by the members of the PT Boat Forum message board)

23

be restricted. BuC&R and BuEng, in considering the problem, favored an experimental program for development of MTB's but on a limited scale only. The Board felt that in the event of a long war, the boats would prove valuable, but that in the early stages of a war, their use would be restricted. The boats would be equipped for mining and anti-submarine work, as well as standard MTB tactical work.[27]

The British company, Vosper, in 1938 took a gamble on a new design of its own and constructed with private means a new type of MTB. The trials on this boat were heartening to the company officials and they sought an Admiralty contract. The gamble paid off when the Admiralty ordered one boat and then upped the order to six. Vosper made an agreement with Thornycroft, and the two companies produced the boats in conjunction. This boat was the first Vosper of the long line of boats that the company has produced for Britain.[28]

It was not until early in 1939 that Scott-Paine finished building the craft that was to be largely responsible for the MTB program in the United States when it finally got under way. His boat was greeted with enthusiasm and curiosity by the yachting and naval world. It was a distinct improvement over his former efforts, and yet managed to keep all their beneficial characteristics. The boat was 70 feet overall and carried two 21 inch torpedoes or four 18 inch torpedoes. Its light armament consisted of two 20mm and one 25mm cannon mounted in power turrets. The boat had a good freeboard and low silhouette. All aerials were built in, and the deck was nearly smooth. For the first time an MTB was constructed largely of plywood with a saving in weight and no loss of strength. The boat was an immediate success, and in little or no time 50 boats had been ordered by England and several other major powers.[29]

On June 15, 1939, this Scott-Paine boat made a trip across the Channel to Brest and back again at an average speed of 42 knots with no engine trouble and with silken smooth riding. There was no longer any doubt; the modern MTB had arrived.[30]

27. Ibid.
28. Naval Institute Proceedings, July 1940.
29. Ibid
30. Naval Institute Proceedings, September 1939.

24

AN ADMINISTRATIVE HISTORY OF PT's IN WORLD WAR II
(Recreated October 25, 2010 by the members of the PT Boat Forum message board)

CHAPTER TWO

DEVELOPMENT 1939 TO 1941

The American developmental work on PT boasts was undertaken with sagacity and forehandedness on paper, and it is an ironic commentary that the two types of PT's which did the bulk of the fighting in World War II were not the result of this earnest paper work. The first, the Elco boat, was an adaptation of an English model, while the other, the Higgins boat, was produced by Andrew Jackson Higgins, of Higgins Industries, Incorporated, New Orleans, Louisiana. Only the rankest naval chauvinist could maintain that United States designs which came as a result of the carefully planned design contest were professionally the equal of the Elco boat or Higgins' craft.

Examination of the processes which turned American designer to high speed torpedo craft shows the government willing and eager to use an American design. Those designers competing for contracts were offered every professional advantage, and the adaptation of the British model and the Higgins boat, came only after this country's naval architects participating in the competition have been given every possible opportunity.

DESIGN COMPETITION

The House Naval Affairs Committee had added to the Second Deficiency Bill for 1938 $15,000,000 for experimental development of small craft.[1] This was the first positive act that this government had taken not to retrieve, but to gain its position as a leader in small craft production and operation. Thus in 1938 the country began to try to catch up on European designers who since the close of World War I, had been continuously drafting plans of small fast boats primarily for torpedo use.[2]

Under the aegis of the White House, plans were made for a design competition, and on 24 June 1938, an outline was submitted to the Chief Constructor by BuC&R which embodied the principles of the competition.[3] This was further modified by BuC&R in a letter of 29 June 1938.[4] The final outline included a 165' steel subchaser, a 110' wood subchaser, a 70' Motor Torpedo Boat and a 54' Motor Torpedo Boat; primarily a torpedo boat and anti-submarine program, and, as will be shown, an attempt was made later in the

---

1. Public Law 528.
2. Chapter I of this volume.
3. BuC&R memorandum of 24 June 1938 to the Chief Constructor.
4. BuC&R memorandum of 29 June 1938 to the Chief Constructor.

AN ADMINISTRATIVE HISTORY OF PT's IN WORLD WAR II
(Recreated October 25, 2010 by the members of the PT Boat Forum message board)

25

program to combine the features of the subchaser (110') with a PT on a PT hull.[5]

To insure more than contractual interest upon the part of the designers, the Navy offered $15,000 for the designs for each of the two types of boat finally accepted, and also offered prizes of $1500 to those designers whose projected boats, although not selected by the Navy, did reach the final stage of design competition. To ease the fears of any small contractors in competing with larger firms, the Navy assured contestants that all designs were to be handled by confidential Navy symbol numbers only, and no where on submitted plans was there to be any other identifying mark.[6]

The navy was looking for originality, for a truly American design, and the rules allowed the greatest possible latitude for competing architects. Department data, included only the required military Characteristics for each type, plus the weight, general location, and space necessary for the military features covered in military characteristics. Thus military inhibitions to design were comparatively few, and if American designers had any new ideas, and if the success of the boat was not sole dependent upon these new ideas, there was ample opportunity for the introduction of new features.[7]

Generally speaking, the Navy in asking for a 70' boat set up reasonable qualifications. The Government wanted a boat not over 80' which would babe operated by two officers and eight men. Although the Navy wanted a quiet boat, maximum speed was set at 40 knots (trial) and minimum cruising radius at 275 miles at top speed plus 275 miles at cruising speed. The hull could be either metal or wood, round or vee, and the selection between gasoline and diesel power was also left to the designer. Minimum armament qualifications called for at least two .50 calibre machine guns, two 21" torpedoes and four depth charges; THE Navy also required suitable torpedo releasing gear.

The boat was to be of good seakeeping qualities and seaworthiness and capable of maneuvering in all kinds of seas. Its hull and propeller design should allow the boat to pass through hump speeds with facility when fully loaded. To ease the load on personnel, the Navy asked for group one man controls and safety devices fitted to the engine for protection against all fire hazards. These safety devices were to be equipped for remote control operation. Space was to be allowed for radio facilities and the boat's watertight integrity was to be implemented by four (minimum) watertight bulkheads. Fresh water tanks were to carry enough for 48 hours running (trial condition).

Machinery, crew, hull and propeller, and radio requirements, were the same for the smaller PT. Its length was limited to 60', and hoisting weight was not to exceed 20 tones (long tons). Armament specifications required only

---

5. Navy contracts 70295 and 72096, 13 December 1939.
6. Invitation for competitive designs of Experimental vessels for the United States Navy: conditions of competition, 11 July 1938.
7. Ibid.

torpedoes and depth charges, but offered as an alternative .50 calibre machine guns and smoke devices. Minimum cruising radius was designated as 120 miles at top speed plus 120 miles at cruising speed (15 knots). An absolutely new specification was added when the Bureau stipulated "Hull structure to be of sufficient strength to permit of hoisting over side by means of slings under moderate weather conditions". Previously the hoisting weight had been limited, but the limitation was explained with a note which excluded from hoisting weight all readily removable items such as ammunition, water, fuel, and stores.[8]

TACTICAL CONSIDERATIONS

The fact that the Navy asked for two sizes of boats and especially the fact that hoisting weight was a stipulation in the design of the smaller craft, makes evident the duo-tactical ideas that the General Board held at the time it set up the qualifications and requirements for the design contest. Basic tactical mission was of course the same: the effective delivery of torpedoes to the firing point, but while the larger craft was designed for off shore work, the 54' boat was to be capable of being transported anywhere by cargo ships or auxiliaries. The former, in short, was a coastal defense craft, while the latter could be used in any area, if means were available to transport it.

In considering the addition to the Navy of the type and in arriving at design requirements, the General Board stated in part "For torpedo carrying motor boats it is clearly evident that because of our strategic situation the type is of much less initial value to our Navy than to most, if not all, of the others. In the early stages of war it I unlikely that small torpedo carrying craft would be useful to us. However, the developments of a prolonged war could easily change this situation in that operating areas of our own and the enemy fleets would come closer together, and . . . motor torpedo boats could replace larger craft which would otherwise have to be employed in defensive missions. Moreover, future situations can occur under which it would be possible for such small craft to be used on directly offensive missions as is no doubt contemplated in certain foreign navies. I should be mentioned that, wherever, employed base facilities will be necessary, and will have to include torpedo depots with skilled assembling and adjusting personnel. . ."[9]

This attitude on the part of the General Board is understandable, for the Navy's budget for experimentation was small in 1937, and expenditures for new types of vessels had to be considered carefully. Despite our strategic position, the Board did envisaged possible use of the boats on offensive missions, and recognized the necessity of a fixed base.

8. Preliminary and Final Design Data for Competitive Designs of Experimental Vessels of the United States Navy; 11 July 1938.

9. BuC&R's S82-3-(18)(DF) 5 December 1936; 4th endorsement General Board, Number No. 420-14 (Serial No. 1740), paragraph 8, 14 April 1937.

AN ADMINISTRATIVE HISTORY OF PT's IN WORLD WAR II
(Recreated October 25, 2010 by the members of the PT Boat Forum message board)

27

The Board does mention that at the time the Navy Department was "assisting the Philippine Government in the development of motor torpedo boats for its own program of defense". [10] Some idea of the efficacy of the aid rendered by the Navy Department can be gleaned from a personal letter of General MacArthur to Admiral Leahy written almost two years later when he asked the Admiral to authorized Captain Chantry of BuC&R to make available to him any information the Navy might have about progress made in motor torpedo boat development. MacArthur included the statement, "It is only natural that if a suitable boat is developed there in the U.S. within our means that we purchase those boats there rather than abroad." [11] In short, at the time MacArthur was not only without help from the Navy Department, he was without any idea of progress being made in the United States on motor torpedo boats, and in the two years between the General Board's letter and the MacArthur letter, the Philippine government had been purchasing "Q" class MTB's from Thornycroft the English builder. [12]

Despite the limited aspect of the Board's consideration of the use of MTB's, it is a fortunate happenstance that basic good judgment approved the introduction of the type into the U.S. Navy, regardless of the contemporary opinions of tactical potentialities. The recommendations of the Board did not go much further than the mere creation of the type, and in summing up its case said as much: "In the initial stages of a war our greatest necessity in the way of small craft to reinforce our present provisions for local defenses will not necessarily include the ability to carry and launch torpedoes. The essential equipment will include depth charges, machine guns and listening gear; moderate speeds combined with fair endurance will be satisfactory. The conversion of many of the smaller motor pleasure boats to meet such purposes will be relatively easy and require less than will be the case if the general run of such craft are fitted to also carry and launch torpedoes.

"As far as concerns small craft to be constructed by of for the Navy during peace,. . . we should not go further than a sufficient expenditure to develop the types." [13] Thus did the Board visualize converted yachts as a primary means of coastal defense in an emergency, and eliminated as a necessity the torpedo carrying function of PT's. This decision all but hamstrings the whole PT concept, although the Board warily keeps from falling from grace by a limited endorsement of type construction.

In its peroration, the General Board does authorize design competition but not without an enjoinder for the Navy to plan on utilization of yachts in case of an emergency. "In view of this prospective value to the United States of the smaller type of motor torpedo boats, the Board believes that there should be available a satisfactory design. A successful type cannot be achieved in a

---

11. Letter from Commonwealth of the Philippines, Officer of the Military Adviser, 29 March 1939.
12. "The Development of the PT" Commander W.C. Specht USN, and Lt.(jg) W.S. Humphrey, USNR as published in "Elco PT's in Action" by the Electric Boat Company.
13. General Board Number 420-14 (Serial No. 1740) 14 April 1937, paragraphs 9 and 10.

single design, and therefore recommends the inaugurations of an experimental development program on a moderate scale.

It is also recommended that at least a part of the development and building be accomplished under contract. Moreover, small boat designers and builders in this country should be kept in touch with our development in order to utilize the very general desire of owners of such craft to have them of use in the event of a national emergency." [14]

The force that upset the Navy is inertia re PT Boats and gave impetus to the General Board's investigation of the matter came in the form of a letter from the Chief of the Bureau of Construction and Repair. Evidently there were two motivating factors; first, the rapid and efficient development of the type by the European navies, and secondly, the appearance of a fundamental interest in the type among the small boat builders and designers of the country, who, from patriotic interest, wished to develop pleasure craft which might be of value for naval functions in the event of a national emergency.

This letter precluded the possibility that PT Boats might be used offensively and suggested that their best use would be to release larger types on defensive duty for action on offensive duty. Because of this possibility, the Bureau suggested the inauguration of the experimental design contest, which the General Board ratified. The Bureau envisaged no extensive program, and planned for the building of two boats each year - one by contract design and one by Departmental design. [15]

The Bureau of Engineering concurred with C&R's plan, and added that is was endeavoring to attain not only gasoline engines, but funds for diesel experimentation in an effort to provide a unit of that type suitable for the boats. [16] CNO recommended referring the plans to the General Board [17] and SecNav passed it to the Board with a request for military characteristics if approved. [18] The Board's action has been recorded fully above, and its decision was ultimately approved on 7 May 1937 by CNO [19] and SecNav. [20] Chief, BuC&R's basic letter had been written on December 5, 1936. The paper work for the inauguration of a PT program had been accomplished in little more than six months.

The paper foundation had been laid carefully and cautiously, but the grass grew and flourished over this foundation while the Navy, perpetually broke in peace time, cast about for funds. A year and ten days after the PT program had been approved, Congress gave the Navy some money to do something about it.

---

14. Ibid, paragraph 13
15. BuC&R's S82-3-(18) (DF) 5 December 1936
16. BuEng's S82-3(12-5-Yg) 16 December 1936
17. CNO's Op-23C-KM, S82-3/L5-2(361216) 5 January 1937
18. SecNav's Ibid.
19. CNO's C/o-23C-KM, S82-3/L5-2(361216) 7 May 1937
20. SecNav's Ibid.

AN ADMINISTRATIVE HISTORY OF PT's IN WORLD WAR II
(Recreated October 25, 2010 by the members of the PT Boat Forum message board)

29

Public Law number 528 appropriated "the sum of $15,000,000 to be expended at the discretion of the President of the United States for the construction of experimental vessels, none of which shall exceed three thousand tons standard displacement". The Navy came into another slice of appropriations by means of HR 10851 which earmarked an extra $9,500,000 for naval construction of all types, including specifically the experimental small craft program. [21]

The grass ceased to grow, and by 29 June 1938, Captain A. J. Chantry had submitted the first draft for an invitation for competitive designs. [22] On 11 July 1938 the Navy Department publicly invited designers to compete for the prize money and the contest was on. Open only to qualified and experienced designers, the competition was divided into two phases.

PRELIMINARY DESIGN

The first phase was a preliminary design stage, expiring August 24, 1938. (This was later extended three times to 30 September 1938). [23] For the preliminary design period the architect was expected to submit a general description covering the principal dimensions, fuel and water capacities, type and material of hull, the armament, the number of propellors, shaft r.p.m., the full power shaft horsepower, the trial speed, the type, size, weight, capacity and manufacture of machinery units, listing the data furnished and describing special features contemplated but not described elsewhere. Lines were to be substantially complete, although not necessarily faired, and material submitted was to include a tabular statement showing principal dimensions and coefficients.

To give The Bureau some idea of stowage and equipage methods, the Navy also asked the designers in the preliminary stage design to submit a small scale general arrangement plan. This plan was to include inboard profile, main deck and engine space plans with just enough detail to show the location of the propulsion units, auxiliary machinery, gearing and the run of the shafting. An outline was to be given, with no details of the location of fuel and water tanks, torpedo tubes and depth charges, living and messing spaces, and the bridge. The contest also stated that the competing designers must submit a general conception of their structural plans, and estimated weights in order to give the Bureau an idea of the structural strength contemplated and the probable weight involved.

After all preliminary designs mailed prior to the expiration of the preliminary design period were received, the Navy Department was to examine the data and design and eliminate all but five competitors for each type of MTB. Selection

---

21. Public Law, 723, 52 Stat. Chapter 681, 25 Jun 1938
22. See Note #4
23. AstNav Letters of 22 July 1938 (S)SED-1A-OM), 5 August 1938 (SOSED-O-OM), and 8 September 1938 (No number).

was to be made of the competitors whose preliminary design included all the preliminary design data, and appeared best to meet the requirements of Department Data and to offer the best prospect of development into a satisfactory final design. Those designers who failed to qualify for the final phase would have their preliminary designs returned and would be eliminated from the competition. No fee was to be paid these designers by the Government. [24]

FINAL DESIGN

For the final design phase, the five remaining competitors in each class were to submit detailed specifications for hull and machinery. These were to be in detail, and the designers were allowed ten weeks in which to complete their final phase plans. The final specifications were to include everything expected in a finished design, and were to be in sufficient enough detail so that, together with the other material to be submitted, they would form a proper basis for placing a contract. Not only were they only to be accurate as to actual details, but also definite as to intent, quality of material and workmanship, work to be done by the

contractor, outfit and equipment to be furnished by the contractor and by the government, inspection, applicable plans and specifications, changes, testing, cleaning, painting and other pertinent material.

At the close of the final design period and upon receipt of all final designs submitted in that period, the Navy Department was to examine all designs and data and select the best, and if necessary, such additional designs as might be elected. The basis for selection would be from those that best included all the final design data, and which best met the requirements of Department Data. These winners would receive the $15,000 prize money, and the other contestants in this stage would receive the $1500 prize money.

As the government was interested in obtaining a design for its own use, the complete designs and patent rights relating to material covered by them, the competition invitation set up express covenants regarding patents and licenses which would be made a condition of any award made by the Navy. The covenants were as usual in a case of this sort, and called for non-exclusive licenses to make or to use designs and material of the winners, while at the same time the use of these patents and licenses would not be construed as an abrogation by the government of any of its patents pending. [25]

Thus the government would have two of the best designs available in the country for motor torpedo boats, if American architects became interested in the competition. Arrangements were made by BuC&R to answer any questions

---

24. Preliminary design data for Competitive Designs of Experimental Vessels for the United States Navy 11 July 1938.

25. Final design data for competitive Designs of Experimental Vessels for the United States Navy, 11 July 1938.

AN ADMINISTRATIVE HISTORY OF PT's IN WORLD WAR II
(Recreated October 25, 2010 by the members of the PT Boat Forum message board)

31

that came up during designing, as long as they were submitted in writing, and as long as the designer agreed to respect the classification of all matter that was entrusted in his hands. It remained now only for the designers to deposit their $100.00 entrance fee checks and begin their preliminary work.

COMPETITION RESULTS

The results were gratifying. The Navy Department received twenty-four designs from 21 designers for the 54' boat, and for the 70' boat 13 designs from 13 designers. In the smaller class, all but three designers were eliminated, and in the other type five designers were authorized to continue into the final design stage. [26]

In evaluating the designs submitted, BuC&R and BuEng working jointly, gave primary consideration to four factors other than responsiveness to the terms of the contest. Initially, the Navy hoped to secure ideas from private designers which give reasonable assurance of definite advantages without obvious or undue prejudice to other important characteristics. Secondly, although the Navy wanted the boats to have the designated speed, it was essential that they be sturdy craft. Rough water service was contemplated for the boats, and although required speed was important up to the designated point specified in the contest data (40 knots) beyond that it was desirable only if obtained at no expense to robustness, reliability, sea-keeping qualities, and operational and maintenance ease. Thirdly, with an eye to potential tactical use, the Navy felt that the final vessels selected should offer reasonable possibilities of satisfactory experiments in operations, tactics and general use. This proviso eliminated from competition any freak designs or extreme types whose utility was highly specialized. Finally, the judging officials made all possible efforts to insure absolute justice and fair play to all the designers in the competition. [27]

Although the Navy was dealing with a new form about which little was known in American military circles, it became evident at the close of the preliminary stage of the contest that a number of the designers (four of the final eight) were seriously under powering their boats, despite the fact that the Navy had made available to all designers information on the latest available Allison engines. [28] Hoping that the designers' new hull forms would make up the evident deficiencies in horsepower, the Bureau chiefs, nevertheless, suggested to the Assistant Secretary that if "no violence will be done the competitive spirit of this design project, it is recommended that all designers selected for the Final Design Stage be warned that sufficient power and fuel capacity must be incorporated in the final designs to meet the speed and radius requirements of the Department Data." [29] Having exerted themselves to give the designers

---

26. Joint letter, BuC&R (S82-3-C18) (CD) and BuEng (AA/S1(C10-26-D) 1 November 1938.
27. Joint letter, BuC&R (S82-3-(18)(DP)) and BuEng (AA/S1(11-16-D)) 28 November 1938.
28. Unnumbered Navy Department letter of 8 September 1938.
29. Joint letter, BuC&R (S82-3-(18)(CD)) and BuEng (AA/S1(10-26-D)) 1 November 1938: Paragraph 5.

every possible advantage, the Navy set the opening date of the final design period as 7 November 1938. The final stage competitors received their guidance specifications and the last part of the competition got under way. [30]

After due deliberation on 21 March 1939 the Navy announced the final winners. Of the three designers in the 54' class all submitted entries, while one competitor, represented originally in both classes, dropped out of competition in the 70' class. Winner in the 54' class was Professor George Crouch who made his design for Hewey B. Nevins, Inc. The winner in the larger boat design was Sparkman and Stevens, a firm of naval architect well known hitherto for their sailing vessel designs. [31]

The Navy now had two civil designs for PT's. The planning stage was over, and the next step was to make building arrangements. The contests had been open to all qualified American designers, thirty-four of them had submitted 37 designs. In short, theoretically speaking the Navy now had the best available American design for PT's. Whether or not these designs would live up to expectations could be determined only by actual construction, and in June of 1939, the Navy Department let the contract for PT 1. [32]

THE ELCO PROGRAM

About the time the Navy Department was receiving plans for the final design stage of their competition another important development was taking place in the evolution of the American PT boat. This was a development whose consequences were to be much more far-reaching than those of the prize contest, and was, in effect, to father eventually a goodly percentage of all American PT boats. It was late in 1938 that the Elco Boat Works of Bayonne, New Jersey, through the efforts of Charles Edison, at that time SecNav, became interested in the possibilities of producing torpedo boats for the United States.

Henry R. Sutphen, Vice President of the Electric Boat Company, and President of the Elco boat works at Bayonne, had kept an eye on European development, and especially on the budding, but far from universally recognized, genius of Hubert Scott-Paine, then in the employ of the British Power Boat Company. At the time, the British had their Thornycroft evolution from the CMB, the Vosper, and the Scott-Paine, as pointed out in the first chapter. All three were superior to US craft, for the simple reason that we had done nothing along these lines, while, to reiterate, all the European powers had been continuously designing and redesigning small, fast, torpedo carrying craft.

If one of these designs could be purchased, or at least an American license for one of these designs, it was reasonable to suppose that there would be a market for the craft with the US government. [33] Although Scott-Paine had yet

---

30. Ibid: paragraph 6.
31. Joint letter, BuC&R (S82-3-(18)(D)) and BuEng(AA/S1(2-20-D) 21 March 1939, paragraph 2.
32. Contract no. NOS 67019.
33. SecNav Op-23C (SC) 382-3, 13 January 1939; General Board No. 426-14.

AN ADMINISTRATIVE HISTORY OF PT's IN WORLD WAR II
(Recreated October 25, 2010 by the members of the PT Boat Forum message board)

33

to make his famous Brest trip with his boat, comparatively speaking, these three British designs were seasoned and proved, while this country had yet to arrive at the completion of the paper stage of design. Nationalism would prove a serious damper on marketing of these boats, but the logic of employing at least one of them as an experimental boat, or as a control for the boats produced by the prize contest, could not be denied. To Elco it seemed like good business speculation and the company made the gamble.

ORIGINS OF THE ELCO PROGRAM

In February, 1939 Sutphen and his designer Irwin Chase embarked for England to check their hearsay information of the Royal Navy's progress with MTB's with actual observation of the types in construction and under comparative performance tests. If the English boats lived up to expectations, Sutphen and Elco were ready to purchase one to take back to the United States. [34]

Exactly what caused Elco's sudden interest in PT's is conjectural, for they did not enter the design contest. Irwin Chase has evidently been asked this question a number of times and offered this plausible reply: "I have often been asked what was the underlying cause of Elco's gambling on the motor torpedo boat as a weapon of this war. In retrospect I suppose the principal reason was because we had long experience in one basic factor in hull design with which the average naval officer was not familiar; namely, that a small high speed motor boat could be so designated so that she would be fit to go to sea and stay there in any weather. We had learned much with the ML's, weathering winter gales in the North Sea, and still more during the prohibition era from a class of fast weight carrying boats which alternately served the rum-runners and the Coast Guard. The latter notorious craft also proved that a converted aviation engine, properly installed and run within its capabilities, could accomplish propulsion miracles. Few commercial installations of high powered light weight engines have been given a real chance to show what they could do, not because of the construction of the engine, but more often because of faulty conversion and shoddy installation." [35]

Chase bases ELCO's gamble, therefore, on the company's superior knowledge and ability to handle the factors of rough water and high speed engines in their relationship to the boats. Reference to converted aviation engines is to the old Liberty engine developed by Packard during World War I. This engine was an outstanding surplus commodity during the 1920's and proved ideal for conversion for rum-runners et al. Although Chase is one of the leading men in his profession and his position on ELCO's gamble seems unassailable, there are other opinions.

---

34. PT 9/L4 (391216) 21 December 1939, Article 7.
35. "The Story Behind 'The Expendables' " by Irwin Chase.

An alternate opinion is furnished in a paper on the development of the PT which was first presented at the Naval War College at Newport, R.I. by Lt. Comdr. W.C. Specht, U.S.N. on 17 March 1943. AT the time Lt. Commander Specht was the Commanding Officer of the nearby Motor Torpedo Boat Squadrons Training Center at Melville, Rhode Island. Specht asserts that Sutphen was asked to go to England by Edison, and moreover, states that Sutphen left for England with assurance from Edison, that the Navy would back whatever boat he bought.[36]

It is possible that the more captious of Mr. Edison's critics, might possibly draw their own inferences from this statement of Specht's, especially, in view of the New Jersey backgrounds of both the Secretary and the ELCO Company. Such a promise seems rather obscure, especially, when a third alternative, offered by reliable Navy officials, is presented.

This version holds that ELCO was interested in the proposition of obtaining one of the British boats, but with the prize competition imminent, the purchase seemed too much of a gamble. ELCO acquainted the former New Jersey Governor with the facts that Chase brings out in his explanation. Edison, knowing the firm to be a reliable one, and impressed by the Chase theories, offered to back the boat as SecNav, if it were recommended to him by the Board of Inspection and Survey.

The story resolves itself in two letters written in January of 1939. One dated 13 January 1939, is from SecNav, and the other is from the chairman of the General Board, at that time Admiral Thomas Hart.

SecNav wrote the General Board that there was a possibility of obtaining a British boat for the US Navy (Sutphen and Chase had just departed for England), and asked the Board, if, in connection with the Board's studies for recommendations on a building program for small craft, it would make a recommendation as to the desirability of obtaining a 70' Motor Torpedo Boat from the British Navy.

GENERAL BOARD'S OPINION

The General Board was aware of the progress had made with the type and three days later on 16 January 1939 replied to SecNav. "Inasmuch as said design is known to be a result of several years' of development", the letter read, "the General Board considers it highly advisable that such a craft be obtained as a check on our own development". The Board that the Navy procure one of the 70' boats if possible, and then went even further by also suggesting " . . . if it can be arranged . . . that a boat be obtained as nearly as possible the size of our own 54' design." It is evident that the General Board, once committed to PT's, was

---

36. "The Motor Torpedo Boat - Past, Present, and Future, History, development, Employment and Tactics Accomplishments to 1943" compiled and written by Ensign W.S. Humphicy, U.S. Navy and Lieutenant Commander W.C. Specht, U.S. Navy.

AN ADMINISTRATIVE HISTORY OF PT's IN WORLD WAR II
(Recreated October 25, 2010 by the members of the PT Boat Forum message board)

35

determined to keep as close a check as possible upon the comparative merits of US and foreign torpedo boats.[37]

This bears the General Board's earlier desire to keep in touch with the developments in private industry and among civilian naval architects. American boat-building industry had watched the situation abroad and realized that Europe was mobilizing powerful weapons with the building of fleets of torpedo boats. ELCO saw the possibility of obtaining one of these craft, and took the lead among civilian designers by going to England for this express purpose. The company had evidently laid their cards on the table before SecNav, while the Secretary, appreciative of the patriotic interest of the company, asked the General Board if the plan were feasible. The General Board's decision ratified the forehandedness and foresight of ELCO in this matter.

On 19 January 1939, the Navy Department invited Mr. Sutphen to preliminary discussion with its representatives concerning the possible purchase of the British boat.[38] Mr. Sutphen accepted 21 January, enclosing a letter to him from Mr. Scott-Paine's representative in New York.[39] The preliminary conference was finally held on 25 January 1939.[40]

ELCO furthered its position on 31 January 1939. The company submitted a memo outlining certain procedures in respect to procurement of the boat. This memo included the suggestion that if the first demonstrator was satisfactory that the Department would obligated itself to purchase five more. The proposition as it stood was turned down, but AstSecNav said he would ask Congress for funds for the purchase of additional boats if the demonstrator justified such action.[41]

At any rate Sutphen and Chase did go to England(at no expense to U.S. Government) on 10 February 1939, with the idea firmly entrenched in the back of their minds that small, seaworthy motor boat capable of high speed would make a useful fighting ship. The preliminary talks resulted in an understanding that if they succeeded in purchasing a Scott-Paine boat the U.S. Navy would buy in accordance with terms of a contract tentatively agreed upon by Elco and the Navy.[42]

The two men were given unusual opportunities by the Royal Navy to observe the boats,[43] and their reaction to Thornycroft, Vickers and Scott-Paine designs was definitely positive. Sutphen and Chase felt without a doubt, the U.S. would be better off with one of these boats, and the problem at the time of selection.

37. SecNavy Op-23C (SC) S82-3, 13 January 1939; General Board No. 420-14
38. R.B. Carney letter of 19 January 1939.
39. Henry Sutphen Letter of 21 January 1939.
40. R.B. Carney memorandum of 26 January 1939. 41. 21 December 1939: Article 6.
42. SecNav's P.T. 9/L4, 21 December 1939: Article 7.

43."THE STORY BEHIND 'THE EXPENDABLES" by Irwin Chase.

SCOTT-PAINE BOAT PROCURED

Once again the idea of seaworthiness won out, for both of the men were primarily interested in the boat that would take the roughest treatment. This proved to be the point which turned the men from Elco to the Scott-Paine's 70' design, for this vessel had a remarkable affinity for rough weather. This factor plus sound and advanced design characteristics convinced the Americans that this was the boat which could be best adapted for use by the United States Navy. Sutphen and the Attaché reported favorably on the performance of the MTB and,[44] Elco then and there made arrangements for the purchase of Scott-Paine's boats.

Negotiations for the Scott-Paine craft were successful, and on 17 March 1939 Mr. Sutphen reported by radio that one Scott-Paine 70 footer had been purchased under favorable terms with shipment in three months.[45]

Figure 1. Scott-Paine's PT 9

44. SecNav's PT 9/L4 (394216) 21 December 1939, paragraph 8.
45. RDC New York 0017 1040 March 1939

The purchase was approved by the President, and his informal endorsement to SecNav's letter on the subject read, "O.K. if the price is as low as the proposed American 70 footer". [46] As engine development costs had raised the price of the American 70' boat, the price of the proposed Scott-Paine design was under the proposed cost of the 70 footers building in this country.

In order to comply with the wording of the appropriation act, Elco, on 25 April 1939 submitted proposal for construction of one 70 foot MTB of Scott-Paine design, and on 29 May SecNav forwarded a contract. [47] This contract was signed on 1 June 1939. To obviate delivery difficulties, the government extended Elco's prospective delivery date to 1 November 1939. [48]

The Scott-Paine boat was delivered to Elco at New York on 4 September 1939 two days after the beginning of World War II, and was lightered to Electric Boat Company plant at Groton, Connecticut. ELCO moved its investment to New London for a series of tests and trails, and SecNav ordered Commodore A. Loring Swasey out of retirement to act as an observer at these trails. Swasey had previously been attached to the Patrol Craft section of BuShips before his retirement at the age of 63, and it was he who built the first five volunteer patrol craft (40' overall) during World War I at the behest of Franklin D. Roosevelt, then AstSecNav. [49]

Scott-Paine intrigued with the possibilities for his craft in the United States, had come over with the boat, and was in charge of its operation. He, together with the Elco company, solicited the Navy to send its representatives up to New London to take trail spins on the boat. The Coast Guard also evinced interest and sent an observer to New London for the trails, although that service finally decided that the potentialities of the craft for a Coast Guard vessel were too limited to warrant investment.

BuShips officials who were intimately acquainted with this phase of the PT Boat program have stated that Scott-Paine personally did as much to sell the Boat to the Navy as the boat did itself. From all evidences, the English designer was an exceptional boat-handler, and he was a non-peril when handling his own design. His performances with the PT 9 were no doubt influential in the ultimate sale of the boat to the government. [50]

BEGINNING OF FIRST BUILDING PROGRAM

The matter introduced by ELCO at the preliminary conference - the acquisition of additional boats - had not been forgotten by the Navy Department. Shortly after delivery of PT 9 the Navy went into the matter

45. RDC New York 0017 1040 March 1939
46. SecNav No. S82/L4 (390119) 3 April 1939 with Presidential approval.
47. SecNav letter AA/S1(380708) of 29 May 1939.
48. Later delayed by BuEng PT9/L4 (390119) OF 10 November 1939.
49. Conversations with Sidney Peters, BuShips architect
50. Ibid.

38

AN ADMINISTRATIVE HISTORY OF PT's IN WORLD WAR II
(Recreated October 25, 2010 by the members of the PT Boat Forum message board)

thoroughly. "Tables of costs, advantages, etc.", of British and American types were studied; the coordinator (of Shipbuilding) submitted estimates of available funds; various technical questions concerning characteristics, armament, equipment, etc. were considered in the Bureaus and Offices concerned. Preliminary discussions, attended by the Acting Secretary of the Navy and representatives of Elco and the Department were held; PT 9 was inspected and observed in operation by a Department Trial Board and by other experienced Department representatives.

It was tentatively decided in late September to acquire a sufficient number of Scott-Paine boats to permit going ahead with the tactical and operational phases of experimentation with the M.T.B. type. Final decision was reserved until PT 9 could be observed in rough water to prove her seakeeping qualities.

"On October 3rd, the Acting Secretary of the Navy informed the President by letter that he wished to go ahead with the project of obtaining additional MTB's of the Scott-Paine design, using unexpended funds of the Experimental Appropriation made available by the second Deficiency Act of 1938, and negotiating the best possible bargain with ELCO – Scott-Paine's licensee in the United States. The President indicated his approval on the face of the original letter, adding "How many?, How much?", to which question The Acting Secretary of the Navy indicating 18 to 20 boats for $271,000 or better".[51]

BuEng and BuC&R in a joint letter set up trial requirements for PT 9. The requirements included standardization, endurance and fuel consumption, astern and maneuver trials; determination of tactical diameter; steering gear inspection; and a post trial examination to ascertain any defects and deficiencies in the boat or its appurtenances which may have been caused by the trials.[52] On 9-10 October 1939. In the presence of sub-board of Board of Inspection and Survey and other Departmental representatives, PT 9 successfully demonstrated its ability to achieve the standards set up by the Board in fulfillment of contract obligations. Despite the fact that PT 9 passed these trials successfully, the Navy withheld approval of the boat and procurement of additional craft pending rough water trials.[53]

ROUGH WATER TRIALS

The heavy weather trials would be decisive as far as the yes or no of further procurement of this type of craft were concerned, for the Navy was interested in the boat only if it was all purpose and uninhibited by bad weather. These trials were held on 1 November 1939 off New London, Connecticut. The results can best be demonstrated by excerpts from the report of the Inspecting Officer. "As a sea boat, PT 9 has my unqualified approval and I have such confidence in the

---

51. SecNav's PT9/L4 (319216) 21 December 1939: Articles 18, 19, & 20.
52. Eng. No. PT9/L4 (8-29-Bc) 30 August 1939. Also AstNav's PT9/S8-2(390966).
53. SecNav's PT9/L4 (341246), Article 19.

AN ADMINISTRATIVE HISTORY OF PT's IN WORLD WAR II
(Recreated October 25, 2010 by the members of the PT Boat Forum message board)

39

boat after observing her in rough water that I would not hesitate to take her anywhere under any conditions.

"I started the trials frankly skeptical about the claims I have heard made for this boat during the past year, and I asked for every condition which I thought might bring out any weakness in the boat's performance...

"I feel sure that any seagoing officer would share my original doubts in the claims for this boat, but I also feel that any experienced officer would agree with me after witnessing the performance that I saw yesterday. On the seaward run I do not believe a destroyer could have maintained the speed PT 9 held with complete comfort for all onboard; on the other hand, the seas which bothered PT 9 would have caused no discomfort for a larger ship."[54]

Evidently the Trial Board felt that a report with such a lyrical peroration and only a tinge of adverse comment was open to criticism, and the boat was again run through rough water for the Trial Board. Although the board's report was not so enthusiastic, there was nothing in it that indicated that unsuitability of the type for tactical training purposes.[55]

In order to expedite contract arrangements in the event satisfactory rough water performances, a series of discussions began on 23 October 1939 to consider points that would appear in any contract for additional boats. On 26 October ELCO submitted a proposal to build additional boats, although at this time, SecNav had reached no decision on this matter. During these preliminary discussions representatives of ELCO and the Department were at odds over the delivery date of PT 9. Elco maintained that it needed PT 9 for a pattern for its work, while the Navy wanted it for its own uses.

The day after the rough water tests had been run, the Acting Secretary, put an end to the atmosphere of suspense which had been hanging over the negotiation by transmitting to the coordinator of shipbuilding decisions to grant ELCO a two months delay in delivering PT 9; to contract with ELCO for as many boats of Scott-Paine design as could be obtained for $5,000,000 figure named to him by the coordinator; to endeavor to secure an increase of the limitation of the Experimental Appropriation from $15,000,000 to $25,000,000; and to expedite contract negotiations.[56]

The Navy ultimately approved the purchase of PT 9, after some confusion as to the price. Elco had originally asked for $283,095 for PT 9, but the government was unable to accept this figure. Details of the sale were worked out in contract NOd-1175, and later accepted by Elco on 4 June 1939. The contract was further modified by the Navy Department in July of 1939, but a final price

---

54. SecNav's PT 9/58-2 (390928) 21 December 1939, articles 17, 18, 19, and 20.
55. SecNav's PT 9/S8-2 (391216) Article 23.
56. SecNav's PT 9/S8-2 (391216) Article 26.
57. SecNav's letter PT/L4 (390119)P 31 May 1940; Navy Department letter PT/S41-3 (390623)1 25 July 1939; contract Nod - 1175, 1 June 1939; Elco letter of 4 June 1939.

40

AN ADMINISTRATIVE HISTORY OF PT's IN WORLD WAR II
(Recreated October 25, 2010 by the members of the PT Boat Forum message board)

agreement was not reached until 31 May 1940. On this date the government agreed to pay Elco $175,000 plus $4,000 for spare parts and accessories.[57]

INTRODUCTION OF PACKARD ENGINE

At the time the boat arrived, it was powered by three Rolls Royce Merlin engines. Colonel J.G. Vincent, Packard's engine designer, felt that an American engine could better the performance of the Rolls Royce product. He convinced Elco with his enthusiasm and capability, and PT 9 was later re-engined with three Packard W-8's.[58]

The boat displaced about 40 tons, and carried eighteen inch torpedoes in four forward launching tubes. With this displacement, the boat had no trouble in reaching the 40 knot minimum speed which the General Board had designated as standard for the prize contest boats then building.[59]

Government acquisition of the boat was slated for 1 November 1939, and a crew was assembled to take over, but delivery date was postponed to 3 January 1940. This delay was to allow the crew to go to Bayonne with the boat for further familiarization. Actually, acquisition was Delayed for more than six months after this latter date, while the Elco company studied the construction and prepared to build its own version of the Scott-Paine design. Delivery ultimately took place 17 June 1940,[60] and the boat was placed in service with Motor Torpedo Boat Squadron ONE on 24 July, 1940.[61]

Elco was to base its first series of boats upon this Scott-Paine model, and the delivery delay gave the people at Bayonne an ample opportunity to examine the boat, look into its construction principles, and adapt or modify the design characteristics of the English boat to best suit the needs of our Navy.

Not all the time was spent at Bayonne, for the boat underwent sea trials, and ordnance materiel tests. The materiel tests were largely in conjunction with torpedo firing at the Naval Torpedo Station, Newport, R.I., and with test machine gun firing on the Belgian designed power turrets installed on the boat.[62]

BUILDING THE PRIZE DESIGNS

The President was pleased that the prize contest had come off so well, but was impatient for actual construction to begin. His experiences as SecNav in World War I had probably made him more familiar with small patrol craft than with any other type of vessel in the Navy in 1939. He conveyed his sentiments to the Navy Department through his aide, at that time Rear Admiral

---

58. "The Story Behind 'The Expendable'" by Irwin Chase.
59. Humphrey and Spechts, see note 36.
60. Op-38-C-MG6/13, PT 9/A4-3 (400615) Serial 93038, 15 June 1940.
61. OpNav dispatch 201345/July 1940.
62. MTB RON ONE's PT/A4-3 (37) 29 August 1940.

AN ADMINISTRATIVE HISTORY OF PT's IN WORLD WAR II
(Recreated October 25, 2010 by the members of the PT Boat Forum message board)

41

D. J. Callaghan, and asked that bids for construction of all the vessels in the preliminary design contest be opened immediately. His keen eye for the technical aspects of small craft came in his warning not to overload the boats, and that he, personally, would keep the navy's efforts at adherence to designers waterline under close surveillance. His foresight concerning overloading was not remiss, for extra weight became a potent problem with PT's.[63]

HIGGINS SIGNS FIRST CONTRACT

The first step in the transition from the designing board to the ways came on 25 May 1939, when the Department let its first PT contract to Andrew Jackson Higgins, head of the Louisiana firm, Higgins Industries, Inc., Higgins thereby became the first American boatbuilder to sign with the government for the construction of motor torpedo boats. His company was assigned the job of building the Sparkman and Stevens design which was the winning entry in the 70' MTB class, although PT's 5 and 6, as the first Higgins craft were designated, both scaled over eighty feet. Higgins price for the boats was $177,006 for PT 5 and $158,300 for PT 6. The difference in price came about with the installation of Packard engines in PT 6 to replace the Vimalerts on PT 5.[64]

The chain of command necessary to put the boats in production began to function, and on 5 June 1939, the Navy Department authorized the first two divisions of PT's. These divisions were designated as "experimental divisions THREE and FOUR" (Experimental Divisions ONE and TWO were larger anti-submarine craft), and were assigned to COM 5 with orders to base at Norfolk Navy Yard "to develop their capabilities and limitations under various sea conditions."[65]

Although at that time only one contract had been let, the numbers of the boats in each division were designated. Experimental Division THREE comprised PT's 1, 2, 3, and 4 while Experimental Division FOUR comprised PT's 5, 6, 7, 8, and 9. Of these, PT 9 was the only boat any nearer the commissioning stage than the drafting board, and at the time the Scott-Paine boat was still in England. Contemplated delivery dates for the boats were: PT's 1, and 2, 15 November 1939; PT 3, 15 December 1939, PT 4, 4 January 1940, PT 5, 25 November 1939, PT 6, 19 January 1940, PT 7, 1 February 1940, and PT 8, February 1940. Acquisition date by the government for PT 9 had at that time not yet been ascertained, but was set tentatively as August of 1940.[66]

Upon completion of the tests and trials at Norfolk Navy Yard, the boats were to be detached from COM 5, and were to proceed under their own power to New

63. Letter from D. J. Callaghan, 18 March 1939.
64. Navy Contract NOS 67021.65. CNO's letter PT/P16-1 (390531) Serial 14775, 5 June 1939.
66. Ibid.

London and there report to the Commanding Officer, NOB, New London for further exercise and tests.

PT's 1 and 2

Final production arrangements were concluded on 8 June 1939 when the Navy awarded the contract for PT's 1 and 2 to the Fogal Boat Yard, Inc. of Miami Florida. The cost of these boats was pegged at $89,874.60.[67] On the same date Contract NOS 67020 awarded the Fisher Boat Works of Detroit, Michigan, the contract for PT's 3 and 4, to be produced at a cost of $102,325. In line with the formulatory ideas of the General Board - some boats civilian built, others Navy built - the Navy Yard, Philadelphia, began work on PT's 7 and 8. The design for this hull was the work of the Bureau of Ships and came as a direct result of their experiments with model hulls.

Building began with PT 2 on 12 July 1939 and with PT 1 on 19 August 1939. These Crouch designed boats were never to see service as PT's, for they were unable to come up to performance expectations. Building was hampered by constant delays.[68] The two boats were commissioned ultimately on 20 December 1941, and on 24 December 1941, the Navy changed their classification to that of small boat (C-6083 and C-6084 respectively). These boats are disposed of rather summarily here, because of their operational contribution to the PT program was nil. Ex-PT 1 is known to many PT men, however, for upon reclassification, the boat was shipped to the Motor Torpedo Boat Squadrons Training Center, Melville, Rhode Island, and was used throughout the war as a familiarization for motor machinists. Ex-PT 2's fate was assignment as an auxiliary craft at the Naval Torpedo Station, Newport, Rhode Island.

These two boats were 58' 11" overall with a 13' 9" beam. Their displacement was 60,850 pounds, and fuel load was 1665 gallons of 87 octane gasoline. The boats were equipped with two stern launching torpedo tubes. Power was provided by two V2500-2 1200 horse power Vimalert engines, although upon transfer to Melville, Ex-PT 1 was reengined with 2 Packard 4M-2500 engines.[69]

PT's 3 and 4

In August, Fisher began to build the second pair of boats in accordance with the bids let on the winning designs. PT's 3 and 4 were essentially of the same design as PT's 1 and 2, but the details had been modified by the Bureau of Ships. The outstanding changes were made in engine type and installation,

67. Navy contract NOS 67019.

68. According to a BuShips official, reorganization of Stirling Engine Company, which produced the Vimalert engine, delayed delivery of the engines to Fogal. This resulted in an overall delay of almost 500 days in the delivery of the boats. The difference between PT's 1 & 2 was in the manner of engine installation.

69. Op 414-C-4's control cards.

AN ADMINISTRATIVE HISTORY OF PT's IN WORLD WAR II
(Recreated October 25, 2010 by the members of the PT Boat Forum message board)

43

Figure 2: PT'S 3 & 4 UNDER CONSTRUCTION

while the lines of the two boats were similar to the Florida built craft. They were 58' - 5" overall with a 13' - 8" beam, and the amazing draft of 3' - 3". They were slightly lighter than the first two boats, displacing 56,600 pounds. Fuel capacity was the same. Two 18" torpedo tubes comprised the main ordnance load.[70]

PT's 5 and 6

Higgins meanwhile was building the larger craft in New Orleans. His Sparkman and Stevens designed boats were to displace 94,230 pounds, and to carry a fuel load of 3500 gallons of 87 octane gasoline. Overall length was 81'-3", beam was 15' - 4 1/4", and draft was 4' - 6".[71]

Thus while Elco was in the process of importing and testing PT 9, Fogal, Fisher and Higgins began their work on the American boats. The Philadelphia

70. Ibid.
71. Ibid.

FIgure 3: Higgins' PT 6

Navy Yard at the same time was commencing construction on PT's 7 and 8, a product of official design and labor. Where Elco was importing a tried and tested type, the American builders were starting out in a new field of naval construction. They did not have the benefit of the years of European experience, nor did they have a pattern by which they could gauge their work. Building directly from the drawing boards these contractors hoped to produce for the navy a satisfactory American built and designed PT.

FIRST ELCO BOATS

On 10 November 1939 CNO was informed of the Secretary's proposed allocation of boats in the additional program - the $5,000,000 given to Elco. The General Board, in turn, was requested to make the recommendation as to armament and equipment for these boats to be built as sub chasers. Finally, on 24 November 1939, the schedules were mailed to Elco, but effective termination of the paper work stage of the building was inhibited by difficulties which Elco was having with Packard in contracting for the twenty-three additional boats. The item was smoothed out and on 7 December 1939, the Navy made an award

AN ADMINISTRATIVE HISTORY OF PT's IN WORLD WAR II
(Recreated October 25, 2010 by the members of the PT Boat Forum message board)

45

Figure 4: 70' Elco PT

to Elco for the construction of 11 motor torpedo boats PT's 10-20, and 12 motor-boat subchasers PTC's 1-12. The $5,000,000 allocation was estimated to be sufficient to cover construction costs.

The award to Elco was the signal for an avalanche of criticism attacking the Department's decision to use an English design. Telegrams of denunciation began to arrive at the White House and at the Navy Department, and the press was far from indifferent on the matter. The nationalistic reaction, not entirely unexpected, had set in.

In replying to its critics, the Department pointed out that construction on the American boats would not be completed until the late spring of 1940, and that even then additional time would be required to allow the navy to evaluate the merits and demerits of the craft that were the result of the design competition. As it was, the American boats then under construction were not being built by production line methods, as the type was new, and there was no basis upon which a construction line could be built. The more sanguinary estimates stated that it would be the latter part of 1940 before

American industry could begin production in quantity of the American designs. Industry in this country was not geared to fast production of such an elaborate commodity.

As it turned out these results were extremely optimistic, for production on the design competition boats was disappointing; but this was a future factor, which the Navy could not use as a defense at the time. The Navy argued that the situation then existing in Europe made the use of all possible speed imperative in construction of motor torpedo boats. In the eyes of our navy (and conjecturally in the eyes of the Axis navies) ordinary procedures - a careful and deliberate examination of the relative merits of American and English boats - would have an immeasurably stultifying effect upon the program.

The Department felt that 1939 and the coming years did not furnish the proper opportunity to make only marginal use of time. The procurement of a capable and proven training type was essential in order to acquaint the navy with the potentialities and tactical uses of the boats. The Scott-Paine was available, seasoned, and satisfactory: hence the selection. "Therefore, the Acting Secretary felt that although he had faith in the ability of the American designers, the interests of National defense demanded that we get to the all-important tactical and operational training without delay and that could only be done by using a proven type, even though that type was British rather than American."[72]

Consequently, despite the furore on the part of the opposing elements, Elco began work on the construction of twenty-three 70' motor torpedo boats, patterned after the Scott-Paine design, and powered with three engines developed especially for the job by the Packard Motor Car Company of Detroit, Michigan.

PROPOSED SQUADRON ORGANIZATION

The letting of the Elco contract meant a new organizational set up for the PT's. Experimental Divisions THREE and FOUR, which never existed off paper, were scrapped, and Motor Torpedo Squadron ONE and TWO were created. To take care of the boats to be constructed as submarine chasers, the Department also created Motor Boat Submarine Chaser Squadron ONE. MTB Squadron ONE comprised MTB Divisions ONE and TWO: PT's 1, 2, 3, and 4 scheduled for the former, and PT's 5, 6, 7, and 8 for the latter. The new boats were to go to MTB Squadron TWO with PT's 10, 11, 12, 13, and 14 in MTB Division THREE, and PT's 15, 16, 17, 18, 19, and 20 in MTB Division FOUR. The boats were to operate directly under CNO, and BuNav had instructions to authorize complements. In designating the operational setup for PT's, the Navy named the squadron as the commissioned adjunct. The boats were not commissioned, and their captains were, technically speaking, not Commanding Officers,

---

72. SecNav's PT9/L4 (391216) 21 December 1939 Articles 28 through 32.

but rather boat captains. This system, adhered to throughout the war, has minimized administrative work and has been highly acceptable. The boats were scheduled to fit out at NOB Norfolk, and then following the fitting out period, the Department contemplated basing the boats at either Key West or Miami (or both) for further tests.[73]

In the middle of 1940, the PT program was still not an actuality. Squadron ONE was assembling personnel, but no boats had been placed in service. PT's 1 and 2 were complete as to hull work but were awaiting engines; PT's 3 and 4 after a trip from Detroit through the Welland Canal into Lake Ontario in to the Erie Barge Canal and thence down the Hudson, were completing trials and outfitting at Norfolk;[74] Higgins expected to deliver PT's 5 and 6 in August and September; and Navy Yard, Philadelphia expected to place its two boats in service at about the same time. The Navy had agreed to deferred delivery of Elco boats at this time because of some additional modifications the Bayonne Company wished to make in the Scott-Paine design.[75]

Plans became actualities on 24 July 1940, when Motor Torpedo Boat Squadron ONE was commissioned. Simultaneously the Officer-in-charge of PT 9 was ordered to report with the boat to the squadron.[76] The squadron at this time included only PT's 3, 4, and 9, and PT 4 had no torpedo tubes. Pending the placing in service of the other boats, PT's 3 and 9 were ordered to carry out tests and trials at Washington and at Newport Torpedo Station. From Newport the boats were to proceed to New York and carry out torpedo exercises and "develop type tactics and tentative standard operations." PT 4 was ordered to Washington Navy Yard for torpedo tubes.[77]

PT 7 was ordered to report on 22 November 1940,[78] and on 24 November 1940, PT 8, the only all aluminum PT developed, was placed in service. Delivery on PT's 5 and 6 was postponed by Higgins pending further trials, which ultimately took place in December.[79] The Philadelphia boats were exceptionally heavy when placed in service, as the Navy yard had used Destroyer fittings on the boats. Speed curves showed that a speed of 40 knots was impossible for PT 7, and her best speed was 36 knots. At the time the excess weight load was estimated at 17,000 pounds.[80] Even with this additional weight, PT 7 exceeded PT 3's acceptance run of 34 knots, which was made without a full military load.[81]

---

73. CNO's PT/P16-1 (390531) Serial 41138, 4 April 1940.
74. SecNav's A2-14 (400418) Serial 54213 (To the Secretary of State).
75. BuEng PT 9/L4 (11-8-Pa) 390119 10 November 1939.
76. OpNav dispatch 201345/July/1940.
77. CNO PT/A4-3 (400731) Ser 137638 10 Sept 1940;CNO's PT/A4-3(400731)
78. CNO PT/A4-1 (401115) Serial 188038 20 November 1940.
79. CNO FF13-1/A43 (401216) Serial 13423
80. W.H. Leadhy's memorandum of 9 December 1940
81. MTB Ron One's PT/A4-2 (02) 13 September 1940

Figure 5: MTBRon TWO 70' Elco

In November, Elco began delivering the first of PT's 10 through 19,[82] when PT 10 was placed in service on 7 November. This would seem to prove the worth of the Scott-Paine performance, for although the Elco contract was not let until six months after the design completion contracts, the company began to produce boats at approximately the same time or ahead of the other builders with the exception of Fisher, whose production time paralleled Elco's. PT's 11 and 12 followed the first boat of the series on 12 November and 14 November respectively.[83]

Winter in New York did not look too enticing to the squadrons, and the cold weather would have seriously hampered operations. The squadron commanders suggested in their proposed itinerary that the boats winter in Florida[84] and the squadrons were ordered south on 16 December 1940. Their scheduled base was

---

82. BuC&R S28-2 (MP) 11 January 1940; SecNav 2nd endorsement Op-38-c-MW,FS/S26-2(380318)
    (C8H #282) 24 March 1938: Navy contract number10296 13 December 1939
83. MTB Ron Two's PT/A4-1, 2c November 1939
84. ComMTD Ron One's PT-23-1 (1b) 2 August 1940; CNO's op-38-lac, Serial 136738 6 September 1940

AN ADMINISTRATIVE HISTORY OF PT's IN WORLD WAR II
(Recreated October 25, 2010 by the members of the PT Boat Forum message board)

49

Key West, but the movement order also proposed a cruise to Guantanamo, San Juan, Puerto Rico, and St. Thomas, Virgin Islands. ComMTBRon One was authorized to base the boats of MTB Div. ONE at Key West during this trip, as their operating capabilities were limited. The boats were to remain in southern waters during the cold weather and were to return to New York on 13 May 1941.[85]

BUILDING OF 77' ELCO's

On the boats constructed from design completion plans, the General Board had recommended installation of 18" torpedo tubes, as there was a large supply of this size torpedo on hand. For the later boats, however, the Board recommended that the builders install 21" tubes. The Bureau of Ordnance, in commenting on this plan in July of 1940, recommended an increase in the length of the boats in order to accommodate four 21" tubes.

The Navy was confronted with the problem of building a larger boat, and before letting contracts for the boat, the Department decided to review its data on PT's and obtain new opinions. CNO in a letter to SecNav on 30 July 1940 recommended that the Department should have the benefit of General Board's opinion awarding contracts, and suggested that this opinion be obtained as expeditiously as possible. The General Boards reply came on 23 August 1940 and presented a set of characteristics arrived through the consideration of prospective employment and design possibilities. The Board recommended an 80' wooden boat powered by reliable gas engines capable of 40 knots with a range of at least 500 miles at 20 knots. Armament was to consist of 4 21" torpedoes and tubes, one smoke screen generator, four .50 caliber machine guns in two twin mounts with 5,000 rounds of ammunition per barrel. The Board also recommended a satisfactory radio for operational use and provision stowage for five days

Construction of the boats was definitely approved by the Board, with the suggestion that the Navy build twenty-four of these boats with funds made available by the $50,000,000 for small craft for the fiscal year beginning 1 July 1940. SecNav approved of these recommendations on 23 September 1940.[86]

The Navy signed a second contract with Elco on 17 September 1940, which was slightly modified on 25 September 1940. This contract called for the construction of PT's 21-32 and PTC's 33-44, 77' overall. The PTC clause of the contract was never fulfilled, for unsuccessful experiments with the earlier type had convinced the Navy that other craft would be more successful as anti submarine vessels, and PTC's 33-44 were built as PT's with the same numbers.[87]

---

85. CNO's FF13-1/A4-3 (401216), Serial 236538, 16 December 1940.
86. Form the files of the General Board on PT's, Serial 420-14.
87. SecNav letter PTC 13/5 28-1 (410234) 24 March 1941.

50

AN ADMINISTRATIVE HISTORY OF PT's IN WORLD WAR II
(Recreated October 25, 2010 by the members of the PT Boat Forum message board)

NEW SQUADRON ORGANIZATION

The building of these new boats called for another organizational set up. Squadron ONE included or was to include PT's 1,2,3,4,5,6,7, and 8 in MTB Divisions ONE and TWO. PT 9 was transferred to Squadron TWO which gave that organization PT's 9-19, divided into MTB Division THREE, PT's 9-14, and the MTB Division FOUR, PT's 15-19. A new squadron THREE was proposed, with PT's 20-32, divided into MTB Division SIX, SEVEN and EIGHT. Squadron FOUR was to include PT's 33-44, comprising Divisions NINE, TEN, and ELEVEN. The PTC's were slated for similar administrative organization. The PTC's were slated for similar administrative organization.[88]

UK TAKES BOATS ON LEND LEASE

Squadrons One and Two with the USS Niagara (ex-Mansfield "Hi-Esmare), assigned as a mother ship, wintered in Florida. It was here that the two Higgins built PT's were delivered. Higgins had held out for New Orleans as a delivery point, despite contract specifications stipulating NOB, Norfolk. In an effort to expedite delivery, the Navy met him a little more than half way, and accepted delivery of the boats at Key West. At Key West ordinance installations were made on both boats as far as practicable before their trip north.[89] The boats made the proposed West Indies cruise which furnished a thorough shakedown.

Plans to remain in Florida until May were cut short when, on 26 March 1941, most of the boats were earmarked for immediate transfer to Great Britain. The boats designated for transfer to the United Kingdom were PT's 3, 4, 5, and 7 from Squadron One, and PT's 9 through 15 from Squadron Two. The letter promulgating the transfer stated that enough additional units to raise the total to 19 would be transferred in the near future. This virtually eliminated Squadron One as an operational element, and made serious inroads into Squadron Two.[90] Delivery dates were set in the first two weeks of April, so the boats started north immediately.

The trip was not without color for PT 18 ran aground, PT 8 failed mechanically and was unable to complete the trip, and all power plants except the Packard's had given the boat captains headaches during the entire trip.[91]

FAMILIARIZATION SCHOOL ESTABLISHED

The boats that were not to be transferred to the United Kingdom had only a brief respite at New York. PT's 6, 8, 16, 17, 18, and 19 were ordered to Newport

---

88. CNO's PT/P16-1 (390531) Serial 48238 18 February 1941.
89. CNO's FF 13-1/A4-3 (401216) Serial 13423, According to MTBRon ONE's PT/A4-1 (70) the trip north started upon completion of ordnance installation onPT 5, thereby designating 29 March 1941 as actual completion date for this boat.
90. CNO's EF 13/L11-3 (22) (410326), Serial 90638, 26 March 1941.
91. MTBRon ONE's PT/A41-1 (70), 9 April 1941. 91. MTBRon ONE's PT/A41-1 (70), 9 April 1941.

AN ADMINISTRATIVE HISTORY OF PT's IN WORLD WAR II
(Recreated October 25, 2010 by the members of the PT Boat Forum message board)

51

to assist in the instruction of new personnel. The Niagara, which had reported to Newport, was to be the center of the familiarization school, and was to be under the command of ComMTBRon Two for training work. The school was the first PT training activity per say, and undertook to indoctrinate newly assigned personnel. General instruction in fundamentals, joint maneuvers with planes, drills, and exercises were the essence of the curriculum. Concurrent classes were scheduled for the torpedo station at Newport, beginning on 21 April, and at the Packard Motor Car Company's marine engine plant. [92]

The Naval Fuel Depot at Melville, Rhode Island, agreed to berth a limited number of PT's at its docks. The prime mover in the establishment of this school was ComMTBRon TWO. [93]

ASSIGNMENT OF NEW CONSTRUCTED ELCO 77's

Although the remaining token force from each squadron was assigned to the Niagara and to the familiarization school, it was evident that with the next transfer of boats to the United Kingdom, Squadron ONE and TWO would revert to their paper status. This called for another reorganization and reassignment of new construction. CnO ordered the two squadrons to fit out and accept PT's

Figure 6: Elco 77 foot PT 20

92. Navy Contract No. 79702, paragraph 15(a), 9 December 1940.
93. MTBRon TWO's PT/P11-1 Serial 68, 14 April 1941.

52

AN ADMINISTRATIVE HISTORY OF PT's IN WORLD WAR II
(Recreated October 25, 2010 by the members of the PT Boat Forum message board)

21 through 32 as delivered from the contractor. The new organizational plan gave Squadron ONE PT's 21, 23, 25, 27, 29, and 31; PT's 20, 22, 24, 26, 28, 30, and 32 composed the new Squadron TWO.[94]

HIGGINS BOAT SHOWS SUPERIORITY

The squadrons were anxious to obtain their new boats, so that the squadron commanders could obtain further comparative data, as the offices in the program at that time believed that the extra seven feet added to the Elco's new production would make a considerable difference in operational qualities. In the spring of 1941, the Higgins production PT 6 was acclaimed most enthusiastically by the operating personnel. The enthusiasm for Andrew Jackson Higgins step child began with the Board of Inspection and survey that observed the boat in preliminary trials. This enthusiasm appears to have been contagious and well founded. The board liked the boat because of its improvements over its predecessor, PT 5, which had been turned down as a type by the General Board. PT 6 was recommended as a type, but the CNO withheld judgment pending a comparative test of all types.[96] PT 6 was superior in speed, maneuverability and access within the boat, and had little or no tendency to yaw in a following sea, a characteristic which had been fatal to PT 5's type chances. The strongest demonstration of PT's 6 potentialities came in the trips made with the other boats. PT 6 remained dry, while accompanying boats were taking heavy seas and spray, and in a trip with PT 19, the Higgins built boat was undamaged while the Elco boat showed definite signs of breaking up because of hull failures. Engined with three Packard's, PT 6 was more satisfactory and economic than the Vim alert powered PT 5, which burned 12 gallons to the mile on this trip up from Florida, as compared to 6 gallons per mile for the other Higgins boats.[96]

ORIGINS OF PT 6

PT 6 was the most successful of the boats fathered by the design competition, but its success came through the efforts of its builder rather than its prize winning designer. Higgins ingenuity and designing know-how made a success of a boat whose potentialities appeared limited, despite the fact that the Navy had awarded top prize to Sparkman and Stevens for the design. It was evident to Higgins when awarded the contract that the actual boat would fall short of design expectations, and he sought to have some characteristics modified. The Navy however, was adamant, and Higgins built the boat with a minimum number of changes. It was no surprise to the officials at the New Orleans plant that the boat-tentatively designated PT 6 - was a resounding failure.

94. CNO's PT/A4-3 (410602), Serial 199838, 2 June 1941.
95. CNO's PT6/S8-2 (401220) Serial 95123 14 April 1941. Fifth endorsement to Board of Inspection and Survey's report on trials of PT 6 held 19 and 20 December 1940.
96. MTBRon ONE's PT/A4-1 (70), 9 April 1941.

AN ADMINISTRATIVE HISTORY OF PT's IN WORLD WAR II
(Recreated October 25, 2010 by the members of the PT Boat Forum message board)

53

Figure 7: Higgins PT 6

On his own initiative and with his own capital, Higgins decided to build a modified version of the unsuccessful boat. This modified boat, which officially became PT 6, incorporated Higgins' own designing ideas on strength and speed, and included other major modifications of the original government approved design. Ultimately the new PT 6 was a Higgins designed craft rather than a modified Sparkman and Stevens. When he undertook the PT work, Higgins had a world of experience in design, and his amphibious craft - outgrowths of his "Eureka" bayou boat - were soon to become justly famous. His work in high speed craft steamed back to Volstead days when the Coast Guard and other agencies made extensive use of fast Higgins designed craft.[97]

GOVERNMENT ACCEPTS HIGGINS DESIGN

The success of the craft as compared to the original Sparkman and Sevens designs became evident by comparing Higgins PT 6 with PT 5, the direct product of design competition. PT 6 had rectified most of the faults of PT 5 and had added strength and speed. Its performance was not limited to certain

97. From an interview with Mr. A. J. Higgins

speeds, as in the case of PT 5, and its Packard engine installation proved much more economical. The principle characteristics of Higgins PT hulls was a bottom composed of concave sections of uniform radius from stem to stern on either side of the keel.[98] The Higgins PT was definitely not a planning boat.

The Higgins PT 6 was accepted by the government, while the original PT was shipped to the United Kingdom, with some 70' boats which Higgins began to deliver to the British in 1940.[99]

The existing squadrons were almost cleaned of their original craft when CNO ordered transfer of PT's 9, 16. 17, 18, and 6 to the United Kingdom. PT 19 had previously been ordered to New York for decommissioning.[100] This left PT 8 as the sole survivor of the original boats, although PT 6's transfer date was later changed to allow it to compete its comparative tests.[101]

DELIVERY OF FIRST ELCO 77's

On 2 June 1941, CNO ordered Squadrons ONE and TWO to accept the new boats Elco was building (PT's 20-44) as soon as delivered by the builder. At the time, plans called for delivery without torpedo tubes or machine gun mounts.[102] Elco delivered the first 77' boat, PT 25, to Squadron ONE on 11 June 1941. This could be called the first Elco boat, for although PT's 10-19 had been built by Elco, they were close to the Scott-Paine design, The new boat still incorporated many of the Scott-Paine features, but its seven additional feet made it capable of carrying greater pay loads, and promised to change performance characteristics.

Upon acceptance, the Squadron immediately made a number of suggestions for modifications. The request for self-sealing gas tanks was the forerunner of many similar complaints about the unprotected tanks, and did eventually result in self-sealing tanks for almost all the operational boats. Other outstanding requests made by the Squadron were for increased pilot house visibility, simplified deck house construction, improvement of midships section to eliminate waste space, and a number of ordnance improvements centered around the mechanical turrets, which were to become a definite nuisance on these boats.[103]

BUILDING PROGRAM UNDERWAY

The United States was now started on a building program of homogenous squadrons of PT's. These first Elco squadrons promised easier administration

98. U.S. Patent 2,369,633, 13 February 1945.

99. From an interview with Mr. A. J. Higgins.

100. CNO's EF13/L11-3 (22) 410519, 7 July 1941.

101. ComsMTBRons ONE and TWO joint letterPT/A4-3 (143), 14 July 1941; Op Nav's dispatch 212251 July 1941.

102. CNO's PT/A4-3 (410602) Serial 199838, 2 June 1941.

103. ComMTBRon TWO's PT/S1-1, Serial 256,11 June 1941.

of engineering work, for such repair and modifications problems as existed were bound to be common to all of the boats. The theory of a homogenous squadron was excellent, but the government wanted to be sure that the Elco Company was the best company to build PT's for the government, and a series of comparative tests were scheduled for the month of July. The need for comparative tests was envisaged during the winter of 1940-41, when CNO wrote "standardization of this type for rapid production if the present limited emergency should become more serious, demands the conduct of comparative service tests without further delay". [104] As the months passed and the operating personnel learned more and more about the various types of craft, then need became more apparent.

As CNO had eliminated the production of any further 70' Elco boats, because of their shortcomings , and because of the greater potentialities in the larger Elco boat, the comparative tests promised to be largely a contest between the new Elco's and the Higgins boats. Both boats had their staunch adherents, and comparative tests were the only way for the Navy to shape an intelligent building policy.

Final arrangements were made for the participation of squadron boats in the tests when ComMTBRon ONE asked for facilities a New London for the tender and nine boats: PT's 6, 8, 20, 21, 23, 25, 27, and 29. [105]

---

104. CNO's FF13-1/A4-3 (401210) serial 134223.
105. ComMTBRon ONE's PT/L5-1 (144) 15 July 1941.

56

AN ADMINISTRATIVE HISTORY OF PT's IN WORLD WAR II
(Recreated October 25, 2010 by the members of the PT Boat Forum message board)

CHAPTER THREE

STANDARDIZATION AND QUALIFICATION (THE "PLYWOOD DERBY")

By mid 1941 the Navy had compiled data on its various extant types of PT's, but there was a fallacy inherent in the figures: none of the information, except in one instance, had been recorded with more than one type at a time. Individual data were available on all the boats, but the amount of collective comparative data, which were needed for a proper type evaluation, was almost nil. The one exception was the reports of Squadron TWO on the performance of its boats on the trip from Key West to New York City. The Squadron ONE report was valuable, for the boats reported on were the PT's 5, 6, 7, 8, 18 and 19. To obtain a complete and accurate table of figures on all types, the Navy authorized trials [1] for standardization and qualification to be held on July 21-24, 1941 off New London, Connecticut.

Five primary types of boat were entered for the trials, [2] which later became affectionately known as the "Plywood Derby". [3] Elco entered 77' boats of the

Figure 8: 72' Huckins PT 69

---

1. The trials were conducted pursuant to CNO's restricted letter Op-23D-KM Serial 150323 dated May 31, 1941, and CNO's restricted dispatches 212338/June 281633/June/41, and 051837/July/41.
2. CNO PT/S8 (410621) Op-38-c-LAC/S/20 25 June 41 President, Board of Inspection and Survey to SecNav PT-S8 (1955-8)
3. The purpose of the test was ". . . to crystallize, as far as possible, opinion as to the suitability of the various designs and to establish criteria for future construction . . ."

AN ADMINISTRATIVE HISTORY OF PT's IN WORLD WAR II
(Recreated October 25, 2010 by the members of the PT Boat Forum message board)

57

PT 20-44 class. Huckins, whose boat was first tested by the Navy earlier in the month, entered his PT 69. The Navy itself was represented by PT 8, an all aluminum boat, designed by BuShips. Higgins entered PT 6, his modified version of the first Higgins MTB, PT 5, and as a second entry, PT 70, a new and improved Higgins craft that was soon dubbed the Higgins Dream Boat". A third Higgins entry, a 70 foot PT built by the Louisianan for the British, was entered for comparison only.

TYPE CHARACTERISTICS[4]

PT 6 was built and designed by Higgins Industries, Incorporated, of New Orleans, Louisiana. It was of wood construction with an over-all length of 81 feet, five inches and a waterline of 75 feet, seven inches; its beam was 16 feet, eight inches. Power was supplied by 3 direct drive Packard 4 M engines. Fuel capacity was 3700 gallons, and water capacity was 200 gallons. It was designed to carry two 21 inch torpedoes in stern launching tubes, four 300 pound depth charges or one smoke screen generator, and two .50 caliber machine guns. This

Figure 9: 80' BuShips Designed PT 8

---

4. All information in this section was taken from "A Report of Comparative Service Tests of Motor Torpedo Boats held July 21-24, 1941 and August 11-12, 1941 at New London, Connecticut by a Board of Inspection and Survey." This report was dated August 14, 1941.

boat was produced after the original Higgins - PT 5 - had been tested, and many earlier structural deficiencies were eliminated in PT 6.

The Navy was to make its bid in these trials with a boat built by the Philadelphia Navy Yard - PT 8. 80 feet, eight inches overall and 75 feet at the water line, this entry was powered by a hermaphroditic power plant of Allisons and one Hall-Scott. There were two Allisons of 2000 hp each, but actually they were four 1000 hp engines mounted on two common blocks. The Hall-Scott was only 550 hp, and was used for slower speeds and backing - all engines featured geared drives. As has been mentioned, the hull was of aluminum alloy throughout, and its beam was 18 feet, eight inches. There were tanks for 3000 gallons of fuel and 400 gallons of water. The designed ordnance installation included two 21 inch torpedoes and tubes, one depth charge rack with a capacity of four 300 pound depth charges, one smoke generator and two .50 caliber machine guns.

Elco had entered several boats in the Derby, but all were of the same specifications. The boats were evolved from the Scott-Painc design, and were built by the Electric Boat Company at their Bayonne plant. Constructed largely from plywood, the boats were 77 feet overall with an 18 foot beam. Like the Higgins, the Elcos were powered with three Packard 4 M's (total horsepower 3600), but only one of these engines drove the shafts directly; the wing engines powered the shafts through a Vee drive, 3000 gallons of fuel were carried and 180 gallons of water. The ordnance installation differed in that the boat was designed to carry four 21 inch torpedoes and tubes, and the two twin .50 caliber machine guns were mounted in power turrets of Belgian design. The Huckins Yacht Corporation of Miami, Florida used four Packard 4 M's in a wooden hull 72 feet overall, 70 feet at the waterline and 16 feet, five inches beam. The additional engine gave the Florida boat builder's craft a total of 4800 hp, and there were tanks for 3430 gallons of gas and 250 gallons of water. Offensive equipment was similar to the other boats – two 21 inch tubes and torpedoes, one depth charge rack with seven depth charges (300 pound) or one smoke generator, and two .50 caliber machine guns.

The Higgins "Dream Boat", PT 70, was 76 feet, 2 inches overall and 70 feet, one inch at the water line. Its beam was 20 feet, 10 inches. The boat was designed and built by Higgins, and its power plant was the same as PT 6. Fuel capacity was 4500 gallons and water 250 gallons. Ordnance installations included four 21 inch tubes and torpedoes, two depth charge racks with 10 depth charges and three twin .50 caliber machine gun mounts.

The Higgins British boat was 70 feet long, and built of wood and aluminum alloy. The waterline length was 64 feet and the beam 17 feet, eight inches. The power plant was 3 Hall-Scott 900 hp engines driving directly, and fuel and water capacities were 2400 and 200 gallons. For ordnance equipment the boat was armed with two 21 inch torpedoes and tubes and three .50 caliber machine guns.

AN ADMINISTRATIVE HISTORY OF PT's IN WORLD WAR II
(Recreated October 25, 2010 by the members of the PT Boat Forum message board)

59

THE FIRST "PLYWOOD DERBY"

The Board of Inspection and survey appointed to judge the PT's in these trials had specified as the main test a run of approximately 190 miles at full throttle in open sea. This would give the Board a chance to observe not only the speed of the boats, but also their sea keeping and structural qualities. The Derby was scheduled for the waters off New London and the course specified started at Sarah's Ledge, from there to the eastern end of Block Island, around Block Island to and around Fire Island Lightship, and thence to Montauk Point whistling buoy. The date was July 24, 1941.

The day was not ideal, but the worst conditions encountered were a moderate swell with a cross chop, a wind of Beaufort force 3, 2 visibility, and generally hazy weather. The boats were to carry an ordnance load of 20,600 pounds comprising two 21 inch tubes and torpedoes, depth charges and racks, two twin .50 caliber machine gun scarf ring mounts, and 4000 rounds per barrel of .50 caliber ammunition. The only boats which had the complete ordnance load aboard were the Elco's, while the Higgins Dream Boat (PT 70) had none of the required ordnance installations. The other boats had some equipment but not the complete load.

Figure 10: 70' Higgins MRB's for Britain

To put the boats on an equal footing, those boats lacking equipment were ballasted to simulate a 20,600 pound ordnance load. The ballast could not be displaced as to give horizontal and vertical moments equal to the load simulated, and this created stresses that were not the same as those which an actual ordnance load would have produced. Although this was definitely an unfortunate condition, there was no method of alleviation if the boat s were to be tested with like loads.

There were nine entries in this first test run. Elco entered PT's 20, 30, 31, and 33; Higgins entered PT's 70 and 6 and his British boat; Huckins entered PT 69 and the Navy was represented by PT 8. Six of these boats managed to finish the run. PT's 33 and 70 suffered structural damage and withdrew, and the Higgins British boat developed engine trouble within five minutes after the start of the race and was forced to retire. Elco had strengthened the hull framing and deck of PT 20, removed the throttle stops and installed special 28 inch propellers; PT 30 equipped with standard wheels also had the throttle stops removed. The Board considered the changes in these two boats made them distinct designs, and so they were considered as two additional Elco entries.

Elco captured top honors in the sea run when PT 20 crossed the finish line first with a 39.72 knot average for the 190 mile course. PT 31 was second,

Figure 11: 76' Higgins PT 70

insuring an Elco victory, with 37.01 knots, and the other finishers scaled down to the Navy's entry, PT 8, which completed the course an inglorious last with a low 30.73 knot average. Four of the boats which entered the run suffered structural damage of varying degrees.

PT 70, whose failures forced withdrawal from the race (see supra), suffered a transverse failure of the main deck accompanied by a shear failure of the frames in the same vicinity. A close inspection of the boat after it had left the race revealed separation of the side planking from the frames due to excessive working. In all fairness to the Higgins design, it must be said that the deck failure was largely caused by the unrepresentative moments set up by the ballast used to simulate the ordnance load. As PT 70 had no ordnance equipment aboard, the complete load, 20,600 pounds, was simulated with deck weights. Without a doubt the boat was grossly handicapped by this unnatural load displacement.

One of the Elco entries, PT 30,[5] competing with a complete natural ordnance load, fared little better. Cracks of a dangerous nature developed at frame forty-five from the forward port corner of the engine room hatch to the rail, and at frame fifty-one the after starboard corner of the engine room hatch. One longitudinal stringer splintered, and three engine room hold-down clamps carried away. The support for the port rudder control lever failed, and the engine room canopy was loose and vibrating. Most of these failures can be accounted for by the old system of interrupted longitudinal used by Elco in its early construction. PT 33's[6] engine room canopy cracked, and on 21 July 1941, PT 26[7] had developed deck failures similar to those of PT 30, mentioned here only for general interest, as the 26 boat was unable to compete in the sea run trials.

In an effort to record one of the factors thought to determine speed, the Board installed accelerometers on four of the boats, in order that a comparison of the pounding of different boats in like sea conditions could be made. Data was taken at previously agreed points on the course. PT 8 registered the least pounding with a reading of 2.5 "g's", while PT 20's "g" reading was the greatest – 9.0; an interesting comparison, suggesting at face value an inverse ratio, for PT 20 finished first and PT 8 finished last. PT 69 registered 3.2 "g's" and PT 6, 4.5. Within a boat the pounding would seem to be a function of the speed, but in comparing many boats at the same speed in like sea conditions, pounding must be considered as a function of hull form.

The sea run had provided the Board with a set of new comparative data from which some study could be made, but because of the weighting of some of the boats to create proper displacement, and because of the need for performance data in different type seas, the Board scheduled another sea run for August.

5. MTBRon TWO's Hull Derangement Serial 2-41, 25 July 1941.

6. MTBRon ONE's PT/L11-1(155) 26 July 1941.

7. MTBRon TWO'S Hull Derangement Serial 1-41, 25 July 1941.

HULL TESTS

Previous to the sea run the Board had made a number of inspections and tests on the various hulls. In structural efficiency tests in light weather using five of the boats, PT's 69, 8 and 6 suffered no damage, and PT's 70 and 21 only minor failures. In the rough weather tests PT 70 was extensively damage, but damage was localized in PT's 69 and 21. Once again unrepresentative ordnance equipment cast doubt as to the creditability of this date.

Habitability, access and communications facilities were inspected with no great differences between boats, except for PT 8. The Board was far from favorably impressed with the habitability of this boat. The Board inspected the boat on a hot New England summer's day, and the aluminum hull had not reflected the heat. Consequently, the inside of the boat was stifling, and the hull itself was hot to the touch. In its report the Board made strong mention of this deficiency, and minced no words. In judging the boats for accessibility, sacrifice of access was allowed if necessary for improvements in other categories.

Final inspection consideration was given to the cost of the boats. The two Higgins entries had been the most inexpensive to construct, while the Navy Yard's boat cost almost three times as much as the most expensive of the others. Table of costs:

BOAT	HULL	MACHINERY	TOTAL
6	61,100	70,500	131,600
70	120,000	70,500	190,500
69	118,000	94,000	212,000
*20	157,600	70,000	228,100
8	268,200	413,200	681,400
*Contract price less allowances, less 1/2 cost of one spare engine per boat.			

SPEED TRIALS

While the 190 mile run had determined the ability of the boats to make a maximum sustained speed in an open sea, measured mile speed runs were held at a separate time, with much better results. The boats were tested with both a heavy and a light ordnance load. The heavy load included four tubes and torpedoes, two twin .50 caliber machine gun mounts, 16,000 rounds of ammunition for the .50's and 10 300 pound depth charges.

Elco once again topped the honors. With a heavy load PT 20 averaged 44.1 knots, and with a light load 45.3 knots. The first speed was made at 2196 rpm's and the second at 2264 rpm's; 28 inch propellers were used on both runs.

Figure 12: MTBRon ONE in Miami Florida

PT 26 turned over 44.2 knots at 2287 rpm's with a heavy load, but suffered structural failures and was unable to make a run with light displacement. The Huckins boat make 41.5 knots at 2061 rpm's with a heavy load, and 43.8 knots at 2145 rpm's with a light load. The Higgins (Dream Boat) was the only other craft in the plus-40 knot class, making 40.9 knots at 2492 rpm's with a heavy load, and 41.2 knots at 2501 revolutions with a light load. The other four entries - PT's 6, 25, and 8 and the Higgins British PT – all failed to make 35 knots. PT 25 was unduly handicapped by stops on the carburetor throttles which limited rpm's to 1800. The Navy's entry once again turned in a bad exhibition. PT 8 could make only 31.1 knots at 2218 rpm's and 31.9 knots at 2250 rpm's. In desperation, the Board sanctioned special trials for the boat. All excess weight that could be stripped was removed, and once again the boat chugged over the measured mile grinding out 2331 rpm's for two extra knots or 33.9 knots.

A comparison between rpm's and speed is interesting, but in this case far from conclusive as many necessary determining factors are not recorded. The winning Elco boat was equipped with 28-inch wheels which tend to spin

64

AN ADMINISTRATIVE HISTORY OF PT's IN WORLD WAR II
(Recreated October 25, 2010 by the members of the PT Boat Forum message board)

slower for speed attained than do those with a 26-inch pitch. This accounts for the seeming discrepancy between rpm's and speed when comparing PT 20's performance to PT 70's. PT 70's construction later proved excessively heavy when examined by BuShips architects who removed more than a ton of dead weight inherent in such structural parts as butt joints and blocks. Despite its four engines, which gave it a 250 horsepower edge over its nearest competitor, PT 8, the Huckins entry was unable to beat the Elco boat, powered by only three engines. This would seem to give the Scott-Paine hull design a definite edge over the Florida hull, for with the same pay load, allowing for engine equipment as set forth above, this superior performance of the Elco was undoubtedly a function of hull form. As far as rpm's were concerned, the Huckins boat failed to top the Elco maximum, although the speed-rpm ratios were similar. It is difficult to offer a case that would hold water concerning the reasons for the range of the various boats' speeds, for this was the first test which had used such a variety of craft, and the Board itself probably had little idea of what speed range to expect. The speed results can be considered happy in that four of the boats cracked better than forty knots with heavy displacement, while on the sea run PT 20 fell short of a 40 knot average by only .28 knots.

MANEUVERABILITY TESTS

The Board ran an exhausting series of tests to determine the maneuverability and tactical qualifications of the boats. Rudder throw tests from hard over, full speed to stop, full astern to full ahead, 180 degree turns – all these and more were the hurdles the entries had to attempt. The tests were extensive and demanded top performance of the boats for the Board was anxious to find out the capabilities of a small boat with reversible high speed engines. The propellers on the boats were right hand turning, which made some difference in timing turns to port and starboard, with the starboard turns naturally quicker.

Maneuverability tests brought out the ability of these boats to spin without gaining or losing in a seaway. This maneuver was accomplished from an under way with no way upon condition: for a starboard spin, the port engine was put ahead, the starboard engine astern and the wheel turned hard to starboard. In the combat area this maneuver was utilized many times in snaking the boats out of tight anchorages and docking areas. The Philadelphia boat lagged sadly behind on many of the tests for maneuverability; because its two huge wing engines were unable to reverse, and backing down was accomplished only with the small Hall-Scott.

The most graphic evidence of the boat's ability to maneuver is afforded by the pictures of the boats turning circles. Running at flank speed the boats made a full 360 degree turn, first to port, then to starboard. A blimp from the Naval Air Station at Lakehurst, New Jersey had been assigned to the tests. While the boats ran their circles, the blimp hovered above them and photographed the

AN ADMINISTRATIVE HISTORY OF PT's IN WORLD WAR II
(Recreated October 25, 2010 by the members of the PT Boat Forum message board)

65

circles, as represented by the wake. By considering altitude, focal plane length, and the size of the resultant print, the Photographic Laboratory at Lakehurst was able to compute the boats' turning circles within two yards. Only four of the boats were able to make arrangements for this test, with the Higgins "Dream Boat" and British entry not participating.

Pt 69 turned the tightest circle to port- against the direction of the revolution of the screws, PT 6's turning diameter was shorter when the turning with the screws. This was probably due to the two Higgins rudders, large spade type affairs, which greatly abetted turns to starboard, as they presented a much greater thrust surface for the screws. PT 69 turned the port circle with a diameter of 336 yards, while PT 6 turned the starboard circle with a 256 yard diameter. Conversely, PT 69's diameter for the starboard circle was 274 yards, while PT 6's diameter for the port circle was 368 yards. PT 8's turning circle to port- 443 yards- was the largest diameter recorded, although to starboard the boat turned inside the Elco entry, PT 20, by registering 340 yard to the Bayonne boats' 382. PT 20's 432 yard port circle gave it the worst average of all the boats. Once again this was no doubt due to the rudder arrangement, for Elco boats featured three small rudders, which made for easy, not close handling at high speeds.

The Board was pleased with the results in the maneuverability tests, except in the case of the boats demonstrating the larger turning circles, and, as has been mentioned, with inability of the Navy's PT to reverse its wing engines, which made its maneuverability almost nil, as far as starting and stopping on more than one engine was concerned. It is worthy of note here that PT 8 had no self starters and depended on the Hall-Scott engine to drag in the larger Allisons, a cumbersome procedure not conducive to quick getaways. At the time the tests were made all boats were steered by hand power and hand power alone. Electric hydraulic systems on the boats had proved to be too cumbersome and too treacherous. Earlier in the year, some of the first Elco boats had met with near disaster in the Potomac travelling among ice flows when the electric steering failed, as there was no stand-by manual system.

The blame cannot be held to the steering mechanism alone. For the early 2.5 KW auxiliary generators on the boats were absolutely undependable, and failure of the generators to supply power meant failure of the steering system. All boats installed a chain and rod linkage system of manual steering which soon became standard equipment on the boats. The main difference lay in the number of turns of the wheel from hard over to hard over. Because of its extremely large rudders, compared to the Elco, the Higgins had twice as many turns on its wheel, but this was later remedied by installing reduction gears in the system which allowed a reduction of turns desired. The Board's decision in laying heavy stress on the maneuverability of the boats was borne out time and again in the operating areas, when tight turns to avoid enemy fire were mandatory. The best example of the advantages of maneuverability came during

66

AN ADMINISTRATIVE HISTORY OF PT's IN WORLD WAR II
(Recreated October 25, 2010 by the members of the PT Boat Forum message board)

the 1944 Philippine campaign when a task unit of Higgins boats engaged in battle with Japanese Kamikaze planes, and maneuverability several times save the boats from complete destruction at the hands of suicide pilots.

THE SECOND PLYWOOD DERBY

The sea run held July 24 had been for the purpose of determining sea-keeping qualities and hull strength, but because of the light sea and weather conditions on the 24th, and because of the handicap of extreme compensating ballast on some of the boats in the first run, neither the board nor the contestants were entirely satisfied with the results. The boats had not shown what they could do in heavy weather, and the performance of some of the boats, notably the Higgins entries, did not seem representative to the individual contestants involved.

A second run, moreover, would give not only additional comparative data among the types of boats, but also a good idea of comparison between data on all types on two runs. If the conditions were radically different a second run, the figures would be that much more satisfying, for it would allow an evaluation of performance extremes.

Following the tests off New London, Rear Admiral J. W. Wilcox received a hurry-up note from Admiral H. R. Stark, then Chief of Naval Operations, asking "what next" as far as the Motor Torpedo Boat program was concerned. Wilcox, who had been president of the Board of Inspection and Survey, wrote a memorandum to CNO on 28 July 1941 containing several recommendations.

As the Higgins "Dream Boat" had sustained casualties during the race which made the immediate running of another set impractical., Wilcox placed repairs for this craft at the head of the list. Secondly he suggested lightening the Philadelphia Navy Yard boat by removing all the battleship fittings. The boat that had been fitted out by the Navy Yard with little or no idea of economic weight in mind, and as a result it was greatly overloaded. The hull design was good, but as Wilcox admitted "The Navy boat is good, but too heavy."

Once these two alteration jobs were completed, the President of the Board suggested that the Navy borrow the British owned Higgins PT again, and run this boat, together with the Dream Boat, PT 8 and the Huckins entry, PT 69 in another set of sea trials. "By conducting one more trial as suggested and loading the Higgins boat differently than it was before, we might obtain valuable data with respect to that design."

In concluding his memorandum, Wilcox went out on a limb and suggested to CNO that "if it is necessary to let contracts for more PT's immediately, I suggest letting some to Huckins Yacht Company." The Admiral's conclusion on this matter is extremely hard to justify off hand in that the Huckins had been unable to demonstrate any great speed in the sea run. On the other hand, structurally the Huckins had proved sound, and its turning circle indicated

AN ADMINISTRATIVE HISTORY OF PT's IN WORLD WAR II
(Recreated October 25, 2010 by the members of the PT Boat Forum message board)

67

great maneuverability. Its cost was reasonable, and in the measured mile it had cracked better than forty knots. The one short coming was the action of the boat in a tight turn; for some reason the Huckins would list toward the outside of a turn whereas the other entries heeled toward the inside. This radical action caused some fear as to broaching possibilities in a high sea.

The memo containing the above recommendations was submitted to Admiral Stark who disposed of the letter by scrawling cryptically and strongly across the letter "Push, Get decision and start new boats." And the second Plywood Derby followed less than three weeks later. [8]

August 12 was set for the date of the second sea run, and the course was approximately the same with the exception that in the second run the boats started at Race Rock instead of Sarah's Ledge. This made no change in total distance run. As the other trials, tests and inspections had satisfied the Board, the sea run was the only feature of the first meeting to be repeated.

The Board was not blind to the disadvantages of the boats with simulated ordinance loads in the first Derby, and had urged replacement by the actual weight before the second derby. Contestants made an effort to install complete equipment on all the boats except the British PT which was shortly to be shipped to England with ordinance as prescribed by the United Kingdom. Thus, many of the strains and stresses which previously had set up fallacious moments were eliminated with the installation of actual equipment instead of ballasting weights. Moments for this run could be considered equal.

THE WEATHER

If the Board wanted rougher conditions for the second sea trial, it was not disappointed. Visibility and actual weather were good, and the wind was not heavy – Beaufort forces 2 to 4. The drastic change in the weather came in the change in surface conditions, for in the August go, the sea was lumpy with heavy cross swell. These heavy swells ran from six to eight feet tall, with occasional swells of ten to twelve feet. The heavies and conditions encountered on the run were short steep seas running as high as fifteen feet.

Ordinarily one would suppose that the fifteen foot seas would have been the hardest on the boats, and well they might have with any other craft except PT's, but these hard chinned shallow draft boats have idiosyncrasies which belie this belief. When seas assume proportions of fifteen feet or larger, the boats will climb up one side and coast down the other. Although this glorified chute-the-chute does not make the best conditions in the world, these ea are definitely preferable to a six to eight foot sea.

In the smaller sea the boat tends to pound, for the waves are of too small a magnitude to allow the boats to ride them like so many ships. Instead PT's will

8. CNO letter: PT/88(2111-s) 28 July 1941.

68

AN ADMINISTRATIVE HISTORY OF PT's IN WORLD WAR II
(Recreated October 25, 2010 by the members of the PT Boat Forum message board)

slap continuously, and the effect is much the same on the crew as driving a light car at high speed over the ties of a railroad bed.

When the boats didn't slap in the lesser seas, some of them had a tendency to nose under, with the result that the decks often ran green. Such conditions called for a watertight topside with all topside hatches equipped with watertight fittings. Salt water could spell sudden death for the engines and discomfort and consequent lowering of morals for the crew, and for these reasons the Board was quick to notice any hold-down clamps or deck fitting that failed during the test. Because of the continual punishment the boats took, the fittings had to be good, not ornate but husky, not fancy but strong. There could be no failures, for if boats were caught in an unfavorable sea and cracks developed or some fitting carried away, the force of the water would exploit the weakness, and without a doubt cause further failures of serious consequences.

Because of these reasons the Board had taken especial notice of the transverse decking fractures on the Elco in the first run, and naturally was eager to see what the consequence of a run in a heavier sea would be upon the same boat. In the first run the jogged longitudinal had definitely proved faulty, and a second run would no doubt help the board shape its final opinion. Where the seas had been more or less favorable during the July trials, it became evident the day of the August trial that if there were any structural weaknesses inherit in any of the boats and which had not yet been brought to light, the weather that day would bring them out.

The Results

For the August Derby there were but six entries: the Higgins British PT, the Elco 77 foot designed as exemplified by PT 21, and PT 29, the governments boat, PT 8, hitherto an absolute Jonah, the Higgins "Dream Boat", PT 70, and Huckins four engine PT 69. Five of these six boats completed the run.

Elco made it definite that it was the superior craft for speed when PT 21 crossed the finish line with an average 27.5 knots. Breathing down the Bayonne entry's neck for average speed was the Higgins PT 70 with 27.3 knots. The aluminum-hulled PT 8 was tied with PT 29 for third spot with 25.1 knots and last came the British PT with an average of 24.8 knots for the 190 mile course. PT 69 was forced to withdraw from the trials when heavy seas took their toll on her structure with resultant fractured bilge stringers.

The effect of rougher weather is self-evident in the tabulation of speeds. The first boat, PT 21, was more than 12 knots behind the average rung up by its sister boat in the first run. It proved without a doubt that seas had a marked affect upon the speed of the boats, but it also proved, and this is of much greater relative importance, that the PT's could operate in weather decidedly unfavorable for that type of vessel. The fact that the boats, or at least five of them, did finish the course was extremely heartening for those who had wondered just how the boats would stack up in a heavy sea.

The tests performed with the accelerometers had been of some success in the first run, and the Boar was anxious to obtain comparative "g" readings in the heavier seas. The results were mildly astounding, for PT 8 hit the amazing maximum of 14.5 g's at the same time PT 29 recorded 4.2 g's. PT 29 had been assigned to accompany PT 8 in order that comparative readings could be obtained for any point on the course.

The board was not anxious to accept these readings as final, for the unusually violent motion of the boats made the instruments unreliable, and many of the readings recorded were far in excess of the normal calibrated range of the instruments. Whether or not these reading were accurate, it was self evident that the boats had undergone a severe pounding, for there were a number of personnel casualties, the number on PT 8 during this test indicated that it definitely had no advantage over the other boats.

The report makes only passing mention of these personnel casualties, and there seems to be no list of the injured aboard in any of the reports. Several of the participants in the Derby corroborated the impression that the casualties were more numerous than expected; the worst casualty sustained seems to be a broken leg.

As has been stated, the main purpose of these tests were to obtain comparative data among the different types of PT boats, but to give an added fillip to the occasion, the Board arrange to have a destroyer, DD441, (USS Wilkes) run over the course with the boats. This would give a rather rough but general idea on the comparative potentialities of the two types.

In order that the test be truly representative, the destroyer was notified of the proposed starting hour and instructed to cross the starting line at full speed. The ship was then to maintain the same speed throughout the course. The arrangements were successful and the destroyer sliced over the line at full speed and churned around the whole course without slackening revolutions. Despite this force draft run the destroyer finished only 25 minutes ahead of the first boat. This gave the Wilkes a 29.8 knot average for the course or only 2.3 knots better than PT 21.

The officers conducting the inspection were truly impressed by this performance on the part of the small boats. The effort of the PT's was noteworthy enough to draw from the Board this conclusion in the reports: ". . . . It appears, therefore, that for the assigned mission, modern destroyers possess no sensible advantage over the motor boats (sic) even under sea conditions highly unfavorable for the latter, and that in areas where limited visibility is not unusual, the motor boat might readily prove much more adaptable than the larger vessels within the limitation of their operating ranges."

70

AN ADMINISTRATIVE HISTORY OF PT's IN WORLD WAR II
(Recreated October 25, 2010 by the members of the PT Boat Forum message board)

Although this may have been true in the case of the Wilkes, "sensible advantage" was gained by the destroyers during the next few years when anti-aircraft protection was added and new design forced much greater speeds from these sleek ships. The "limited visibility" factor lost much of its import with improvements in electronics, but in 1943, there was talk of towing PT's from Attu to Paramishiru so that the boats might penetrate the harbor and attack shipping undercover of the more or less ubiquitous bad weather conditions, and then return to Attu under their own power. The distance and the bad water between Attu and Paramishiru made the plan prohibitive at the time, but it might well have been worked out, and would have borne out the Board's prognostications almost to the letter. As it was, the main discordant element in this scheme – distance – was provided for by the addition of "within the limitations of their operating ranges" to the last sentence of the Board.

FINDINGS OF THE BOARD

The Board began its peroration by summing up its finding concerning each of the boats. These were not conclusions nor recommendations, but simply a compilation of the data the Board had accumulated during the July and August tests.

The Board found that the Elco 77 foot boat demonstrated ability to make a maximum sustained speed of 39.7 knots and a maximum speed of 44.1 knots with a heavy ordnance load. The boat's maneuverability was satisfactory except for a large turning circle. Structural weaknesses had resulted in transverse fractures of the deck planking. The cost to the government fully equipped (hull and machinery plus $75,000 ordnance allowance) was $302,100. On the debit side the boat had a tendency to pound heavily in a seaway and its fittings and finish were unnecessarily refined.

The Huckins 72' designed demonstrated a maximum sustainable speed of 33.8 knots and a maximum speed of 43.8 knots with a light ordnance load. Its maneuverability was satisfactory with a good turning circle, and it was able to carry two 21 inch torpedoes and tubes and ten 300 pound depth charges, although structural weaknesses appeared when the bilge stringers fractured. Its fittings and finish were approximate and there was little tendency for the boat to pound in a seaway. The cost of this boat to the government fully equipped was $263,000.

The maximum sustained speed demonstrated by PT 8 was 30.7 knots and the maximum speed was 33.9 knots and this with a light ordnance load. The boat could not maneuver satisfactorily, it pounded too much, and its fittings were too cumbersome and heavy for the type. It was strong and managed to carry two 21 inch torpedoes and tubes and then 300 pound depth charges. The cost to the government was $756,400.

Higgins first entry, PT 6 made a maximum sustained speed of 31.4 knots and a maximum speed of 34.3 knots with a heavy ordnance load. Fittings, finish, structural strength, and maneuverability were satisfactory, and the boat was able to carry four torpedoes and tubes. It had a moderate tendency to pound in a seaway. The cost to the government was $206,000 fully equipped.

The Higgins "Dream Boat" made a maximum sustained speed of 27.2 knots, but this figure is taken from the rough water run. The highest speed with heavy ordnance load was 40.9 knots. Although the turning circle was not photographed, it was estimated at three hundred yards, and otherwise maneuverability was completely satisfactory. This boat also carried four tubes and torpedoes. Although the Board termed fittings and finish satisfactory, it noted that the boat had only a moderate tendency to pound in a seaway, it was designated structurally weak, for there were failures in transverse bottom framing, separation of side planking from framing, and extensive failures of deck fastenings. The cost of this boat fully equipped was $265,500.

Although the Higgins 70 foot design had been built for the British, the Board found from unofficial estimates and information that such a boat could probably be purchased for around $200,000, and consequently entered its findings on this craft. The boat was able to make a sustained speed of 24.8 knots, this was also in the rough seas test, and a maximum speed of 34.7 knots with a light ordnance load. The maneuverability was satisfactory, and although not photographed, turning circle was estimated at 150 yards. The boat carried two 21 inch tubes and fish and its structural strength was judged adequate. It had a moderate pounding tendency and satisfactory fittings and finish.

CONCLUSIONS OF THE BOARD

All the above the Board issued as its findings, and as can be plainly seen is nothing more or less than a recapitulation of information that has gone before. When it came to conclusions, the Board issued only three:

#1. That the Packard power plant has proved highly satisfactory.

#2. That the hulls of these boats have in general demonstrated their ability to withstand operations in a heavy sea to the limits of the endurance of their crews.

#3. That Motor Torpedo Boats are suited only for operations in protected water and in such operations are superior to destroyers. Motor Torpedo Boats should normally operate from a shore base.

The final conclusion is an evidence of the open-mindedness of the board and in itself is extremely visionary. Every phrase of this last conclusion was born out. The boats proved their superiority to destroyers especially with the anti-barge patrols run in New Guinea in 1943 and 1944. Later, in the Philippines the boats, used in protected water, carried out a number of missions it would have been unfeasible for destroyers to undertake; scouting operations close in shore, rescue missions, close strafing and small convoy work. Although tenders were introduced into the PT program, and did prove successful, there is little doubt that a shore base was more efficient and much better for morale.

The personnel casualties sustained during the second sea run were evidently in mind when this report was written, for the second conclusion is qualified by the inclusion of "to the limits of the endurance of their crews." There was some concern at the time about how much punishment the crews of these boats would take, and several ideas á la Buck Rogers were advanced for protective uniforms and harnesses. In the long run, no special PT equipment was adopted for personnel, and the men managed to stand the pounding fairly well. Injuries occurred on the boats, but not with the incidence that the public seemed to expect. If the patrols were of normal length, i.e., no more than twenty-four hours, the crews' stamina saw them through with little or no trouble. Longer patrols had a definite fatiguing effect upon personnel.

The Packard engines were the logical choice for the Board, as the Hall-Scott's and Allisons offerings involved in the tests had not shown themselves superior to the Packard equipped boats. The Packard demonstrated its ability to perform capably either with direct or geared drives.

RECOMMENDATIONS OF THE BOARD

The report on the tests and trials closed with six recommendations which are self-explanatory. Though terse, these six recommendations involved much work, and are the first concrete recommendations that PT builders were able to use as a criterion.

The Board made the following recommendations:

#1. That the Packard power plant having been found highly satisfactory be adopted as a standard for future construction.

#2. That the ordnance installation of future Motor Torpedo Boats consist of two torpedo tubes and torpedoes, depth charges and machine guns.

#3. That the Huckins 72 foot design be considered acceptable for immediate construction.

#4. That the Higgins 81 foot design, suitably reduced in size to carry such ordnance loads as are required by our navy be considered acceptable for immediate construction.

#5. That the Elco 77 foot design be considered acceptable for future construction provided changes in the lines are made to reduce the tendency to pound in a seaway and the structure is strengthened in a manner suitable to the Bureau of Ships.

AN ADMINISTRATIVE HISTORY OF PT's IN WORLD WAR II
(Recreated October 25, 2010 by the members of the PT Boat Forum message board)

73

#6. That the Philadelphia 81 foot boat (PT 8) be stripped of excess weight and be re-engined with three Packard engines."

Thus a firm base was established for future construction of PT boats, a program that was to start moving swiftly within the next few months, and was to establish the United States as the leading Motor Torpedo Boat nation in the world.

CHAPTER FOUR

DEVELOPMENT FROM 1941

The boats that did the fighting in the latter part of World War II were the Elco eighty foot boat and the Higgins seventy-eight foot boat. Although these boats were the most important of the PT"s, there is little on file about their development, for most of the design and specification work was done in off-the-record conferences.

This is not too surprising in that the evolution from seventy-seven feet to eighty feet on the part of the Elco Company and the parallel growth from seventy-six to seventy-eight feet by Higgins Industries is much less significant than the early attempts at designing a PT boat. After the test off New London, the Navy had a good idea of just what it wanted for a PT boat, and by this time the Navy had also had enough experience with various builders to know which firms would be satisfactory as possible constructors for the boats.

At a meeting of BuShips and CNO representatives in the fall of 1941, a decision was reached to enlarge the size of the boats. BuShips was requested by CNO to write up specifications for a new boat, and then to invite representatives of Huckins, Higgins and Elco to Washington for a conference on the possibility of contracting for the boats. Each company was to submit designs and bid for its proposed boat.

The business of changing the design was a rush matter and Captain Swasey and Mr. Peters of BuShips worked day and night for two days drawing up specifications for the projected craft.[1] On 6 October 1941, Captain E. L. Cochrane, USN, called the preliminary conference at the Navy Department.

Buships was represented by Captains Cochrane and Swasey, Commander J. O. Huse, Lt. Comdr. J. C. Guillot, Lt. W. H. Leahy, Mr. S. A. Peters, and Mr. W. C. Karl. The Electric Boat Company (Elco) was represented by Mr. H. R. Sutphen and Mr. Irwin Chase; Higgins Industries, Inc. by Mr. Eaton and Mr. Frank Higgins and Huckins Yacht Corporation by Mr. Baldwin and Mr. F. P. Huckins.

In explaining the reason why it was felt necessary to start on a new design, Captain Cochrane said in part: " . . . Of course we are reluctant to start at this stage of the game in the development of new designs, and yes, that appears to be the best course to arrive at is a point (sic) where we will have the means of satisfactory quantity production, when and if this becomes imperative . . . We

---

1. Conversations with Mr. Sidney Peters, BuShips.

AN ADMINISTRATIVE HISTORY OF PT's IN WORLD WAR II
(Recreated October 25, 2010 by the members of the PT Boat Forum message board)

75

are convinced that the boat isn't big enough to do the things we want it to do, and we need a heavier, more effective, more powerful boat; . . ."

It is evident that BuShips was looking ahead to the possibility of war time mass production of PT"s. The Electric Boat Company (Elco) had shown a complete mastering of the intricacies of high speed mass production of small craft in World War I, when it built and launched 550 ML's in 488 days. The men responsible for this feat – Irwin Chase and H. R. Sutphen – were at the conference, and were prepared to duplicate that production record, only this time with PT's. Higgins Industries were well schooled in the production of landing craft, and the company appeared admirably suited for rapid building of PT's. Although the Huckins Yacht Corporation did not have as extensive experience as Elco and Higgins, its building potential and previous work made the inclusion of the company in the contract conference suitable in the eyes of the Navy.

Captain Cochrane further outlined the background to the meeting and explained what he hoped would be accomplished: "Representatives of the three companies have demonstrated their ability to design and construct these boats, namely, the Electric Boat, The Huckins Yacht and Higgins Industries, and they have been called to discuss the particular requirements in detail. Companies listed above may submit designs which in their opinion conform to the requirements. The Design Division will study the designs and comment upon them; the Shipbuilding Division will then issue proposal for boats in lots of 12, 20 and 32 - - there are 32 boats which funds are immediately available . . . . Each company can then submit bids based on its own design and on the basis of these designs, the Shipbuilding Division can make awards. . .

"Now that was the background behind this meeting. It is a competition not only of building problems but of designing sagacity. . ."

While explaining the purpose of the meeting and the basis for calling it, Captain Cochrane touched once again on problems of production. He called for a boat that would incorporate within its design no novelties or features which could not be readily reproduced in a plant other than the original designer's. In making this request, he was motivated by the knowledge of the effects of bombing on industry in Europe. He desired a plan which would enable the boats to be built in any plant in case of an emergency. He made this point unmistakably clear by saying ". . . we don't want to be put in a position where having once developed the type, something happens to the plant – it may run into fire casualty or something like that – something which has happened abroad in a good many places, and we don't want to be stuck until that plant can build a new plant. . . henceforth, we'll be able to, or must be able to, order boats of any one of the designs built this time from any of the yards. . . "

Thus, although industry was not hit by any enemy attacks during the course of the war, BuShips, two months before Pearl Harbor was gearing the

76

AN ADMINISTRATIVE HISTORY OF PT's IN WORLD WAR II
(Recreated October 25, 2010 by the members of the PT Boat Forum message board)

PT program to a production schedule that could be maintained even if one of the plants had been damaged. Whether or not this plan would have worked successfully once the three plants began producing their own designs is somewhat conjectural, but at any rate, the forehandedness of BuShips in this matter is commendable.

The specifications set up for the boats were general, but had enough stringency so that designs would be similar. The overall length was set at between seventy-five and eight-two feet. Seventy-five feet was considered the smallest overall length that would fulfill BuShips expectations, and eighty-two feet was the maximum length which could be transported easily and successfully.

The power plant was standardized with Packard engines, which had performed successfully with Squadrons ONE and TWO on the Atlantic Coast . Three engines were specified, although Huckins had previously experimented with four. Silent operation at low power was another feature incorporated in the specifications, and this introduced the problem of mufflers. At the time of the conference, Irwin Chase, Elco's designer, was the expert on mufflers, as he had just completed designing three types for the British which were satisfactory to them. The possibility of using an auxiliary for low power operation, with the advantage of less noise, was ruled out. Fuel capacity was set at three thousand gallons, although there was some question of the location of the tanks, and three designers went their own separate ways on that problem.

Trial speed was set at forty knots fully loaded, and this speed was to be sustained for an hour. Accommodations were to be provided for one officer and a crew of eight men, with spare accommodations for one officer, and forty-eight hours supply of provisions. Cruising radius was set at 500 miles.

The ordnance load did not vary greatly from the load already aboard some of the boats. The specifications called for four 21 inch torpedo tubes, four .50 caliber A.A. machine guns; one thirty-two gallon smoke generator, and stowage capacity for 1000 round per barrel of .50 caliber ammunition.

BuShips set up the following specifications for the hull: "The hull shall be the hard chine stepless bottom type with lines formed with a view to minimizing stress on the hull and fatigue of crew under all conditions and to assure a suitable platform for torpedo and gun fire. The lines shall also be formed to insure easy maneuvering of the boat and a small turning circle at full speed and ability to change direction quickly. The sides shall flare outward from chine to gunwale." The Bureau was trying to help the designers to strike a happy medium between too low and too high a chine.

"The hull construction shall be of the lightest weight, consistent with adequate strength, stiffness and durability for the service intended, with an eye to simplicity for mass production." Once again the Bureau is keeping an eye on production methods. The boat that Elco produced as a result of this conference was greatly speeded up in production with "an eye to simplicity for mass production" by eliminating the molded day room which had been a feature of the Elco seventy-seven foot boats.

For the various members of the boat the specifications stated, "The keel, stem and stern post frames, deck beams, longitudinals, clamps, shelves, and chine shall be securely through-bolted or riveted and not screwed. Deck longitudinals and side keelsons shall run continuously the entire length of the boat, as nearly as possible, with adequate butt joints, and no discontinuities. The arrangement of the engine hatches and opening for trunk and cabin house shall be made to suit the deck longitudinals. The side and bottom planking shall be made in two layers mahogany with muslin between. The decking shall be laid in two layers with the upper courses running fore and aft, with muslin between."

This long quotation of technical specifications is important because it reflects clearly the desire of BuShips for a stronger boat. The emphasis on the proper fastening, the elimination of the jogged longitudinal, and primary stress placed upon the importance of a structural deck all point to a stronger boat. But strength alone was not the answer and the double decking with its consequent resilience are indications of the efforts of BuShips to make a better riding boat.

For arrangements the specifications asked for an engine room with forward and after bulkhead and watertight, and with boundary strips connected to the bulkhead and the frame with staggered rivets, which eliminated any unnecessary fastening to the plywood of the hull itself. The engine foundations were to run as far forward and aft in the engine room as possible. Forward of the engine room, the trunk charthouse was to be secured to the hull with through bolts, and the gunwale guards were also to be bolted to the hull and clamps and deep beveled into the flare of the sides.

With the exception of the trunk charthouse the boats were to be flush decked, as it was believed that this gave the best arrangement with the greatest extend of effective deck material and the best arrangement for the operation of the boats at sea. The bridge was to be located directly behind the charthouse, and was in effect a part of the charthouse. A wheel was to be installed on the port side, with throttles and tachometers near the wheel, with a windshield in front of the whole bridge. The machine gun turrets were to be within easy communication, and preferable near the after end of the bridge.

The matter of fittings, location of equipment in the chartroom, furnishings of the living spaces, arrangement of clutch signals, etc., were also generally covered by the specifications.

The Bureau included two items at the end of the specifications which more or less qualified some of the ideas which had gone before. The first had to do with possible changes in the boats: "Tactical employment of certain of these

Figure 13: Turning an Elco PT during construction – both Elco and Higgins hulls are constructed upside down and then righted for completion

craft may make it desirable to effect a substitution by the installation of depth charges and racks. It is necessary to keep this in mind when constructing the boat. It is to be noted that only one outside steering and control station is called for instead of the inside and outside locations that have been commonly used." This meant that the torpedo tubes should be readily removable if the need for installing depth charges should arise.

The second general requirement amplified methods and materials to be used in the job of building: "Utmost care must be taken to secure highest quality workmanship in fitting and fastening the hull structure to prevent working of joints. Everdur or equivalent bronze shall be used and fastening holes shall be suitably drilled to assure tight fit without unduly bruising wood fibers. The use of resin base waterproof glues in making up good joints is invited. Casein based glues will not be accepted. Metal fastening into end grain or into the edges of plywood will not be accepted."

The three companies were invited to adapt their plans to suit the specifications, and then to submit plans and a bid to BuShips. In an effort to straighten out any misunderstandings and to answer any new questions, BuShips representatives met individually with each of the designers on 6 and 7 October 1941.[2]

As a result of this conference, Higgins was awarded a contract for PT's 71 thorough 94 and Huckins was scheduled to build PT's 95 through 102. These contracts were let before Pearl Harbor, and comprised the entire thirty-two boats for which funds were available. Immediately after the beginning of the war, the Navy Department let a large contract to Elco for PT's 103 through 196, and these boats and their successors were to become the preponderant type in the operating areas.[3]

Elco led the way in production by turning out its first new squadron, FIVE, in the late spring of 1942. Higgins followed with his initial outfit, Squadron THIRTEEN, in the fall of 1942. Huckins first squadron, FOURTEEN, was commissioned in February 1943 and went to Panama, where Squadron FIVE was on duty. Huckins completed his building program with Squadron TWENTY-SIX, and none of these boats were ever used in combat work.[4]

As these types were not developed until after Pearl Harbor, the "Expendables" in the Philippines and the boats at Pearl Harbor at the time of the attack were seventy-seven foot Elco boats of Squadrons ONE and THREE. On 31 January 1942, the General Board adopted the Elco PT 103 class as a standard for any increased building.[5]

With three new types of boats and with the old seventy-seven footers still in service there was bound to be a difference of opinion regarding the merits of the boats, and although this matter was never definitely settled in the minds of many of the officers in the PT program, several efforts were made to determine which of the boats was superior.

In reply to a letter from VCNO,[6] the Commanding Officer, MTBSTC, made a survey of the relative suitability of the types of PT boats in use as of 7 September 1942. As a criterion he took the opinions of experienced motor torpedo boat officers under his command who had had the opportunity to observe the capabilities of the four major types – the eight-foot Elco (PT 103 Class), the seventy-seven foot Elco (PT 59 Class), the seventy-eight foot Huckins (PY 95 Class) and the seventy-eight foot Higgins (PT 71 Class).

There was some difference of opinion as to whether the eighty-foot Elco boat was an improvement over the strengthened and reinforced boats of the PT 59 Class. The consensus, however, considered the boats in the order given above. In an effort to sum up the factors involved in the decision, the Commanding

2. The foregoing is from the minutes of a meeting held 6 October 1941 at the Navy Department.
3. Conversations with Mr. Sidney Peters, BuShips
4. Op-414-C-4 control cards.
5. GB No. 420-14 (Serial No. 202) 31 January 1942.
6. VCNO restr. Ltr. OP-23D-MEM/SO S241046; Serial 284323 of 24 Aug. 1942.

Figure 14: Higgins Production Line

Officer, MTBSTC offered the following arguments for the PT 59 Class boat: It was lighter and smaller, and consequently easier to transport; it was three to five knots faster; it had a longer cruising radius; its shallow draft allowed the boat access in shallower waters; the silhouette was lower, and acceleration was faster. The advantages of the PT 103 class were a heavier and stronger boat, probably permitting higher sustained seeds in rough seas; softer riding and drier; firepower ahead; smaller turning circle; superior arrangement of below deck spaces; and armor on the steering station.

As it was the unanimous opinion of the officers consulted at Melville that the PT 71 Class and the PT 95 Class were decidedly inferior in every respect to either of the two Elco classes, the Commanding Officer felt that if eighty feet was to be adopted as a standard size, the PT 103 Class was the most likely candidate.

To support his contention he claimed that not only would adoption of the 103 Class standardize the type, but it would also standardize training, maintenance, equipage and spare parts, interchangeability of parts, manufacture of equipment, and procurement of material.

AN ADMINISTRATIVE HISTORY OF PT's IN WORLD WAR II
(Recreated October 25, 2010 by the members of the PT Boat Forum message board)

81

In arriving at the conclusion that the Higgins and the Huckins products were decidedly inferior to the Elco boats, the report considered speed, silhouette and target presentment, arc of gun fire, arrangement and accessibility of below deck spaces, workmanship and machinery installation, displacement and cruising radius and stability.

In the matter of speed, preliminary trials in 1942 indicated that with a full military load, the PT 95 type was one to three knots slower than the PT 103 type, and the PT 71 class was from eight to ten knots slower. Both PT 71 and PT 95 has larger silhouettes than PT 103, and of the three, the "cigar box" profile of PT 95 was the largest.

The criticism of the arc of guns on both the Higgins and the Huckins boats was based on the inability of the boats to bring firepower to bear dead ahead. On the PT 71, gunfire could not be brought to bear within about thirty degrees on each side of the bow except at high angles of elevation. On the PT 95, fire could not be brought to bear within about twenty degrees on either bow, while on PT 103 fire could easily be brought to bear dead ahead.

Arrangement of the below deck spaces on the PT 103 Class had always been an outstanding feature of these boats. Accommodations for personnel were roomy and comfortable, and the arrangement of spaces for communications, navigation and engine operation was considered superior. The bilges in the boats of this class were also much more accessible for inspection and cleaning.

The main difference in the below deck spaces presented itself in the fact that all compartments in the two Elco boats were connected while on the Higgins and Huckins boats, it was necessary to come topside to enter different compartments. The Elco compartments were connected by a series of watertight doors, and this arrangement was felt to be much better.

The officers consulted in the preparation of the report submitted by MTBSTC felt that the workmanship and the materials in the PT 103 class stood out as superior to those used in the other boats. On the boats on the PT 103 type electrical wiring was enclosed in gas type conduits; bonding was used to route to eliminate sparking and reduce radial interference; and hull construction showed great care and consideration of safety factors and a successful effort to eliminate excess weight. None of these claims was brought forth for the Higgins and Huckins boat.

PT's 95 and 103 were of the same displacement - 106,000 pounds - but PT 71 displaced 126,000 pounds. The extra ten tons on PT 71 showed up in the cruising radius of the boats, for while PT 103's radius was seventy-five miles greater than PT 95, the Elco boat had a 150 mile advantage over PT 71. In considering maneuverability, the report pointed out that although PT 71 had the smallest turning circle, it was considered less maneuverable in view of its low top speed. The turning circles of PT's 95 and 103 were approximately the same, but the Huckins boat exhibited a tendency towards instability and top-

Figure 15: 78' Huckins PT 95

heaviness, evidenced by an outboard heel on full rudder turns.

Thus, the report demonstrated logically that PT 103 was superior in speed, silhouette and target presentment, arc of gun fire, arrangement of below deck space, workmanship and machinery installation, displacement and maneuverability and stability. Several changes were recommended on the 103 type in an effort to improve its already superior military characteristics. The hull design was satisfactory, but in order to reduce the silhouette, the report recommended a reduction in length to seventy feet. Also on the recommended list were the installation of auxiliary tanks for 1000 gallons of fuel in the crews day room; the installation of a light 20mm gun mount; removal of steering station armor and replacement with lighter, better grade armor; the installation of radar, and Mark 13 torpedoes; the installation of a satisfactory compass; and the modification of several pieces of engineering equipment.

In commenting on the Huckins PT 95 type, the report suggested first an improvement in the strength of the hull and the deck and its stability, coupled with a reduction in the size of the silhouette. Mark 13 torpedoes, radar, and a light 20mm gun mount were recommended for the Huckins as well as for the Elco. Smaller details included the removal of superfluous luxury equipment – showers and electrical fresh water pumps for the lavatories – and the semi-enclosed canopy on the steering station. This canopy was to be replaced with a low windshield.

As for the Higgins boat, the Commanding Officer, MTBSTC felt that the best thing to do was to forget it. He felt that a redesign of the hull was required since so much of the weight was concentrated in the hull structure.

In advocating redesign he did not men alteration, for he felt that efforts to alter the type would not achieve the necessary results. He recommended that the boats of that class be converted into PC vessels for inshore and offshore patrol.

The conclusion of the report included some interesting comments concerning the effect of torpedo supply on the development of the boats:

"In commenting on the suitability of Motor Torpedo Boat types and changes in design to improve their military characteristics, it is considered appropriate to point out that the increase in their size and length from the original 70 feet to the present 80 feet has gained little and lost much in their capabilities. The real reason for the increased size, length and displacement is not known. It is believed that one dominating factor was because our Navy has no satisfactory lightweight 18 inch torpedoes, for which the original 70 foot boats were designed to carry for, and it was felt a larger boat was necessary to carry the larger, heavier 21 inch torpedoes. This apparently led to the construction of the 77 foot boats, and later the 80 foot boats, all of which now carry four (4) Mark 8-3c&d torpedoes. (These torpedoes are very slow, extremely heavy except in explosive content, and of quite long range.) This development has adversely affected the capabilities of our Motor Torpedo Boats in reducing those vital qualities which insure effectiveness, namely speed, acceleration, maneuverability and cruising radius. It is believed that a 70 foot boat constructed along the same lines as the PT 103 and carrying four Mark 13 torpedoes, together with the present gun armament, would be a more effective weapon than anything developed to date.

The need for extremely long range torpedoes on Motor Torpedo Boats cannot be visualized. In order to deliver an effective attack, these boats must drive in to short decisive ranges, whether it be under conditions of high or low visibility. They will be most effective during darkness or low visibility, where it has been proved possible for them to get into decisive ranges, in view of their high speed and small silhouette. The Mark 13 torpedo is relatively fast and light, carries a high explosive charge and requires but a small portion of deck space. It seems to be the ideal torpedo for these boats. Four of these torpedoes carried on board would result in savings of approximately 5000 lbs. in weight from torpedoes alone, and considerable more in the shorter torpedo tubes that would be required." [7]

---

7. The foregoing was quoted from or based on CO, MTBSTC's NC129/S82 Serial 303 (jhb), 2 September 1942.

84

AN ADMINISTRATIVE HISTORY OF PT's IN WORLD WAR II
(Recreated October 25, 2010 by the members of the PT Boat Forum message board)

COMPARATIVE TESTS IN 1943

More than a year went by after the Commanding Officer, MTBSTC made his report on the various PT types before a Board of Inspection and Survey conducted official comparative test with an eighty foot Elco boat and a seventy-eight foot Higgins boat. The trials were run in the open sea off Miami Beach, Florida on 4, 5, and 6 November 1943, and the report of these tests was somewhat different from the Melville survey in its conclusions.

Two boats were obtained from the current production of each builder. The Elco Company was represented by PT's 552 and 553, and the Higgins outfit was represented by PT's 295 and 296. One boat from each builder was equipped with Packard W-8 engines, and the other boat was fitted with Packard W-14 engines. Just before the trials all boats were docked for bottom inspection, and a fresh coat of Coperoyd bottom paint was applied to each boat.

The bottoms themselves were in excellent condition. Daily checks insured a full military load on each boat, and recorded displacements. Where actual military equipment was not available, adjustments of fuel and personnel compensated for the difference. The Elco boat carrying 2500 gallons of gasoline, four torpedoes with warheads in side launching racks and a full allowance of machine guns and ammunition was taken to be the standard reference load. The boats equipped with W-14 engines also ran tests at lighter displacement with the torpedoes removed, thus simulating the conditions that might be expected to exist upon the completion of an attack mission. The purpose of using the two displacements was to develop data which would indicate possible differences in performance between a fully loaded boat and one conduction evasive maneuvers after an attack.

When ready for the tests, the Higgins boat with the W-8 engine (PT 296) displaced 106,500 pounds, while the similarly equipped Elco boat (PT 553) displaced 106,000 pounds. The W-14 equipped Higgins displaced 105,100 pounds at heavy displacement and 94,300 pounds at light displacement. The readings for the Elco boat with the W-14 power plant were 106,000 and 94,500 pounds for similar displacements. For the endurance runs the displacements were PT 296, 106,100 pounds; PT 553, 105,700 pounds; PT 295, 104,600 pounds; and PT 552, 105,900 pounds.

Elco, Higgins, Packard, and BuShips were all represented at the trials, and at the conclusion of the tests, both Elco and Higgins expressed their satisfaction with the manner in which the trials had been conducted. Besides the company and Bureau representatives, Commander A. R. Montgomery, USN, OIC of PT Shakedown, SCTC Miami, Florida and Lieut. Commander D. J. Walsh, USNR, Commanding Officer MTBSTC were on hand to witness the trials.

The trials included tests for acceleration, retirement maneuvers, reverse course at top speed, turning tests (complete turning circle), speed tests over a measured mile, and a fuel economy run of 77.6 miles.

AN ADMINISTRATIVE HISTORY OF PT's IN WORLD WAR II
(Recreated October 25, 2010 by the members of the PT Boat Forum message board)

85

REPLACEMENT PHOTO - FROM "AT CLOSE QUARTERS"

Figure 16: 78 foot Higgins PT

Both Higgins boats showed superiority over the Elcos in acceleration, retirement maneuver, reverse course at top speed, and in turning tests at speeds of 600 rpm, 2000 rpm and full speed. The success of the Higgins boats in the turning tests came largely as a result of the large rudders which are a distinctive feature of the boats while the Elco boats were equipped with rudders of a much smaller area. In the acceleration tests, the difference in equipment once again should be taken into consideration, for the Elco boats were equipped with 28 x 29 or 28 x 29.1 propellors on the wing shafts and a 28 x 28 propellor on the center shaft, while the Higgins boats mounted 29 x 26 propellors across the board.

The speed tests were a different story. The Elco boat with the W-8 installation turned up to 40.00 knots at 2272 rpm's, and 42.5" mg, while its Higgins running mate was clocked at 41.49 knots at 2355 rpm's and 43.3" mg. The Elco was the faster of the two boats mounting W-14 engines, registering 45.14 knots at 2658 rpms and 50.1" mg. The W-14 Higgins boat recorded 43.90 knots at 2615 rpms and 49.2" mg. In the light displacement check run, the Elco

86

AN ADMINISTRATIVE HISTORY OF PT's IN WORLD WAR II
(Recreated October 25, 2010 by the members of the PT Boat Forum message board)

again outran the Higgins, and its speed over the mile was 45.83 knots at 2679 rpm's and 50.2" mg, while the Higgins boat went the distance at an average speed of 44.91 knots at 49.4" mg. and 2626 rpm's.

On the fuel economy run the Higgins PT 295 used 5.80 gallons of gasoline per mile as compared to its competitor's 6.25.

This gave the PT 552 an estimated cruising radius of 480 miles at 27.71 knots and PT 295 a radius of 491 miles at the same speed. The W-8 boats were a little closer in fuel consumption; PT 296 burned 5.93 gallon per hour and PT 553, 6.18 gallons per hour which gave the boats cruising radii of 485 and 481 miles respectively.

The Board drew several pertinent conclusions from the data which it had gathered during these tests. As there was no substantial difference in displacement between the boats carrying full military loads, the Board concluded:

"In the speed tests . . . no significant difference between hull designs could be detected . . . the hull making the higher speed showed higher average engine rpm and higher manifold pressure, indicating that engine performance was the controlling factor in this test.

"In the fuel economy run . . . the Higgins boats showed somewhat lower fuel consumption per mile . . . However the validity of these figures may be open to question since the calibration of tanks and measuring sticks was not checked and levelometers were demonstrated to be unreliable. . . .

"In the acceleration test . . . the Higgins boats indicated that engine revolutions increased faster than in the Elco boats. This might have been expected in view of the lower pitch of the propellors on the Higgins boats. However, this test was not considered conclusive, and the boats with W-14 engines were therefore run over a measured course. The times to pass fixed marks indicated no significant difference in boat acceleration, and confirmed the previous observations that engine acceleration in the Higgins boats is greater than in the Elco boats, though in the second test the difference was not as marked as in the first.

"In all tests involving turns the Higgins boats demonstrated an ability to turn more quickly than the Elco boats."

Not satisfied to base its conclusions on what had taken place at the trials, the members of the Board queried veteran officers as to their opinions on various aspects of boat operation which the trials did not bring out. The consensus showed that visibility from the conning station on both boats was limited, but that in this matter the Elco was the superior of the two. The officers consulted also pointed out that the Higgins was somewhat rougher riding than the Elco, and much wetter at low speeds in rough water, with consequent reduction in the effectiveness of conning. The silhouettes on both boats were

Figure 17: 80 foot Elco PT

held to be too large, and all officers pointed out that a differential of eight to ten knots was to be expected between trial and operating speeds.

The officers present with the most comprehensive war experience suggested that the essential characteristics of a PT boat should be sneak ability, torpedo punch, ability to get away (which meant a service speed of forty knots and consequently a trial speed of around fifty knots), as great a cruising range as possible with full military load (1000 miles at about twenty to twenty-two knots was suggested), an auxiliary battery of two twin .50 caliber mounts and one .20 mm mount, unrestricted vision from dead ahead to at least thirty degrees abaft either beam for all personnel at the conning station, seaworthiness, and only emergency living quarters and facilities.

The Board was of the opinion that all of the boats tested fulfilled contract provisions and that the only substantial difference between the two types lay in the shorter turning time of the Higgins boat. The Board suggested that turning characteristics of Elco boats be studied in an effort to improve this shortcoming. Finally, the Board stated that although both types lived up to contract specifications, neither of the types matched the performance of the Higgins experimental seventy foot boat PT 564. (More appears about this boat

88

AN ADMINISTRATIVE HISTORY OF PT's IN WORLD WAR II
(Recreated October 25, 2010 by the members of the PT Boat Forum message board)

later in the chapter.) The Board said of the PT 564 "That vessel much more nearly approximates those characteristics, and appears to embody substantial improvement over current models. It is recommended that both builders be invited to develop designs to meet the essential characteristics set forth above, and that the improved designs replace current construction at the earliest possible date."[8]

These tests proved the worth of the Higgins seventy-eight foot boat which had been highly criticized, and the type continued in production, although not on such a large scale as the Elco eighty foot boat.

COMPANY PROJECTS

Although Elco and Higgins production was confined to the eighty and seventy-eight foot boats for the rest of the war, both companies experimented with modifications on their successful design. The Elco Company altered the bottom design of their boats by adding a series of five steps, while Higgins designed an entirely new boat. For various reason neither of these types was put in production for combat use, but they are worthy of consideration here as examples of the efforts of these two companies to improve their products.

There had been feeling among PT officers that the boats could be made smaller and still serve their purpose with no loss of efficiency,[9] and in an effort to achieve a satisfactory design Higgins submitted plans for a seventy foot boat, known unofficially as the Higgins "Hellcat", to BuShips. It is interesting to note that although Higgins and Elco had been through an evolutionary period during which both companies increased the length of their boats, that the overall length of the new Higgins was the same as the original Scott-Paine boat.

THE HIGGINS "HELLCAT"

Higgins launched the boat in March and gave it its first trials on Lake Pontchartrain 30 June 1943. At this time the company had no contract from BuShips for the boat, and it was still the property of Higgins Industries, Inc. These trials were witnessed by officers from the PT Shakedown Division of the Submarine Chaser Training Center, who were extremely enthusiastic about the boat's potentialities.

In a report to CotCLant, one of the officers who witnessed the trials summed up the qualities of the boat neatly:

"The three vital characteristics of a PT boat are: (a) SNEAK ABILITY; the ability to reach attack position undetected; (b) TORPEDO PUNCH; four fast torpedoes with large warheads; and (c) SPEED; giving the boat the ability to get

---

8. The foregoing quotations and information were taken from Board of Inspection and Survey, RLP, PT/ S8(4657-S) Serial 197721, 7 November 1943.

9. VOPNAV conf. ltr. file Op-23D-MEM (SC) LU-3/PT serial 04654323 of 9 October 1943.]

AN ADMINISTRATIVE HISTORY OF PT's IN WORLD WAR II
(Recreated October 25, 2010 by the members of the PT Boat Forum message board)

89

away. The "HELL CAT" has all three of these vital requisites. First, the boat has "SNEAK ABILITY", extremely low silhouette, good idling speed (about 12 knots) with very little wake, effective mufflers at idling speed, and clear vision almost 360 degrees.

Second, the boat when equipped with four side-launching Mark 13 torpedoes will have "TORPEDO PUNCH". Third, the boat has "SPEED". This together with the Fu smoke she carries enables her to outrun and elude any enemy vessel encountered. The present PT boats now being built with their doubtful 33 knots have none of the above three requisites. (They could have "Torpedo Punch" if quipped with proper torpedoes.)"

During these tests the boat (which was 70'6" long, 17'10" at the widest point, and 5'9" in draft) turned up forty-six knots at top speed, and was able to reverse course in nine seconds, while a similar turn at top speed on a seventy-eight foot Higgins boat took twenty-two seconds. The trials were conducted with a full military load, and the boat was powered by three 4M 1350 hp Packard engines. [10]

The Commanding Officer, Submarine Chaser Training Center, Miami was strongly impressed by the report of the trials, and urged CotCLant to take steps to bring about cancellation of the contract for the Higgins seventy-eight foot boats in favor of the new seventy foot type boat. [11]

CotCLant, in turn, referred the matter to MTBSTC for comment by the Commanding Officer, [12] who concurred with the remarks made concerning the lack of "Sneak Ability, Torpedo Punch and Speed", especially as far as the Higgins and Huckins types were concerned. He said in part: "The increase in size of PT's from 70 to 80 feet has resulted in adding more equipment and armament to a point where present boats are actually a combination motor torpedo and gunboat. This increase in size and load has been effected without an increase in engine power, resulting in larger silhouette, sluggishness, loss of speed and maneuverability."

He closed by adding that the Higgins Hellcat appeared to have most of the basic requisites of an effective PT boat, and that at any rate the seventy foot boat "would undoubtedly be a great improvement over the present Higgins 78 foot type." [13]

COMINCH directed that arrangements be made to test the boat at Miami, and asked VCNO to appoint a Board of Bureau representatives conversant with motor torpedo boat requirements to determine the service capabilities of the boat and to make recommendations concerning its procurement and adoption

---

10. Lieut. Comdr. A. R. Montgomery's ltr. NC130/L6-2 to CocTLant, 5 July 1943.
11. Commanding Officer, Submarine Chaser Training Center's 1st Endorsement (Serial 0905) to above letter; 7 July 1943.
12. COTCLant's Second Endorsement to above letter; COTCLant/L5, (11-ww), Serial 01002,14 July 1943.
13. CO, MTBSTC's Third Endorsement to ltr. cited in footnote No. 10, Serial 0-64(rmf), 21 July 1943.

as a substitute for the seventy-eight foot Higgins boat.[14] On 26 August 1943 the Navy purchased the boat for $100,000 and ordered Higgins to deliver it for tests before 19 September 1943.[15]

From 9 to 13 September 1943, a Board of Inspection and Survey conducted tests to determine service capabilities of PT 564, as the Hellcat had been designated. The tests were made with PT 282, a seventy-eight foot Higgins boat, for comparison. Displacement of the boat was approximately 80,000 pounds, and on its best run, 13 September 1943, the 564 attained a speed of 47.825 knots.

Although no rough water was encountered during the tests, the Board was able to draw comparisons between the two Higgins boats. The seventy foot boat averaged 47.8 knots on a full throttle run as compared with 40.12 knots for the seventy-eight foot boat; the seventy foot boat was more maneuverable than the seventy-eight foot boat; the smaller boat required less material and was cheaper and quicker to build; the elimination of the galley, refrigerator and other equipment was considered justifiable in the seventy foot boat, as it was felt that emergency rations could be used for extended operations; the bridge of the seventy foot boat was considered superior to that of the seventy-eight foot boat in regard to visibility and lowered superstructure; and the silhouette of the seventy foot boat was less than the seventy-eight foot boat, especially in the bow-on or stern-on views.

The seventy foot boat was equipped to carry 4000 gallons of gas as opposed to 3000 on the seventy-eight foot boat, and this greatly extended the cruising radius of the smaller craft.

The Board recommended rough water tests of the boat, and if those tests proved successful, the Board further recommended that the seventy foot boat be put into immediate production and that construction of the seventy-eight foot Higgins boat be stopped.[16]

The general effect of the trials was favorable to a change from the seventy-eight foot boat, and the Commanding Officer, MTBSTC wrote "The trials (of PT 564) were observed by the undersigned . . . . In the opinion of this command, it is far superior to any PT boats in service."[17] BuShips, in a more conservative tone, offered: "If the operating forces are assured that a smaller, faster boat is required and are satisfied to accept the lesser armament and accommodations which can be built into a smaller boat, the Bureau is assured that Higgins and other PT boat builders could build such a boat."[18]

---

14. COMINCH Fifth Endorsement to ltr. cited in footnote No. 10, COMINCH File FF1/S1-1PT, Serial 02742, 12 August 1943.

15. BuShips PT564/L4 (155sa) 26 August 1943. 16. Board of Inspection and Survey's PT564/S8 (3831-5) Serial 159821, 13 September, 1943.

17. CO, MTBSTC's NC129/S1, Serial 0114 (glb).

18. BuShips C-PT/S1-1 (516b), 15 November 1943.

AN ADMINISTRATIVE HISTORY OF PT's IN WORLD WAR II
(Recreated October 25, 2010 by the members of the PT Boat Forum message board)

91

Commander A. R. Montgomery of the PT Shakedown Center at Miami wrote: "It is urgently recommended that construction of the PT 564 Class be started immediately and that all construction of 78 foot and 80 foot boats be stopped as soon as changeover in construction can be affected."[19]

But despite all this enthusiasm, the future of the 564 as a prototype for a new class of PT's was short-lived. At a conference at the Navy Department on 23 November 1943, representatives from the headquarters of COMINCH, CNO, BuShips, BuOrd, CotCLant and the I.C. Board met to discuss the possibility of producing this boat in numbers. The change was finally turned down as "it was considered undesirable to proceed with the design of an entirely new type PT."[20]

This decision could be criticized sharply, for as a torpedo boat PT 564 was certainly superior to the extant type, as reports quoted above have indicated. But the conditions in the field must be taken into consideration when drawing conclusions on this decision. At the time, PT's were encountering heavy barge traffic in all South Pacific areas, and it would have been impossible to equip the 564 with heavy enough guns to put the boat in the same class with PT's then operating, which were, in effect, fast gunboats. Another section of the report of this conference stated that no immediate changes were envisaged in enemy operating techniques, and with these conditions in mind, the abandoning of production plans for PT 564 seems logical if the type was to be used as a gunboat, but a token construction of pure torpedo boats might have been authorized.

The fastest run ever made by any PT and the quickest turns ever made at high speed were undoubtedly accomplished by Elco's PT 487, which hit 55.95 knots during trials for the Board of Inspection and Survey, and made a 180 degree turn at top speed in about six seconds – a turn so fast that at its completion the boat had sternway on! The secret of this amazing performance was the addition by Elco of five steps to the bottom of a standard eighty foot boat.[21]

The tests on the boat took place on 26 December 1943, and although this was the first time that a PT had ever been equipped with Elcoplanes, as the steps were named, the principle of multiple steps on Elco boats had been conceived more than thirty years before. On 14 January 1913, Irwin Chase, Elco's design genius, was granted a patent for a hydroplane-boat which was "a boat comprising a buoyant hull having an unbroken surface skimming hydroplane, secured to said bottom surface . . . " The sketches accompanying the patent show a boat with a series of steps similar to those employed on the PT boat thirty years later.[22]

19. Commander A. R. Montgomery's letter NC130/S8-2, 18 September 1943.
20. Record of conference on 23 November 1943. 21. Board of Inspection and Survey's PT487/S8(6154-S) Serial 230821, 16 December 1943.
22. U. S. Patent 1,050517.

Figure 18: Detail of Elco Plane on PT 487

Newark Bay was the scene of this record run, which was part of general standardization and maneuvering trials. The 487 was equipped with three Packard W-14 engines, and was tested twice, once with a displacement of 109,300 and once with a displacement of 90,300. It was on a light displacement run that the boat hit the high figure, although on a heavy displacement run the 487 turned up 53.62 knots.

The Board was impressed by the performance of the boat equipped with the Elcoplanes, and in one section commented: "Running at top speed, threw helm hard over and reversed course. Turning both right and left, the boat turned 180 degrees in about 6 seconds, and completed the turn with sternway on. At all times during the turn, the boat banked inboard. The performance in this maneuver was spectacular." The boat went on to impress the Board with these results: Maximum speed was increased by about eight knots; maximum engine speed at heavy displacement was increased by 120 rpm and by 170 rpm at light displacement; engine acceleration was greatly increased; turning time (for 180 degrees) was decreased; and manifold pressures were lower than those on the standard Elco boat at comparable speeds, except for full power operation.

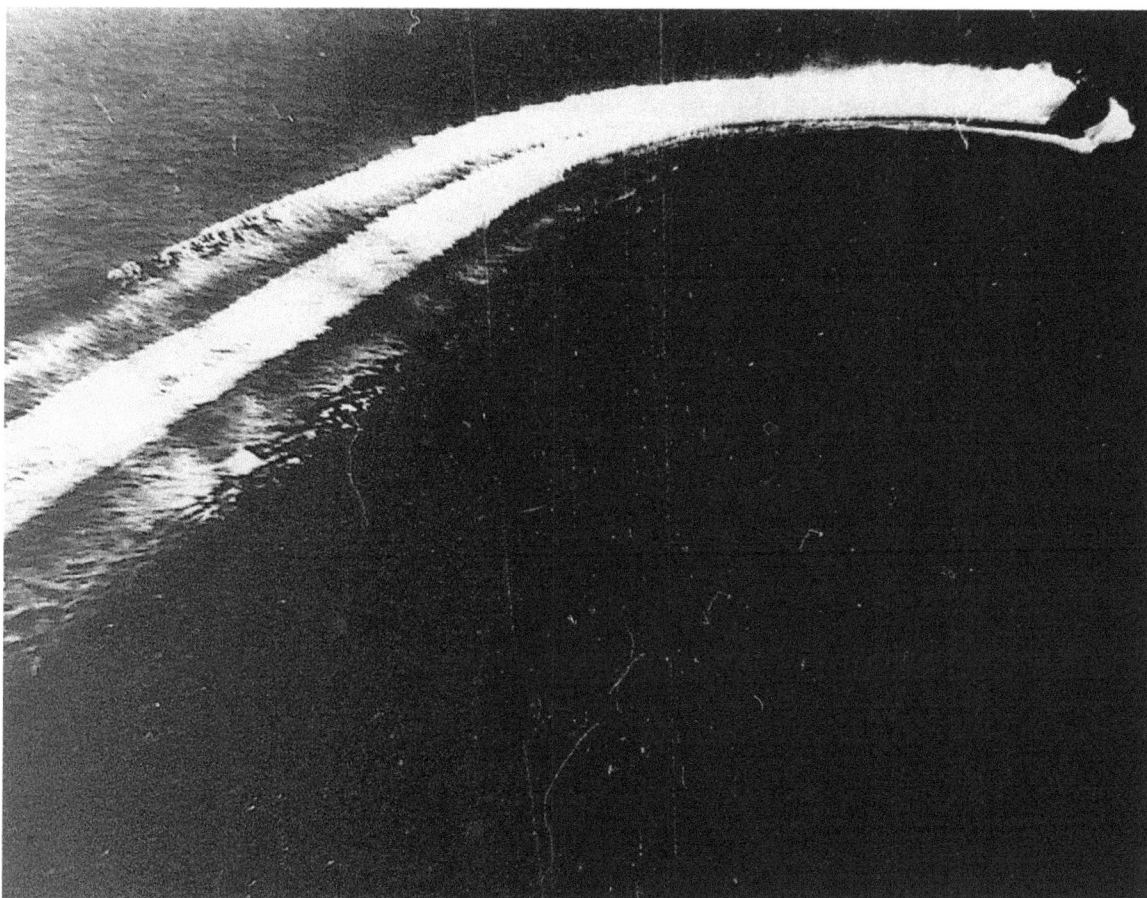

Figure 19: Graphic portrait of PT 487's turning ability

In summing up its report, the Board concluded that " . . . the "Elcoplanes" confer such benefits on the model to which they have been applied that effort should be made to incorporate them as early as possible in the regular production of this company." The Board also recommended that as the Elcoplane offered advantages to new construction, substantial improvement could be expected from the older boats if equipped with the steps, and suggested experimentation with test installations. This recommendation included not only older Elco boats but boats of other builders as well. [23]

BuShips was also favorably impressed with the report, and was requested by CNO to make further action on the matter and to make tests to determine whether large scale installation of the steps on boats in service would be feasible. If the project proved practicable, BuShips planned to send kits to the field to convert the operating boats. [24] As a part of this series of tests PT's 560 through 563, which were units of MTB Squadron TWENTY-NINE, were scheduled for installation of the planes. [25]

23. Board of Inspection and Survey's PT487/S8(6154-S) Serial 230821, 16 December 1943.
24. CNO's Op-23D-MEM, Serial 368735, 29 December 1943.
25. BuShips C-PT546-563/S1-3(516f-772), C-NXS-14560; 31 December 1943.

94

AN ADMINISTRATIVE HISTORY OF PT's IN WORLD WAR II
(Recreated October 25, 2010 by the members of the PT Boat Forum message board)

Figure 20: "PPS"

So sure was the Bureau of the success of the steps on the boats of Squadron TWENTY-NINE that on 29 January 1944 it ordered Supervisor of Shipbuilding at Bayonne to expedite the procurement of kits to enable the "forces afloat" to make installations of the planes. The contract was altered to include this conversion, and all the Bureau needed to complete the picture was approval from the Commanding Officer, MTB Squadron TWENTY-NINE of the performance of the steps under service conditions. [26]

But when the word did come from Squadron TWENTY-NINE, it threw cold water on BuShips' hopes of using the steps extensively. The Elcoplanes were installed on PT's 560-563 and were tested on a trip from New York to Miami, and it was on this long, comparatively slow, cruise that the faults showed up. While the planes were excellent for high speed operation, at optimum or cruising speeds, the boats equipped with planes burned 25% more fuel and 75% more lube oil. [27]

---

26. BuShips C-PT450-545/S1-3(516f); 30 January 1944.
27. SupShips, Bayonne, N. J. ltr. of 10 February 1944 BuShips.

A SIMILAR PHOTO -REPLACEMENT- PROVIDE BY TED WALTHER

Figure 21: Stern view of Eclo with ELCCOPLANE

With the installation of the steps, it had been necessary to redesign the scoops which admitted cooling water. These scoops did not have a sufficient capacity, and as a result the engines on the plane-equipped boats overheated. The planed boats also tended to root into heavy seas, steering was more difficult and acceleration dropped off. The louvers attached to the boats' sides warped, and the supporting brackets cracked and loosened. The boats were sensitive to additional weights and correct trim was an absolute necessity. Because of these shortcomings, Squadron TWENTY-NINE was allowed to remove the planes before proceeding to the combat area.[28]

Shortly after the Florida trip by Squadron TWENTY-NINE, MTBSTC ran rough water trials with PT 487, the original stepped boat. The tests showed that at speeds below 2200 rpm, the standard Elco boat was superior to the planed boat in maneuvering and steering, and at 2200 rpm, the standard boat was faster over a straight course.[29]

28. MTBRonTWENTY-NINE's FC8-29/S1 Serial (02a); 6 February 1944.
29. MTBSTC's NC129/S8, Serial 194 (rmf); 9 February 1944.

After considering the results obtained with PT's 560-563 on the Florida trip, as well as the report of the rough water trials of 487, BuShips held up its projected kit-construction program pending a final decision, and on 4 March 1944, the Bureau decided to abandon the project altogether: In view of the experience with motor torpedo boat PT 487 together with that gathered during the shakedown of PT 560-563, the Bureau was of the opinion that multi-steps as installed on these five ships had not been developed to a sufficient degree of effectiveness to warrant further experimentation by the constructor at Government expense."[30] An experimental installation of Elcoplanes on a Higgins PT, PT 485, also proved unsuccessful.[31]

But because the Elcoplane was turned down as a modification does not necessarily mean that the device was a complete failure. It was useful for high speed operation, and had the boats been able to confine themselves to this type of work, an Elcoplane installation would probably have been a valuable addition. As the cruising speed of PT's was below that at which the Elcoplane operated most effectively, installation in the boats at that time would have been impractical.

The Elcoplane was more than a theory, as the report of the Board of Inspection shows, but the speed obtained by the 487 in these trials was not representative of the speed it would probably have obtained in the operating areas of the South Pacific. During the Newark tests, intake temperature was 32 degrees and air temperature was 16 degrees.[32] In the tropics these figures would be more than doubled, with a consequent loss of efficiency.

Mr. Andrew Jackson Higgins had some rather pungent comments to make concerning the "Hellcat" and the Elcoplane, and his letter is considered worthy of inclusion in an Appendix as an apt and unique commentary upon the administration of the PT program.

---

30. BuShips' C-PT450-545/S1-3(516f); 4 March 1944.
31. Higgins Industries, Inc. ltr. to BuShips with SupShips endorsement; 6 May 1944.

CHAPTER FIVE

MOTOR TORPEDO BOAT SQUADRON TRAINING CENTER

MELVILLE, RHODE ISLAND

The early boats of the PT program had based at Newport with their tender, the USS NIAGARA, and ComMTBRon TWO had established a familiarization school on the tender for prospective PT boat personnel. The highly effective use of PT's in the Philippine campaign made their future employment as a type certain, and in order to provide thorough training for prospective crews and officers, SecNav created the Motor Torpedo Boat Squadron Training Center at Melville, Rhode Island. Operations at the new activity were scheduled to begin on 16 March 1942.[1]

ADMINISTRATIVE RELATIONSHIP

The Training Center was established on Area One of the Government Reservation at Newport (Melville), Rhode Island. The reservation comprised four other areas occupied by the Naval Net Depot and Fuel Annex of the Navy Supply Depot. Although prior to the establishment of the Training Center the Fuel Annex had provided berthing space for several boats, it came to serve the PT school only in a supply capacity, and no interrelationship existed between the technical work of each activity.

For logistics, communications and some administrative matters, MTBSTC came under the cognizance of the Commandant, First Naval District. For matters nearer at hand, the base came under cognizance of the Commandant, Naval Operating Base, Newport. In all matters relating to training, however, the activity was directly responsible to Commander, Fleet Operational Training Command, U. S. Atlantic Fleet, Task Force 23. Task Group 23.4 functioned as the Training Center's operational training command, [2]

MISSION AND FACILITIES

The mission of MTBSTC was to provide instruction and shore facilities for the preparation, indoctrination, and training of officer and enlisted personnel in the fundamentals of sound motor torpedo boat operations, maintenance and upkeep, and to provide an operating base with facilities for

---

1. SecNav's Op-38-c-BuF/2/15, NB31(1) A4-2(420217) Serial 42238, 17 Feb. 1942.
2. COTCLant P16-4/00 (13/fdh), Serial 507, 10 June 1943.

A SIMILAR PHOTO - REPLACEMENT - PROVIDE BY CHARLIE JONES.

Figure 22: Area outlined indicates site of MTBSTC. Note conditions of lagoon before dredging. The existing facility is the Net Fuel Depot.

upkeep, repair, maintenance, overhaul, servicing and supply of all motor torpedo boats assigned or based at MTBSTC, as well as berthing and messing accommodations for personnel attached to such vessels.

Normally, the Training Center was equipped to handle 860 enlisted students and ninety student officers. To handle the concurrent work in administration and instruction, the staff comprised forty-six officers and 187 enlisted men. This number was substantially bolstered by officers and men returning from the operating areas who were retained in a temporary duty status pending further assignment to combat duty.

Physically the base was composed of 286 buildings: Thirteen structures devoted to office space, thirty-four classrooms, forty-two maintenance buildings and 197 living quarter huts.

EARLY DEVELOPMENT

The nucleus of experienced officers assigned as the initial staff for MTBSTC were faced with the immediate problems of setting up a suitable curriculum

AN ADMINISTRATIVE HISTORY OF PT's IN WORLD WAR II
(*Recreated October 25, 2010 by the members of the PT Boat Forum message board*)

99

and of providing adequate housing and training facilities. Instruction was to be provided in the operation, maintenance and overhaul of ordnance and engineering equipment, in communications, in squadron doctrine and tactics, in torpedo, depth charge and gunnery procedures, and in such other matters necessary or desirable to insure the efficient and skillful operation of the various squadrons, and also to insure standard organization and practice in all motor torpedo boat squadrons. Navy Department Bureaus provided the necessary equipment for instruction purposes and the construction of necessary buildings.

By 27 March 1942, forty-seven Quonset huts were in various stages of completion, a request had been submitted for the building of forty-four additional huts,[3] and ten boats of Motor Torpedo Boat Squadron FOUR had reported to the Training Center to provide basic operational training for personnel under instruction. Squadron FOUR boats were to provide underway training for student officers and crews throughout the history of the Training Center.[4] In order to shelter the boats of Squadron FOUR, work was begun on dredging the lagoon adjacent to the Center. This project was completed over a year later in July of 1943.

During the early stages of the development of MTBSTC, especially during the first month, berthing and training facilities were meager, and the Training Center fell back on the better equipped facilities of Price's Neck Anti-Aircraft Training Center, the Naval Torpedo Station at Newport, the small bore rifle range at the Naval Training Station, Newport, the Packard Engine School at Detroit, Michigan, and the Electric Boat Company, Bayonne, New Jersey.

By April, fifty-one officers and 177 enlisted men were under instruction, and BuPers ordered that personnel for approximately one and one-half squadrons per month (about 240 men and officers) be sent to Melville for instruction.[5]

Construction progressed at a steady rate, and by June of 1943, living accommodations were stabilized at 1400 men and 300 officers, and building of these accommodations was completed with the approval by BuPers of the erection of seventy-nine additional huts.

The development of the Training Center was not painless. Reading of the progress reports reveals a long delay between the dates of requisitions and the dates of deliveries. Many of the slowdowns in the delivery of material can be blamed on the exigencies of the critical days in which MTBSTC was founded, or upon the magnitude of the requested work. More often than not, however, delays were brought about by the time it took requests to pass through official

3. Progress report of MTBSTC, 26 March 1942.
4. The terms Melville, Training Center and MTBSTC are used interchangeably throughout this chapter to designate Motor Torpedo Boat Squadrons Training Center.
5. Progress report of MTBSTC dated 7 April 1942.

Figure 23: Little more than a year later, the entrance to the lagoon has been widened, shots (1) living quarters and administrative buildings (2) erected, a quay wall and finger piers (3) built, and a fuel dock (4) constructed, also visible are the excavations (5) for the foundations of drill hall.

channels [6] or by shortages of labor and material. In some of the projects there was also the element of time because of the special nature of the task at hand.

TRAINING POLICY

The training offered at Melville was mainly MTB indoctrination, but general naval subjects, not only as applied to PT's but in the broader sense, held a place in the Melville curriculum. The basic courses for officers and enlisted men were Communications, Engineering, Gunnery, Torpedo Training, Chemical Warfare, Seamanship and Navigation, Recognition, and underway operational training.

The original course for both officers and enlisted men encompassed two months. In this time, the officers and crews were expected to learn the whys

---

6. On 1 April 1943 MTBSTC came under the complete jurisdiction of COTCLant. COMINCH letter FF1/ A3-1, Serial 3464; 11 June 1943.

AN ADMINISTRATIVE HISTORY OF PT's IN WORLD WAR II
(Recreated October 25, 2010 by the members of the PT Boat Forum message board)

101

and wherefores of the boats, responsibilities of their rates on PT's, and in the case of the men; a general idea of what every man on the crew did; boat operation and torpedo firing; and a general knowledge of how the Navy worked, for a majority of the men and officers were very new in the Navy at the time they reported to Melville.

This was much more than a two-month course, and in 1943 another month was added to the officers' training period and to the instruction time of certain experienced student rates. This still was not enough time, for the students were expected to assimilate too much. As has been pointed out before, the majority of personnel reporting to Melville for the first time were green, and there were few petty officers or commissioned officers with any amount of sea duty. The Training Center, instead of using almost all the allowed instruction time in teaching these men their rates, tried desperately to make each man a jack-of-all-trades. The result was inevitable; the caliber of the men turned out was lowered by inefficient training.

The theory behind this exposure to all subjects was excellent, for on a small craft like a PT, it was advantageous to have men who could fill the place of any casualties if the need arises. But it was also necessary to have men thoroughly trained in their own specialties. Semaphore was about as important to a Fireman or Motor Machinist's Mate as set and drift were to a Ship's Cook, but the Training Center continued to ignore the practice and conform to the theory.

When the word finally did come back from the operating areas, it made some change in the Melville curriculum, and more attention was paid to specialization. This economical use of the time available for instruction consequently boosted the capabilities and potentialities of the men turned out by the Training Center. There was still room for improvement, however, when hostilities ended.

These difficulties were, of course, encountered only with the enlisted men, for all officers took the same course together, specializing in no subject, but rather being exposed to them all. The retention by the officers of the subjects studied at MTBSTC was slight, except for those subjects whose learning was intensely physical: Boat handling alongside a pier or station-keeping in formations. Melville's greatest asset was that it gave its student officers and men a background of sorts in the practice and theory of MTB's, and consequently, it was easier for personnel reporting to operating squadrons to absorb the lessons of practice.

MTBSTC cannot be held entirely responsible for the poor training that evidenced itself in MTB personnel. Often it was imperative that general courses be given at the Training Center, even at the expense of MTB indoctrination, for the basic training of arriving students was generally poor. Melville was then confronted not only with its own task of training men to become efficient PT boat operators, but it was also necessary to give them grounding in subjects which should have been assimilated in boot camp or indoctrination schools.

102

AN ADMINISTRATIVE HISTORY OF PT's IN WORLD WAR II
(Recreated October 25, 2010 by the members of the PT Boat Forum message board)

PERSONNEL ORGANIZATION

The Training Center was started with a nucleus of experienced personnel from Squadrons ONE and TWO, and when veterans began to return from the combat areas they were assimilated into the faculty on a rotating basis. Officers-in-Charge of training departments were permanently assigned to the Training Center, and they were assisted by a few other officers and petty officers, some of them combat veterans, also on permanent duty. Returning officers and men filled out the departments on a rotating basis, and their average stay as instructors was about three months. Many of the temporary instructors received a short course at the Teacher Training Division at NOB, Newport.

To take care of the needs of those officers and men not assigned to jobs as instructors, the Training Center inaugurated a program of refresher courses in April of 1944 in order to bring returning personnel up to date on recent developments in MTB operation and equipment. This was a necessity, for modifications in equipment were legion, and operating procedures underwent a series of changes as conditions in the field presented different problems. In addition, the period of refresher training was supposed to provide opportunity for personnel to strengthen mental efficiency and aggressiveness before returning to combat work. A projected reshaping and extension of the officers' refresher course was short circuited by V-J day, when training at Melville ground to an immediate halt.

Upon completion of the refresher courses, personnel were assigned temporary billets in the various departments for the duration of their stay at the Training Center.

Thus personnel at MTBSTC could be divided into distinct categories. They were the permanent staff, the students, the men assigned to temporary teaching or other departmental billets and the men in the refresher courses. There was a constant undercurrent of antagonism among the men in these different categories, which can largely be traced to the fact that all personnel with the exception of the permanent staff were facing immediate sea duty. Boat officers and crews, after initial training, would be shipped to the operating areas, complete a tour of duty, return to the United States, take a 30 day leave, and then report to the Training Center for reassignment only to be greeted by some of the same men and officers who had been holding down jobs behind desks at the Training Center eighteen months before. One junior officer set a record in this category by remaining at Melville just short of three years.

This is not quit the proper light from which to view the whole matter, for there is another facet of the situation which must be considered. PT men were fortunate in that they were able to remain within the United States for any time at all after the expiration of their leave. Personnel on most other combatant ships reported for immediate reassignment at the termination of their leave,

AN ADMINISTRATIVE HISTORY OF PT's IN WORLD WAR II
(Recreated October 25, 2010 by the members of the PT Boat Forum message board)

103

Figure 24: A view in October of the same year showing expansion of living facilities to the point. The drill hall (1) is now completed and the athletic field (2) in use. A swimming pool was later built on the site marked (3) and a mess hall on the site marked (4).

and for them the three month respite at the Training Center would have been unusually pleasant. During this period before reassignment, duties were light and liberty was plentiful, but as this period was common to all returning PT personnel, and as PT personnel administration was carried on almost autonomously by Melville rather than by BuPers, there was no opportunity for corrective comparisons between the advantages of PT personnel and those of other fleet units.

TRAINING FACILITIES

By August of 1945, MTBSTC had grown from an organization consisting of a few pioneer personnel with the most elementary equipment to a large, well-equipped base with extended possibilities for further expansion in training facilities. The large-scale use and introduction of synthetic training devices did not appear until the final stages of the Training Center's existence, and had the war continued, there is no doubt that the caliber and scope of training would have been greatly enhanced by the use of these devices.

Operational or underway training was probably the most valuable course offered at the Training Center, and effective training in tactical techniques called for continual use of a sizable number of vessels, including other types than PT's. The PT's themselves, of course, furnished the primary vehicle for operational training, and boats were made available to the Training Center by the assignment of Squadron FOUR to Melville. This squadron burgeoned to twenty-eight boats, and included simultaneously 78' Higgins, 80' Elco, and 78' Huckins boats. At one time Squadron FOUR was composed entirely of 77' Elco boats, but these were gradually replaced by later models. The result of having such a varied number of boats available for training was not always beneficial. Students often took all their underway training on one type of boat and were sent to squadrons composed of another type. As there were no Huckins squadrons in the operating areas with the exception of Panama and Pearl Harbor, there was little follow-through value in Huckins training except for the more general aspects which would apply with any type. The boats were underway daily, except during the more severe winter weather, on various training operations, but despite the aggravating conditions which could have been brought about by continuous and heavy use, the attrition rate was kept down by use of the extensive maintenance facilities of the base.

Besides the PT boats there had been a number of auxiliary and a few heavier vessels attached to the training Center for varying periods in connection with training for night operations and for use as target vessels. These had included USCGC WICOMICO, USCGC UNALGA, USS FELCIA (PYc 35), USS VAGRANT, USS BIDDLE, (DD 151 and later AC 114), USS SC 642, USS SC 449, USS PC 1984, and USS NEUNZER (DE 150).

Training operations have also been carried out with larger fleet units, when their operational assignments brought them in the vicinity of the southern New England coast.

Gunner's mates were extremely important ratings on PT boats, and the facilities provided for their training were of necessity extensive and specialized. Classroom training in 40mm, 37mm, 20mm and .50 cal. guns was accomplished by using the actual weapons in teaching breakdown and cleaning. For instruction in operation and firing cycle of these guns, mock-ups and sectionalized wooden units capable of simulated operation, were employed.

For training in stoppages and in general trouble shooting, the students had the advantage of a small .50 cal. and 20mm machine gun range located at the northern end of the base. The range area was in constant use and afforded some of the most practical training that student gunners at Melville received, although personnel fresh from the operating areas often failed to appreciate the

AN ADMINISTRATIVE HISTORY OF PT's IN WORLD WAR II
(Recreated October 25, 2010 by the members of the PT Boat Forum message board)

105

irregular auditory evidences of the gunners' work. For handgun and general small arms training, an indoor range was available.

Gunnery students also used one of the earliest synthetic training devices obtained by the Training Center: the Polaroid Trainer. This device taught the principles of tracer fire control with reality, and helped students to understand the problems involved in this method of firing. Because it was realistic, because it was actually pleasant to operate the device, and because its operation and the understanding of the principles involved were inherent functions of each other, the Polaroid Trainer was probably the most successful training device on the base.

The base maintains a large torpedo workshop in which all the torpedoes fired by the boats of Squadron FOUR are overhauled. One section of the shop is devoted to stowage of ready torpedoes, another to classrooms, and the remainder of the shop to overhaul facilities. The work on the torpedoes by men assigned to the permanent staff of the torpedo workshop is combined with instruction of student officers and torpedomen. The shop is equipped with the usual mobile cranes, cherry-pickers, and demonstration models of racks and torpedoes.

The Engineering Department had a large number of classrooms, both in the main departmental building and several huts about the base. Surveyed engines were used for instruction in engine tear-down and assembly, and surveyed parts were used to enable student engineers to make correct diagnosis when trouble shooting. Film strips with synchronized recordings were later used for classroom work. The Engineering Department also maintained a complete overhaul shop, with facilities for performing major overhaul work on Packard engines.

Communications became an increasingly important subject when radar was added to the electronic equipment on PT's. Originally, the department gave instruction in the operation of TCS radio, and several sets were fitted out in a class room in order to enable the students to practice setting up on various frequencies. VHF created new problems in training when this equipment was added to the boats, and the Training Center had to set up a VHF unit for the purposes of instruction. Communications was able to absorb radar in the early stages of development, but modifications came in such rapid succession that the radar branch of the Department operated separately.

Several types of the detecting equipment were available for teaching, and ultimately several buildings were devoted to radar overhaul, instruction and operation. Teaching of the principles of the gyro flux gate compass also came under the Communications Department, and a mobile training unit was assembled for classroom purposes.

Miscellaneous facilities included an Austin torpedo fire control trainer, which never functioned properly, a night look out trainer, Renshaw recognition

106

AN ADMINISTRATIVE HISTORY OF PT's IN WORLD WAR II
(Recreated October 25, 2010 by the members of the PT Boat Forum message board)

equipment and a swimming pool. The swimming pool is listed under training facilities, for shallow water diving and under water repair were both taught with success in the pool.

TRAINING PROBLEMS

The Engineering Department was hard hit by the heterogeneousness of the training as outlined in the early programs of the Training Center. It was difficult to give a Fireman enough instruction in Engineering in two months or even three, but diversified instruction in Seamanship, Navigation, Communications and Gunnery made the job even harder. The only emphasis which instructors could give in the limited time available in the field of engineering was on the theoretical side of the problem, for time was not available for long periods of practical work. Although there was limited instruction in practical work, during 1942 and the first half of 1943, student engineers received the bulk of their instruction from the film strips and from lectures.

This situation was alleviated in the Engineering Department, as well as in the other departments when the emphasis of the training shifted, in August of 1943, from general knowledge to specialized training. More time was given to Engineering, and the extraneous subjects were either curtailed or eliminated from the curriculum of the engineers. In June 1944, the focus on Engineering was further sharpened, and extensive courses of full instruction in engine operation, auxiliary generators, refrigeration, electricity and dry cell operation were introduced.

The caliber of the graduates took an upswing, and those men who were trained during the last two years of the Training Center's history, were generally better equipped when they left Melville than had been their predecessors. The one great fault in the training of Firemen, however, was the lack of sufficient emphasis on maintenance. Unfortunately, this manifested itself in the operating areas and the end product was a loss of operating efficiency among the boats. Many failures could have been prevented and the life of much equipment extended had proper emphasis been placed upon this all important factor by the Engineering Department at Melville.

The problem of how to indoctrinate Communications personnel with a general idea of their duties and responsibilities aboard a PT was further complicated by the fact that it was first necessary to teach many of the men the fundamentals of radio. This meant that the Communications Department was forced to subordinate the teaching of the peculiar duties of a radioman aboard a PT to the more general type of instruction. A compromise was effected, and the course for radioman strikers included enough fundamentals to equip the prospective rates for the more specialized problems of PT communications.

This Department was also hard put by the constant changes which took place in the electronic equipment on the boats. Instruction in gyro flux gate compass and TCS radio changed little during the war, but instruction in the various types of radar and VHF was constantly changing. With little or no idea of to which squadron a man would be assigned, it was necessary to instruct him in all types then in use. Procurement in the field was slow, and it was not unusual to have boats with several different types of electronic equipment in one squadron.

The Communications Department was short on training devices and aids, for all radar equipment was needed for actual operation and any devices employed were of the home grown variety. A final hampering factor was a drag on the program of instruction: because of the high classification of all radar equipment and information pertaining to it, the students were allowed to take no permanent notes. The extreme disadvantages of this method of instruction are self-explanatory.

Training in the rate of Radioman (and later, Radarman) was for PT's always difficult, for the Radiomen on the boats performed many duties ordinarily delegated to Electrician's mates. Operation and maintenance were about on a par on the boats, but too often a squadron's Radar and Radio Officer found it necessary to teach Melville trained men the essentials of preventative maintenance after they were attached to an operating squadron.

The Gunnery Department forestalled possible criticism of its training techniques when it installed the machine gun range which dealt exclusively in the problems which occur in battle. Because of the deliberateness with which changes in ordnance installations were made, the Department at Melville was able to keep abreast with modifications.

In a Gunnery sub-department, Torpedo Fire Control, problems did arise. This was the problem of instructing officers in the proper methods and procedure of accurate torpedo firing. From August of 1943 to October of 1944, PT's in the Pacific fired few torpedoes, although the boats were designed primarily for that purpose. Instead they became high speed gun boats. In the European theatre, on the other hand, torpedo firing was common, and the boats continued to carry out their prime function as notably exemplified by the performance of MTB Squadron FIFTEEN in the Mediterranean. As a majority of the boats were in the Pacific, re-education for most of the returning boat officers in torpedo fire control was essential. In addition, all student officers were educated in this part of the Gunnery Department's program.

A Mark 4 Mod 0 torpedo attack trainer was procured from the Austin Company under a BuOrd contract in May 1944, but the trainer never proved successful. Limited training was possible, but either because of faulty installation or construction, this device never lived up to expectations. Efforts were still being made in August of 1945 to correct the deficiencies existing in the equation solving units of the device, for it was felt that these units were the seat of all the trouble.

Figure 25: Austin Trainer's bridge constructed at Elco

The Training Center also possessed a British Torpedo Director Trainer which was used from the earlier days of the program. This Trainer is in no way similar to the Austin Trainer, and affords practice for torpedo shots made with seaman's eye. There is no plotting element, and the training given is effective only for basic visual attacks.

BuAer made available to MTBSTC one of its Special Device Section's Mechanical Torpedo Attack Teachers. This is a self-propelled cart which launches a self–propelled torpedo at a self-propelled target. This trainer requires a large area of smooth decking, and its use at Melville was limited.

Basic training in Torpedo Fire Control therefore devolved upon the maneuvering board, and this method of plotting and fire control was generally stressed throughout the program. It was probably the only generally satisfactory method of plotting radar data with the equipment that was on the boats.

Early procurement of synthetic training devices would have been an improvement in this department, and no doubt would have resulted in a better brand of torpedo firing than was exhibited by the PT's at Surigaio Straits. Another retarding factor in the teaching program was the size of the classes, seldom less than thirty and running as high as seventy. Because of the lack of

AN ADMINISTRATIVE HISTORY OF PT's IN WORLD WAR II
(*Recreated October 25, 2010 by the members of the PT Boat Forum message board*)

109

individual instruction in such large classes, and because a majority of the class was left inactive while a handful were using some device as the British trainer, instruction suffered. In all fairness, this is not solely a criticism of the Torpedo Fire Control sub-Department, but of many of the Departments at Melville.

The only problems of administration and training in the Seamanship and Navigation Departments were occasioned by the lack of previous training on the part of the students, and in some instances by the size of the classes.

The instruction material of the Recognition Department has at times lagged behind the construction and combat use of planes and ships, especially enemy equipment, but this has been the only valid criticism of the program, which proceeded at a more or less neutral level. Personnel undergoing training at Melville were all given the fundamentals of plane and ship recognition. A "slot machine" type device was given limited use in this program with great success.

The liaison between MTBSTC and the operating areas was too poor to enable Melville to make immediate use in the curriculum of lessons in tactical doctrine learned by the boats in combat. There were no provisions for a relay of such pertinent information by any official channels, and the few unofficial means of obtaining this information were not expeditious.

If the squadrons in the field had forwarded copies of all their action reports directly to Melville, the training Center could have kept its curriculum ideally up to date. With this in mind, MTBSTC requested permission from ComInCh for this service but failed to get approval.

While permission was not forthcoming on the plan of receiving direct copies of all action reports, Melville did receive photostatic copies of the reports after they reached Washington. The delay was abortive, for the reports were anywhere from three to six months old by the time they reached the Training Center. This meant that after the lesson pointed out in the report had been incorporated in the curriculum and taught to the students, the time lapse (including the time the students were enroute to a squadron after graduation) was too great to enable new officers to show in their work any benefit from the instruction. In some case, by the time the officers arrived in an area, the conditions that brought about the original report had changed, and the squadrons were faced with an entirely new problem.

There was another way of obtaining the information, but this was even slower than waiting for the photostatic copies of the action reports. It was simply the word-of- mouth information of combat veterans who returned to Melville. This system left the actuality even further behind, for it was difficult to sort fact from opinion. Methods were improved early in 1945 when a system of questionnaires was introduced at Melville. These questionnaires were given to all returning personnel, and embraced questions on Tactics ("What approach do you feel to be most successful for a type B barge?"), Gunnery ("What gun do you believe to be most useful and why?"), Communications ("What was your policy on dividing radar watches when on patrol?") and Engineering ("Did you have any trouble with your auxiliary generator?"). General questions ("How long do you think a tour of duty should be?") rounded out the questionnaire.

The questionnaires were checked and analyzed each month. In the checking and analyzing, the problem of fact vs. opinion again presented itself, and the analyzers also tried to take into consideration the obvious fact that some of the "questionees" did not know what they were talking about. Conclusions arrived at with the help of the questionnaires were general, and the effect of conclusions upon the Training program was to determine the amount of emphasis necessary for the various phases of each subject.

Liaison at the command level would have eliminated this unnecessary rehashing of second hand information, and had squadron commanders been directly responsible to Melville for accounts of actions and material failures or improvements, the training program would have been more effective. [7]

MOTOR TORPEDO BOAT SQUADRON FOUR

On 27 March 1942, Motor Torpedo Boat Squadron FOUR reported to the Commandant, NOB, Newport, for the dual purpose of conducting operations against enemy vessels and providing the newly established Training Center with boats necessary for underway training. The squadron set up its own organization at the Net and Fuel Depot. A training curriculum was established in April, and the burdon of the most of the teachings fell upon the shoulders of the Squadron FOUR personnel. This included both underway and classroom instruction.

These officers and the men that succeeded them were responsible for many of the improvements in the administration of the training program. Outstanding among the suggestions offered by Squadron FOUR officers (and subsequently adopted by the Training Center) were: The establishment of a restricted area for all PT's for training exercises; the introduction of regular operations with planes; the organization of student personnel into training crews; and the practice of scheduling more and shorter training cruises.

By June of 1942, 17 boats had reported to Squadron FOUR. With these boats, and in conjunction with USS SHAD, personnel of the Squadron and of the Training Center were able to work out the basis for an anti-submarine doctrine for PT's. This doctrine was later developed and included in the training program in 1943. Planes from Quonset aided in the evolution of evasive tactics

---

7. Commander T. G. WARFIELD, USN offered valuable information for this section and several other parts of this chapter. Commander WARFIELD was the Commanding Officer at MTBSTC at the cessation of hostilities.

AN ADMINISTRATIVE HISTORY OF PT's IN WORLD WAR II
(Recreated October 25, 2010 by the members of the PT Boat Forum message board)

111

by PT's against aircraft, and the USS JAMESTOWN helped the boats develop towing and refueling underway procedures.

Maintenance posed a particular problem in the early days of the squadron, and boats requiring more than minor repairs were sent to Elco at Bayonne or to Fyfe's Shipyard at Glen Cove, Long Island. The Herreshof Company of Bristol, Rhode Island dry docked the boats when only one dry dock was available at MTBSTC, and new equipment was installed by Navy Yard, Boston and by NRL, Annapolis, Maryland. Both Elco and Higgins provided instruction in hull repair and in installation, maintenance and repair of equipment.

As the Training Center expanded, it was able to provide all maintenance facilities necessary for the boats, but at the same time the number of boats was increasing. This meant a constant strain upon the repair facilities, but they were up to the task. To augment the Squadron FOUR boats, new squadrons in New York sent up boats on pre-shakedown trips for short stays at the Training Center. This relieved the strain on Squadron FOUR, provided more boats for training, and gave the personnel of the new squadrons valuable experience. By 1943 this plan was working well.

In considering the operations of Squadron FOUR, one of the greatest shortcomings of the Training Center comes to light. This was the frequent cancellation of operations because of weather conditions. New England winters were not kind, and sub-zero operations in PT boats are not pleasant and many not practical. The lack of underway training of personnel attending Melville during the winter months could not be replaced by classroom work, and the consequent effect was a lack of proficiency in boat handling upon the part of personnel reporting to the operating squadrons. Eventually, this meant that a squadron in an active area had to employ boats, men and time which could have been used on combat patrols, to conduct underway training of reporting officers.

The only solution for this problem is a move to a more favorable climate, and the PT Shakedown Center at Miami was a step in the right direction. Miami is not troubled with problems of icing or cold weather, and its climate was close to that of the operating areas (with the natural exception of the Aleutians). The success of the activity at Miami suggests that a PT school could have been set up much more efficiently in Florida. Weather caused the cancellation of at least thirty percent of scheduled underway operations at Melville.

SPECIAL PROJECTS

Three special projects were established by the Training Center: Shakedown Training, the Experimental Department, and the Repair Training Unit. Each of these three sub-activities improved the standards of training at the Center.

New squadrons were usually composed of a nucleus of veteran officers, when available, and a balance of new officers fresh from Melville. To weld a firm squadron organization, and to indoctrinate new officers in the duties of their particular jobs, each squadron participated in several weeks of Shakedown Training. In April of 1943, Melville undertook the responsibility of basing the Elco boats during this period of training.

While at Melville, boats participating in Shakedown Training took short cruises along the New England coast and practiced harbor penetration, anti-aircraft firing, torpedo techniques, and anti-barge techniques. Mechanical difficulties in the boats due to construction cropped up and were remedied during this period. Not only the boat crews, but also student personnel were able to take advantage of the training offered by this period.

Higgins boats had the advantage of better weather, for their Shakedown Training was conducted at Miami, and weather cancellations of operations were few. The Elco boats soon found it necessary to move to Miami for winter training work, and in the winter of 1944-45 all Shakedown Training was transferred to Florida.

In the initial program of the Training Center, no provision was made for experimentation. The program was organized with the assumption that the various departments would initiate their own developmental work. This resulted in duplication of effort on the part of several of the departments and in lack of coordination between the departments. No standardized records were kept of the work done in each department, and in an effort to coordinate all work of this type, the Commanding Officer designated an Experimental Officer from among the rotating personnel.

This was not successful, for Experimental Officers changed so rapidly that projects could not be followed through by one man, and indoctrination of successive officers in the post took up too much time. Another tack was tried when the Commanding Officer gave the head of the Engineering Department collateral duties as Experimental Officer. This plan also failed because the Engineering Officer regarded his duties in his new capacity as subordinate rather than collateral. Effective liaison was not established with the other departments, and there was no improvement in coordination of effort.

Finally, in May of 1944 the Experimental Department was established as a full-fledged unit responsible to the Executive Officer and responsible for all experimental work on the base. Various departments, however, still continued with their own experimental work on the boats, and it was not until June of 1945 that this situation was suitably settled.

The problem was solved by appointing an Experimental Board, consisting of the heads of the Gunnery, Engineering, Communications and Experimental Departments, the Commanding Officer of Squadron FOUR, the Executive Officer of the Repair Training Unit, the Commanding Officer of the Training Center and his Executive Officer. This board passed on all experimental projects and then handed them over to the Experimental Department for development.

AN ADMINISTRATIVE HISTORY OF PT's IN WORLD WAR II
(Recreated October 25, 2010 by the members of the PT Boat Forum message board)

113

No other experimental work was to be conducted on the base. A filing system of records of various projects was standardized, and the Experimental Department was ready to function efficiently, but the metamorphosis had come too late.

The third special project, the Repair Training Unit (RTU), came into being on 8 March 1944. [8] The need for such a unit came with the realization that personnel more competently trained in maintenance, repair and upkeep could affect a great economy of material in the combat areas. This organization maintained its own faculty, which taught a curriculum which pointed more at maintenance than operation.

Specialized courses in upkeep and repair gave the students the background necessary for the successful performance of their duties as base or tender personnel. Trainees included both officers and men, and those who were not assigned to AGP's upon completion of their courses were formed into E-11 and E-12 units. These units are advanced base functional components, and were used in operations where the immediate establishment of a large base was not feasible.

The courses, in fact the whole idea of a Repair Training Unit, indicated the trend toward higher standards in preventative maintenance and repair. This factor, which should have been taken into consideration in establishing the PT program, came to the fore only after a slow developmental period filled with maintenance headaches and heartaches.

PERSONNEL PROBLEMS

Originally most of the enlisted personnel assigned to MTBSTC were graduates of class "A" service schools, and the overall average of "A" school graduates among the student crews had been about seventy-five percent. The training courses were predicated upon the belief that the majority of the students would be able to spend time adapting their rates to PT work and undergoing PT indoctrination. The fallacy in this premise lay in the fact that, as has been pointed out above, retention by many of the men of subjects taught in the "A" schools was not outstanding.

The program was extended to three months to allow for the extra training that such a situation made necessary, but an effort was made to obtain better qualified men. Standards for PT men were set up by BuPers for personnel volunteering for PT service. These two steps raised the caliber of personnel several notches, but the problem was never completely solved.

Another big problem presented itself in 1943, when personnel awaiting assignment to MTBSTC began to pile up at the Receiving Station in Boston. Melville was able to accommodate a limited number at one time, and consequently the steady influx of new personnel built up a constant back log.

---

8. CNO's OP13c-jc, Serial 63813, sO23-168; 12 February 1944.

What to do with personnel until vacancies at the Training Center opened up became a prime problem.

The situation was eased in August of 1943 when a program of pre-Melville training was introduced at the Receiving Station. Courses were introduced in Communications, Gunnery and Physical Fitness. Engineers among the men waiting assignment were sent to Wentworth Institute in Boston for training; Torpedomen were detailed to Naval Air Station, Squantum, Massachusetts, and Radiomen, Radio Technicians, Quartermasters and Radarmen were sent to the Ratheon Manufacturing Company at Waltham, Massachusetts, producers of the radar sets used on the boats, and to the Radar Laboratory of the Navy Yard Annex at Boston.

The main contingent of prospective PT students occupied the fifth deck of the Fargo Building in Boston, but overflow personnel were handled by the Navy Rest Camp at Suncook, New Hampshire, which also maintained a program of instruction in Communications, Gunnery, and Physical Training, paralleling the program in effect at the Receiving Station.

Another problem arose with enlisted men upon their return from combat areas. Many men had advanced either one or two ratings while overseas, but their work had been confined to the special demands of their rates aboard PT's. In an effort to determine whether or not the men were qualified to hold their ratings, the departments at Melville tested the men after completion of the Refresher Course.

It the men were deficient in qualifications, these tests indicated where further instruction was needed, and further training reeducated the men. A second test determined definitely whether or not the men were qualified, and a second failure meant reduction in rate.

The greatest personnel problem faced by MTBSTC was the training of a sufficiently large number of men. The Training Center was hard pressed to keep the volume of men trained up to field demands. It was necessary, in 1944, for ComServForPac to transfer approximately 1000 non-rated general detail men to MTBRons 7th Fleet. This situation was brought about by operational exigencies which demanded the transfer of large numbers of men on the west coast to general detail. Although men had a PT designation in their service record, several times it was necessary to use them to reinforce the fleet units whose numbers had been depleted by casualties.

The transfer of these 1000 men was actually an indirect replacement of PT men who had been sent to other duty while awaiting transportation on the west coast.

This dilemma could have been avoided only by a tremendous expansion of MTBSTC, or by an earlier appraisal on the part of the Navy of the potential value of PT's.

AN ADMINISTRATIVE HISTORY OF PT's IN WORLD WAR II
(Recreated October 25, 2010 by the members of the PT Boat Forum message board)

115

With officer personnel there were other problems besides the problem of poor basic training, which at that time had been considered rather too redundantly to warrant further mention. The initial problem was the control of assignment of officers, and this problem had its severe ramifications.

Because of rapid expansion in the PT program, it was difficult for the Training Center to nominate officers for orders through the usual method of consulting fitness reports. Thus for all practical purposes, the Training Center was in complete charge of officer distribution and control. Nominally, BuPers would have been in charge of the planning and control of officer flow, but in the case of PT personnel, field rotation was determined by assignments from Melville.

This system can be criticized from both side, but it did work during the war, although its principles should not be considered as models. The fitness report system was entirely bypassed, and judgments on officers were made with knowledge obtained from an informal word-of-mouth system, in this case of officers who had completed a tour of duty in the area. Squadron Commanders were requested by Melville to submit letters outlining the qualifications of officers upon receipt of their orders back to the United States, and these letters were used to furnish pseudo-fitness report material for the officers' next assignments.

Although a little irregular for men versed in strict adherence to Navy methods, this informal assignment arrangement worked because a large percentage of officers, once in the PT program, remained until the end of the war. Had there been an interchange of officer personnel between the fleet and PT's, the situation would have worked out much less favorably. This brings up the separate question of channeling men in PT's.

There was little or no interchange of officer personnel between the fleet and PT's. The change was all one way, and it was detrimental to PT's. Officers who were transferred from PT's to other fleet units, left the boats with combat experience. To replace these men, PT's should have received from the fleet the same, number of officers with a corresponding amount of combat experience. Instead, replacements for veteran PT men who were transferred out of the program came from midshipman and indoctrination schools. This meant that seasoned operators were exchanged for green officers, and this exchange was, of course, detrimental to operating efficiency.

Another problem with officer personnel had been the selection of the best age group for PT duty. In the early days of the program, the student officers averaged twenty-three or twenty-four years of age, and although many of these officers had worthy operating records, a change was made in the age grouping. Later classes were composed of officers twenty-eight to thirty-five years of age. The purpose of the sharp boost in the age category was to obtain officers with more experience in handling men and with a greater overall sense of

116

AN ADMINISTRATIVE HISTORY OF PT's IN WORLD WAR II
(Recreated October 25, 2010 by the members of the PT Boat Forum message board)

responsibility. In 1945, the Training Center's policy reversed course and began to draw on young officers, fresh from midshipman schools, from twenty-one to twenty-four, for student officers.

The shifts in the age groupings were no doubt caused by efforts on the part of Melville to try to determine the age grouping which produced the best combination of stamina and leadership. The perfect combination was never found, and many of the officers, especially during the periods when officers from the lower age groupings were part of the student body, were notably lacking in qualities of leadership.

The solution offered by Melville to this dilemma was a honest effort to bring about improvement in the officers by letting them find out for themselves just was qualities they lacked. This was brought about by the formation of crews for training from student personnel. Student enlisted men were put under the jurisdiction of student officers on training cruises and operations, and usually this arrangement was beneficial to both officers and men. In many instances neither the officers nor the men were sure of the responsibilities of the other, or of the interrelationship of the various duties aboard the boats. The formation of these training crews was a stimulant for self-improvement among the students.

Prospective commanding officers for new squadrons and relief officers for the commanding officers of squadron in the field were selected at Melville. In order to train experienced officers as reliefs, steps were taken in November of 1944 to set up a Command Course eight weeks in length, but the course was taught only when there was a demand for competent reliefs. Potential commanding officers were often given a short tour of duty in Squadron FOUR before assignment to their own commands.

The earlier squadrons were commanded by regular Navy officers with a background of fleet experience. Although most of the Naval Reserve officers who commanded squadrons had excellent battle records, the administration of most PT squadrons had left something to be desired. Squadrons often suffered from poor discipline, and lack of organization. The use of Naval Reserve officers is not criticized here because of their lack of potential ability, but rather because there had been little or no time to give Reserve officers training for the highly responsible jobs to which they were entrusted. The criticisms of Reserve Officers themselves are, for this reason, unjust, but at the same time, the criticism of their training is largely valid.

Conclusions

In reviewing the history of the Training Center, numerous criticisms have been made of policy and method, but the failings which brought about these criticisms could be avoided if the occasion should again arise for the establishment of a Motor Torpedo Boat Squadrons Training Center.

AN ADMINISTRATIVE HISTORY OF PT's IN WORLD WAR II
(Recreated October 25, 2010 by the members of the PT Boat Forum message board)

117

This review of the history of MTBSTC leads to the following conclusions:

1. Officers and men ordered to the Training Center should have had a thorough and complete basic training. The activity at Melville was commissioned for the purpose of indoctrinating officers and men in the theory and practice of PT's, not in general Navy subjects.

2. Enlisted men should have been given sufficient training in their own rates as applied to PT's. The training in the specialties of the individual rates was often sacrificed for diversified training. Secondary training should not be a function of the Training Center.

3. Synthetic training devices should have been used more extensively and to a better advantage. More devices should have been obtained, and an efficient system of scheduling classes for these devices should have been introduced.

4. Another Training Center for the PT Boats should be set up in an area whose climactic conditions are similar to those in the projected field of operations.

5. Experienced fleet personnel could be used to advantage in all rates to form at least a nucleus for each squadron.

6. The Training Center staff should be composed of seasoned personnel, and their tour of duty at the Training Center should not exceed one year or eighteen months.

7. Personnel administration should be better coordinated with BuPers. Definite policy on the use of fitness reports, the inter-change of personnel with the fleet, and efficient rotation should be established.

8. Complete and thorough instruction should be given to enlisted men and officers in upkeep and repair, with special emphasis on preventive maintenance.

9. If PT's are to be used tactically as torpedo boats, intelligent emphasis should be placed upon Torpedo Fire Control instruction.

10. If a future program finds more than one type of boat in use in combat areas, as the Higgins and the Elco were used in the past war, personnel should either be instructed entirely in the functions of one of the types, or else equal emphasis should be given to both. Officers and men who reported to Higgins squadrons during the war were often ill-equipped to assume their duties because instruction at Melville leaned preponderantly toward the Elco boat.

11. Classes should be small, especially for practical work. Large classes often become unwieldy when work entailing the use of devices or equipment by a small percentage of the class, leaves the majority with nothing to do.

12. Shakedown Training is a logical function of the Training Center, and in addition, student personnel can be trained on shakedown boats, but weather makes Shakedown in New England impractical.

118

AN ADMINISTRATIVE HISTORY OF PT's IN WORLD WAR II
(Recreated October 25, 2010 by the members of the PT Boat Forum message board)

13. A well organized Experimental Department, with a competent staff, is a valuable part of the Training Center. A separate allocation of boats for experimental work should be made to this Department so that operational training and experimentation will not interfere with each other.

14. Tender and functional component unit personnel need specialized training. The Repair Training Unit is an admirable effort at a solution for this problem.

15. There should be definite liaison through official channels between MTBSTC and commands in the operating area in order to incorporate in the training program changes in operational tactics and maintenance methods.

16. During the period from the opening of the Training Center to 14 August 1945; 12,500 enlisted men and 2,017 officers were indoctrinated in motor torpedo boat operation. The result of this training has been a continuous flow of replacements to the operating areas and a liberal supply of men for new squadrons. [9]

---

9. Most of the information in this chapter was taken either from reports submitted by MTBSTC to COTCLant and ComONE or from the writer's personal experiences at the Training Center.

AN ADMINISTRATIVE HISTORY OF PT's IN WORLD WAR II
(*Recreated October 25, 2010 by the members of the PT Boat Forum message board*)

119

CHAPTER SIX

MIAMI PT SHAKEDOWN DETAIL

To fully understand the administrative structure of the PT Shakedown Detail a brief review of the U.S.N.T.C., Miami (designated as S.C.T.C.until 9 June 1944) is presented.

On 16 march 1942, Cominch requested "BuNav establish a training center for the purpose of training nucleus crews for submarine chasers".[1] Administration of Submarine Chaser Training Center was to remain a function of BuNav, and vessels of the training squadrons were directed by Cominch to report to ComGulfSeaFron for duty.

The purpose of the activity could be interpreted as follows: To provide men and officers properly trained for PC's and SC's, and to provide a shakedown organization which would send the ships out prepared to efficiently perform their duties of escort and patrol.

German subs were patrolling right off the beach, and the need for SC's was tremendous and immediate. Commander E. F. McDANIEL, USN became the PCO of the training program, and he went to work with a directness that was most productive and refreshing to observe. His persistence soon had the S.C.T.C. in an operating status.

On the authority designated by BuNav, the PCO allocated warehouses, offices, and docking space at Pier #2 from the city of Miami. The activity mushroomed, and the existing facilities proved far from adequate. Most of the contracting had to be done through Com 7 ND who was, at that time, located in Key West, Florida. This ultimately, caused delays and friction which hindered the growth and efficiency of the activity.

HOUSING AND SUBSISTENCE

The Training Center was forced to take over some of the local hotels in order to provide barracks for the increasing number of EM in training.

Messing was contracted for with private concerns, but in spite of regular inspections by staff officers the system proved highly unsatisfactory and expensive. The command finally established a general mess in some of the Navy controlled hotels and in a converted garage.

---

1. COMINCH ltr. Serial 0393 of 16 March 1942.

In the early phase of the Training Center, the were no B.O.Q.'s or established officer's mess, and student and staff officers had to find quarters and meals through whatever private means the could.

Throughout 1942 this was not too difficult, but later it became almost prohibitive because of increasing prices. The situation grew progressively worse, and in March 1943, local hotels were taken over for B.O.Q.'s.

A small sick bay was set up on Pier #2, but was quickly outgrown. As soon as the Everglades Hotel was acquired, sick bay was transferred there. The additional space was much better for such purposes and removed many of the problems which had arisen out of the original cramped sick bay.

STAFF OFFICERS

The CO, S.C.T.C. personally selected his staff officers, and his policy was to limit a tour of duty at the Training Center to six months. This constant turnover of instructors brought in officers whose sea duty and experience added in keeping the classroom instruction abreast with the very latest developments.

INTRODUCTION OF COTCLANT

On the 11th of June 1943, CNO assigned direct command of certain shore based operational training activities to the newly established operational training commands Atlantic and Pacific Fleets through the C's-in-C of these fleets. S.C.T.C., Miami, and M.T.B.S.T.C. were included under the jurisdiction of CotcLant (Rear Adm. D.B. Beary, USN)[2]

The Fleets were to control the curricula, training methods, equipment and organization of the activities; but should not become involved in their administration or maintenance. District Commandants were urged to extend all possible assistance support, and freedom of action to Fleet Operational Training Commands in connection with their tasks. In matters pertaining to actual operations or training for district defense, CO's of the activities will be governed by orders of the district commandants; but the fleet duty of the activity and ships attached was regarded as paramount.

INCEPTION OF THE PT SHAKEDOWN DETAIL

STAFF ORGANIZATION

In early 1943, COTCLant investigated the possibilities for establishing a PT shakedown Detail for PT's built by Higgins. By April 1943, the CO, SCTC presented to him a summary of existing facilities necessary for this proposed program. The situation was summarized as follows:

2. E. J. KING's res. Ltr. Serial 3464 of 11 June 1943.

AN ADMINISTRATIVE HISTORY OF PT's IN WORLD WAR II
(Recreated October 25, 2010 by the members of the PT Boat Forum message board)

121

All the facilities necessary for shaking down PT's were available in the Miami Area. No officers or EM at the Training Center were familiar with that type of boat, and it would be necessary for BuPers to supply additional personnel for these duties. It is suggested that the personnel should be:

One (1) CO or O-in-C of PT Shakedown, one (1) Engineering Officer, One (1) Gunnery and Torpedo Officer, one (1) Officer for Shiphandling Instruction, two (2) Chief Torpedomen, two (2) Chief Gunner's Mates, Two (2) Chief Motor Machinist's Mates.

Necessary radiomen could be supplied by SCTC. All the officers should have had operating experience prior to reporting to the Shakedown Detail.

It was further suggested that a minimum of two weeks be allowed in which to shakedown the boats. The program would include:

Piloting and navigation
Firing at surface and AA targets
At least one torpedo firing exercise
Extensive operation in group tactics both day and night[3]

PHYSICAL FACILITIES

In order to incorporate PT shakedown, the command had to expand its water front holdings. A careful study was made of the facilities existing and required, and the CO, SCTC requested COM 7 to acquire all fingerpiers of the Miami Yacht Basin located south of Pier #3 and turn them over to the Training Center. COM 7 was further requested to authorize the Training Center to construct a building approximately 80' x 30' along the sea wall above Finger Pier #2. This structure was necessary for housing a torpedo overhaul shop, PT overhaul facilities, and offices.

By the 21st of April 1943, the Shakedown Detail was considered ready for business, and CO, SCTC informed COM MTB RON 17 (The first squadron assigned to the activity) that the Detail was established and offered the following facilities:

"(a) Ample berthing space is available in local hotel used as enlisted barracks.

(b) Complete machine shop facilities are available.

(c) A torpedo workshop with complete overhaul facilities is at present in process of construction and would be used entirely by PT shakedown. Torpedoes are available.

(d) Ample facilities exist for obtaining provisions and supplies.

---

3. CO, SCTC ltr. to COTCLant, Serial 429 of 8 April 1943.

(e) Office space for base and transient personnel can be assigned as desired.

(f) Five finger piers in the City Yacht Basin are being leased by the Navy, and approximately 36 boats could be moored there

All the above facilities are in convenient walking distance of these piers. An electric shore connection is available on the piers, and fuel can be obtained from a YOG across the channel. Office space for paymasters will be assigned as desired, and complete hospital facilities are available within easy walking distance."[4]

Lieutenant Commander A. R. MONTGOMERY, USN was in charge of the Shakedown Detail, and three additional officers and six Chiefs and 1st Class Petty Officers reported in from MTBSTC, Melville, R.I. to fill out the base force.

SHAKEDOWN SYLLABUS

Commander McDANIEL organized and presented for COTCLant's approval a fourteen day shakedown syllabus that included all phases of operating and testing. The accepted program was installed in both Miami and Melville shakedown details, and became the bible for all future shakedowns.

At the completion of three months operations under this program, the CO realized that two weeks was not sufficient time to effectively shakedown the boats. The 7th of August 1943, COTCLant informed CINCLant that he had lengthened the PT Shakedown period to three weeks. The same syllabus was adhered to, and the additional time was used to offset the vagaries of the delay imposed by weather and material difficulties. Reports from Melville and Miami had strongly indicated that the prescribed two week period was all too short a time in which to effectively follow the Shakedown Syllabus. The complaints did not, apparently, fall on deaf ears, and a change was effected as previously mentioned.

The shakedown syllabus as employed by both shakedown details is presented.

NORMAL OPERATING STATUS

For more than two years PT's had operated in northern waters, and CO, MTBSTC finally realized that the severe winter weather was just too much for efficient shakedown. Lt. Comdr. D.J. WALSH, USNR, CO of Melville Shakedown and Training Center, suggested to COTCLant that Elco PT's shakedown in Miami commencing with RON 29. Ron 28 was then shaking down at Melville and would complete the program there, being the last squadron to shakedown at MTBSTC. On the 1st October 1943, COTCLant notified CO, SCTC that all PT's would shakedown at Miami, and the first Elco squadron would arrive about

---

4. CO, SCTC conf. ltr. to COM MTB RON 17 of 21 April 1943.

14 December 1943. Commander McDANIEL, after a quick survey of the facilities available for handling additional boats, informed COTCLant that his command would accommodate all the PT's if the proposed building program was adhered to.

The first Elco squadron arriving at Miami PT Shakedown found the following facilities and conditions as of the end of 1943.

(a) A torpedo workshop supplied complete overhaul facilities.

(b) The main building housed a machine shop, gunnery shack, electricians' shack, shakedown office and radio shack, four offices available for squadron gear, double bunks topside for base force personnel, and a small assembly room where training films were sown and classes held for squadron engineers. (From 15 January 1944 to 15 March 1944 SCTC held classes on Packard marine engine for the Shakedown Detail).

(c) A small building sufficed as a sickbay where transient squadrons' doctors and Pharmacist's Mates could hold sick call. The Base Sick Bay was located in the "Everglades", some distance from the Base.

(d) S.C.T.C. disbursing paid all hands in shakedown on the 1st and 15th of the month right at the activity.

(e) The Miami Shipbuilding Corporation furnished marine railways for as many as three boats at a time for effecting underwater repairs.

(f) A small shack housed the Coxswains who ran the six retriever boats moored at the pier.

(g) Recreation and welfare facilities furnished by S.C.T.C. and a nearby park were available for athletics.

(h) Supply requests went through the S.C.T.C. Supply Office to Mechanicsburg, and open market purchasing was authorized. (The supply activity was taken over by Pier #3 Supply Depot in July 1945).

(i) Housing and messing were obtainable in local hotels under Navy control, and laundry service was available in these hotels.

(j) An average of eleven officers and sixty-six EM were the normal compliment for the Detail.

The original staff officers of the Shakedown Detail were:

Lt. Cdr. A. Montgomery, USN O-in-C, Senior Instructor

Lt. D. Agnew, USNR Communications Officer

Lt. R. Searles, USNR Gunnery Officer

Lt. (jg) L. Nikoloric, USNR Hull & Engineering Officer

Ens. J. M. Flachman, USNR Seamanship & Navigation Instructor

The successive O's-in-C were

    Comdr. B. K. Atkins,

    Comdr. R. B. Kelly,

    Comdr. R. H. Smith,

    Comdr. J. Harlee,

    and Lt. R. W. Orrei,

The later officer secured the Detail in mid December 1945 with a staff of seven officers and forty-one EM.

EXPERIMENTAL PROGRAM

In addition to supervising the shakedown of boats and conducting inspections, the various commanding officers of the Shakedown Detail did a good deal of experimental work. Comparative tests between the Higgins 70' and 78' and the Elco 80' boats were run, and Lt. Cdr. Montgomery became so enthusiastic with the results of the 70' boat that he recommended to BuI&S that this boat become the prototype for all future production. This same boat, the "Hellcat", was recently decommissioned in New York.

All manner of armament combinations were developed and experimented with, and some valuable results were obtained. Gun installations that were originally considered as fantastic often times became standard compliment for some of the boats as a result of the experimental work conducted.

From time to time, the O-in-C of shakedown submitted reports to the Commissioning Detail in New Orleans and the Supervisor of Shipbuilding at Higgins Industries. The nature of the reports was in the form of constructive criticisms and suggestions arrived at from testing and operating the boats during the shakedown period. The reports were honest evaluations of what was lacking in the boats and their supervision at time of construction. Apparently they were not received in New Orleans with the same spirit with which they were submitted, because friction arose between the two activities. CO, SCTC could not understand the attitude nor the readiness with which the SupShips accepted the reports of employees of Higgins Industries over and above official reports of his command. In no uncertain terms he informed the parties concerned that there would be some changes in attitude made if the program was to function efficiently. Harmony was eventually restored, and much valuable criticism brought about improvements at the production point rather than at the Shakedown Detail.

The experimental program stemmed from two sources, one being the Shakedown Detail itself and the other the Training Center in R. I. MTBSTC had a well-established experimental department in the closing phases of its existence, and conducted the major portion of equipment experiments.

BuShips authorized the various experimental programs and Melville acted upon them. The work was done either at Melville, Miami, or both, depending upon the nature of the experiment. For example, BuShips authorized the testing of flippers (horizontal fins extending beyond the transom).

Melville received several of the installation kits and forwarded some to Miami. Miami Shakedown tested the kits and forwarded their results and recommendations to the proper authorities.

In addition to programs forwarded from Melville, the Shakedown Detail initiated a great many of its own programs for testing and developing. The weather conditions made the Detail an ideal location for testing grounds and many improvements were forthcoming from the activity.

SUMMARY

Since its inception, the PT Shakedown Detail's mission has been categorized as follows:

1. To discover and correct defects in the construction and supply program which would otherwise pass unnoticed until the boats reach combat areas.

2. To speed delivery of the boats to combat areas.

3. To train officers and men for combat operating, and to weed the misfits from the PT program.

To these ends, the Detail has been gratifyingly successful.

Little or no publicity has accompanied the growth of the activity, and one of the chief factors contributing to the success is its location. The climactic and sea conditions are ideal in the Miami area, and are representative of the combat areas to which the boats are ultimately assigned. These same two factors, climatic and sea conditions, were the determining cause of Melville's failure as a shakedown base. The rough winter weather made operating almost impossible. The crews were more concerned about hanging on and keeping warm than they were about learning their duties. Squadrons could not follow the training syllabus in the prescribed time, and the results were not as favorable as they should and could have been.

As a division of the Naval Training Center, the Shakedown Detail functioned efficiently and quietly. There was little or no friction within the organization, and the Detail appeared almost as a separate activity divorced from the Naval Training Center.

SYLLABUS FOR PT SHAKEDOWN PERIOD

FIRST DAY

Inspect all boats using check-off list to determine:

(a) Deficiencies in material and equipment.

(b) Excess or superfluous material or equipment.

(c) Satisfactory operation of equipment.

(d) That operating personnel are familiar with proper operation of equipment.

(e) That routine tests, inspections and upkeep of equipment are being carried out.

PT shakedown group will supervise these inspections assisted by squadron officers.

SECOND DAY

(a) Correct deficiencies noted in first day's inspections.

(b) Calibrate compasses

(c) Calibrate radios, RDF and Radar

(d) Fuel consumption and speed calibration runs over measured mile for heavy and light loads. (none – To obtain worthwhile results, fuel flow meters and revolution counters must be used. Several days will be necessary to obtain this information and should be worked in as opportunity permits throughout the shakedown period. Full load calibration will be made with boat fueled to capacity and a full war load. Light load calibration will be made with 50% fuel and no torpedoes.)

THIRD DAY

(a) Conduct day cruising exercises. This is to include harbor, channel, torpedo ranges, operating areas and inter-island piloting in order to familiarize PT personnel with local waters.

(b) While en route conduct simple tactics, exercise at visual and radio communications, test radar, hold emergency and general drills, and make use of RDF.

AN ADMINISTRATIVE HISTORY OF PT's IN WORLD WAR II
(Recreated October 25, 2010 by the members of the PT Boat Forum message board)

127

FOURTH DAY

(a) Complete calibration tests (except fuel consumption and speed runs).

(b) Hold surface gunnery exercises for .50 cal. and 20mm at moving surface target.

(c) Hold surface firing of small arms at stationary target.

FOURTH DAY - NIGHT EXERCISES

(a) Conduct night cruising exercises similar to day cruising exercises making use of Radar, RDF, and all night communications.

FIFTH DAY

(a) Hold AA gunnery exercises for .50 cal. and 20mm at towed sleeves.

(b) Each boat exercise at taking another PT in tow, astern and alongside.

(c) Exercise at boat handling upon return to dock.

FIFTH DAY – NIGHT EXERCISES

(a) Conduct night search and attack by PT striking force against surface targets, using radar to locate targets and searchlights to simulate torpedo fire. After breakaway, regroup PT's and repeat. Surface targets will flash searchlights to simulate gunfire as soon as PT's are observed.

SIXTH DAY

(a) Hold AA gunnery exercises for .50 cal. and 20mm at towed sleeves.

(b) Exercise at being towed astern from larger surface vessel singly and in pairs.

(c) Conduct emergency drills en route to and from area.

(d) Exercise at boat handling upon returning to dock.

SIXTH DAY – NIGHT EXERCISES

(a) Conduct night search and attack by PT striking force against moving surface targets using Radar to locate targets and searchlight to simulate torpedo fire. Surface target will illuminate and chase

PT's as soon as they are observed, simulating enemy destroyers. PT's will use evasive tactics and smoke to cover retirement.

SEVENTH DAY

(a) Hold AA gunnery exercises for .50 cal. and 20mm at towed sleeve.

(b) Exercise at fueling at sea from larger surface vessel.

(c) Conduct emergency drills en route to and from area.

(d) Exercise at boat handling upon returning to dock.

SEVENTH DAY – NIGHT OPERATIONS

(a) Conduct cruise out of sight of land with assigned mission to simulate mining a designated area.

EIGHTH, NINTH AND TENTH DAY

(a) Conduct torpedo firing against surface targets. Each boat will fire three torpedo practices during this period. The eighth and ninth days, boats will make independent attacks in succession first making dummy runs followed by firing runs. Each boat will fire one torpedo, slow and then follow our torpedo. On the tenth day, group attacks will be made, they will consist of two or more dummy runs followed by a firing run. All available torpedoes will be fired on this run. After break away boats will follow torpedoes.

(b) Study the torpedo war head with its attachments and exploder mechanism.

EIGHTH, NINTH AND TENTH DAY – NIGHT EXERCISES

(a) Conduct night search and attack by PT patrols and PT striking force against moving surface targets using Radar to locate target, simulate torpedo fire. Surface targets will illuminate and chase PT's as soon as they are observed. PT's will use evasive tactics and smoke to make their getaway. PT's return to base immediately.

ELEVENTH AND TWELFTH DAY

(a) Conduct squadron and Division tactics.

(b) Conduct squadron and Division torpedo attacks against larger moving surface target, attacking under cover of smoke.

(c) Conduct exercise with aircraft. Aircraft to simulate dive bombing and strafing attacks. PT's to use standard evasive tactics, scatter plan, defensive formation and smoke.

(d) Each boat drop one live depth charge simulating attack on a submarine which was observed to submerge.

AN ADMINISTRATIVE HISTORY OF PT's IN WORLD WAR II
(Recreated October 25, 2010 by the members of the PT Boat Forum message board)

129

ELEVENTH AND TWELFTH DAY – NIGHT EXERCISES

(a) Conduct night search and attack against moving surface target by PT divisions. Use Radar to locate target. Simulate torpedo fire. Surface targets will illuminate and chase PT's as soon as they are observed. PT's will use evasive tactics and smoke to make their getaway. Use experimental surface flares to silhouette target. Reform.

(b) Conduct exercises with Army to test ability of PT boats to enter and raid coastal area.

THIRTEENTH DAY AND NIGHT

(a) Make up uncompleted work schedule.

FOURTEENTH DAY

(a) Make preparations for departure.

All boats will be required to keep accurate DR tracks whenever exercises are conducted outside the harbor. These tracks will be compared after each exercise, errors pointed out and the importance of accurate DR stressed.

At every opportunity en route to and from operating areas boats will be exercised at deployment, simulated torpedo attack and breakaway.

All available time at the dock will be devoted to boat handling.

130

AN ADMINISTRATIVE HISTORY OF PT's IN WORLD WAR II
(Recreated October 25, 2010 by the members of the PT Boat Forum message board)

CHAPTER SEVEN

COMMISSIONING DETAILS

Like all Naval vessels, PT's required the facilities and assistance of commissioning details to prepare them for sea duty.

When sources of production had been definitely established, CNO authorized the establishment of Commissioning Details in the New York area and the New Orleans or Gulf area. These two areas were decided upon after Elco and Higgins had been selected to produce PT's.

The same officer established both the Details and to Lt. R. J. Dressling, USN goes credit for a fine job in both activities. In conjunction with the Commissioning Detail in New Orleans, a PT Ferrying Command was established in March of 1945. This newly established activity was short-lived, but in its functional organization were included the duties of a commissioning detail to handle the boats earmarked for Russia. A short account of this activity has been included in the following discussion on commissioning details.

MTB COMMISSIONING DETAIL NEW YORK

The early Elco squadrons accepted their boats from the builder in an almost finished condition, but there were always a number of government furnished items, necessary to the boats, which the contractor was not obliged to furnish. These items were furnished by the Navy Yard at Brooklyn, and it was the responsibility of the squadron commander to assure procurement of these items for his organization.

This arrangement was not satisfactory in that it heaped on the squadron commander's shoulders a myriad of minuscule details, which by sheer weight of numbers, could claim a majority of his time. He, of course, could detail this work to his officers, and very naturally did; but this made the boat captains and executive officers of the squadron primarily concerned with supply duties rather than operational duties.

ESTABLISHMENT OF COMMISSIONING DETAIL

In an effort to alleviate this situation, an officer was sent to Brooklyn to be in charge of the outfitting of PT boats when delivered from the

AN ADMINISTRATIVE HISTORY OF PT's IN WORLD WAR II
(Recreated October 25, 2010 by the members of the PT Boat Forum message board)

131

Elco company.[1] His official position was Officer In Charge of YR 28, for this vessel had been procured to hold PT spares.[2]

Thus, the Motor Torpedo Boat Commissioning Detail, Navy Yard, New York came into existence on 12 June 1942. The staff of the Officer in Charge included a junior line officer, a junior supply officer, two storekeepers and two yeomen.

BuShips allowed the Commissioning Detail $18,000 to prepare the YR 28 to act as stowage barge, workshop and cafeteria.[3] The stowage work involved arrangement of bins for squadron spares. Hitherto, all spares had just been dumped on the barge without much thought as to category, but the BuShips allowance enabled the construction of separate bins for hull, engineering, torpedo and gunnery gear. In addition to this, each squadron was given twelve bins for boat spares, thereby creating a supply locker for each boat. Finally, an "I" beam was installed from the shore end to the seaward end of the barge. This allowed the handling of heavy equipment by means of chain hoists, while the "I" beam extended out to the seaward side far enough to handle the removal or installation of torpedoes and engines.

As in all the modifications, it was necessary to start from scratch on the workshop. A large shop was not needed, but a good shop was a necessity for the small jobs necessary on the boats following delivery. The Officer-in-Charge installed a carpenter's work bench and a machinist's work bench, a storage battery charging outfit, a small air compressor for cleaning purposes, and various electrical machinery such as grinding wheels, drill presses and saws. In addition to this it was necessary to rewire the barge to handle all electrical equipment (including the soon-to-be-installed galley gear) plus twelve switch boxes to provide power for the 110-volt circuits of the boats alongside.

A cafeteria was laid out and completely equipped with galley utensils, serving platters, stoves, boilers, and a large electrical icebox. Because the PT program was expanding at this time, the facilities were made adequate for the feeding of 300 officers and men. Experience bore out this forehandedness.[4]

With this work accomplished the Commissioning Detail was set to function as such, and it was necessary to take stock of the shortcomings of the previous methods of handling the outfitting of the boats. This was necessary, for the Detail was expected to handle MTB Squadron FIVE, then in production at Elco. A look at the record showed that previously, equipment had not been ordered

---

1. BuPers orders Pers-31-RB 82664, 17 June 1942, Commandant, Navy Yard, New York's YR28/P16-3/00, Serial 5, 12 June 1942. Discrepancy between the date of the orders and the date of reporting is caused by telephone transmission of the orders prior to the date they were written out.

2. Commandant, Navy Yard New York's PT/PT4/ND3/A4-1/YR28, 16 January 1942; CNO's FC8-4/A4-1 (420107) Serial 3938, 8 January 1942.

3. BuShips project order 795/41; BuShips S32/YR28(275).

4. Letter from Lt. Cdr. R. J. Dressling, USN, First Officer-in-Charge of MTB Commissioning Detail, Navy Yard, New York, to Office of Naval History, 17 September 1945.

far enough in advance. Secondly, after requisitions had been made out to the builder or to Packard by the Supply Officer, the Navy Procurement Office at the Navy Yard, rather than follow through with the original requisition, would substitute the requested item with a similar item that could be obtained more cheaply! This situation reached its nadir when one of the squadrons ordered a 24-volt unit and the Naval Procurement Office substituted a 110-volt unit in order to give the boats more power! Thirdly, delivery of requisitioned items was held up because there was such a large inspection turnover. This was the main bottleneck.

Finally, after a squadron left the yard, parts that were delivered tardily were not forwarded immediately, but sat around the yard for an indefinite period. When they finally were forwarded, they were addressed simply to "PT Boats" with no squadron designation. Many times the Yard had no information at all as to where the boats went after leaving the Yard.

Remedial measures suggested for these deficiencies were, first, bulk orders for the boats proposed under the existing Elco contract (PT's 103-196). Secondly, a request for the Supply Department to order directly from the builder or from the company designated in the requisition of the squadron (or, as would be the case in the future, the requisition of the Commissioning Detail). Thirdly, another request to the Supply Department to allow incoming shipments for the Commissioning Detail to be delivered directly to the activity without prior inspection, and to allow the Supply Officer of the Commissioning Detail to make the necessary checks. Finally, the Commissioning Detail offered to undertake the responsibility for the shipment of any straggling items which arrived after a squadron had left. These items would be shipped directly to the operating base to which the squadron had been assigned. [5]

BASIC TASK

With these difficulties out of the way, the Commissioning Detail set up for its basic task. The Detail would order in advance all squadron spares and boat spares that were not standard stock material. When a boat arrived in the Yard, all standard stock boat spares would be ordered. When a squadron went into commission, all standard stock squadron spares would be ordered. The Detail would prepare and recommend changes in the allowance lists for the approval of the Bureau of Ships. The Detail's personnel would assist squadron commanders and squadron department heads by advising them as to what material they would receive, what material they should carry with them and what material they should ship. When the squadron departed, remaining spares would be shipped to the destination ordered by the Bureau of Ships.

Together with these major duties, the Detail planned to perform several comparatively minor functions. Disbursing records for all officers and men

---

5. Memo of R. J. Dressling to Commander E. D. Snow, 18 June 1942.

AN ADMINISTRATIVE HISTORY OF PT's IN WORLD WAR II
(Recreated October 25, 2010 by the members of the PT Boat Forum message board)

133

would be handled by the Commissioning Detail's disbursing officer until such time as the squadron was commissioned. (Later this was extended until such time as the squadron left the Yard). The Commissioning Detail's personnel officer would assist the squadrons in obtaining their compliment of officers and men by constant contact with BuPers and MTBSTC, Melville, Rhode Island. The executive officer of the Commissioning Detail would assist the squadrons in obtaining training for personnel at activities provided by CotClant. The Detail would also prepare job orders on various repairs and authorized work on the boats after delivery. Lastly, the Detail undertook to expedite delivery of contractor boat material, where necessary, through the Supervisor of Shipbuilding at the Elco plant in Bayonne.[6]

EXPANSION OF FACILITIES

The first boats of MTBRon FIVE arrived at the Commissioning Detail in June of 1942, and Squadron FIVE became the first organization to be completely outfitted by the Commissioning Detail.

The next six squadrons of the contract followed on the heels of FIVE, and the Commissioning Detail handled every Elco squadron from that time on through Squadron FORTY-TWO, the last Elco squadron, which was commissioned after the cessation of hostilities.

The high rate of production maintained at Elco often brought about a situation that found the last boats of one squadron and the first boats of the following squadron at the Commissioning Detail at the same time. Influx of personnel was constant, and all the facilities of the organization were taxed to the limit.

This situation was greatly moderated in January of 1943, when the U.S.S. WHEELING was assigned to the Commissioning Detail to take over berthing and messing of all personnel, thus leaving the YR 28 entirely for stowage and work.[7] The "Wheeling" also provided much more satisfactory offices for the administrative staff of the Detail. At the same time, space for squadron offices was procured on the fourth floor of Building 292. This expansion facilitated work, and eliminated any worries about living or office spaces.

REORGANIZATIONS[8]

The expansion in facilities and the rate at which squadrons were being delivered from Elco made the original organization of the MTB Commissioning

6. R. J. Dresslings, letter of 17 September 1945

7. Commandant, Third Naval District's letter of 11 January 1943; OpNav Serial 500038, 29 December 1942.

8. The following information on the reorganization of the administration of the MTB Commissioning Detail is taken from a plan for reorganization promulgated 12 May 1943 by commandant, Navy Yard, New York's, PT/A4-1.

Detail anachronistic. To handle the personnel successfully, and to provide the greatest possible assistance to the new squadrons, the Commissioning Detail had to reorganize. The final plan of this reorganization was promulgated in March of 1943, shortly after the expansion of the Detail had been completed.

GENERAL

The Commanding Officer of the Detail was responsible to the Commandant, and assumed additional responsibilities as Commanding Officer of the YR 28 and the "Wheeling". The Detail itself was to act as the Navy Yard's fitting out section for PT's and to perform all the functions that would normally be carried out by such a section. Boats delivered to a squadron prior to the arrival of the squadron's prospective Commanding Officer were also under the command of the Commanding Officer of the Detail.

Definite procedure for the handling of boats and for the commissioning of the squadrons was established. A squadron was to be commissioned after the delivery of either its third or fourth boat (12 boats comprised a squadron), and the boats were to be outfitted by the Detail within fourteen days. Every effort was to be made to speed the delivery of the boats, and new commanding officers were to be supplied all pertinent information which might aid in expediting the completion of the squadron.

PERSONNEL

When new squadrons formed at New York, personnel offered a considerable problem, as no definite policy had been adopted as to reporting dates. Under the reorganization, a new squadron was to supply its prospective Commanding Officer and Supply Officer one week prior to the delivery of the first boat; its Executive Officer and six prospective Boat Captains one day prior to the delivery of the first boat; department head within one week after the delivery of the first boat; two additional officers intended for assignment to boats for duty one day prior to the delivery of the fourth boat; and two more officers one day prior to the delivery of each subsequent boat.

As for the enlisted men, the squadron was expected to have on hand thirty enlisted men two weeks prior to the delivery of the first boat. One yeoman and two storekeepers were to report one week before delivery of the first boats, and boat crews were to report one day in advance of the delivery dates of their boats. In all these cases, dates given were the deadline; and, naturally, personnel could be accepted before these dates.

Fitting-out was the prime function of the squadron while in the Yard, and to assist in successful fitting-out, each squadron was asked to furnish a fitting-out detail comprising Personnel, Engineering, Hull, Ordnance, Supply and Disbursing, Navigation and Stores Officers. These officers were responsible for the fitting-out of the squadron, and were not to be shifted to other duties

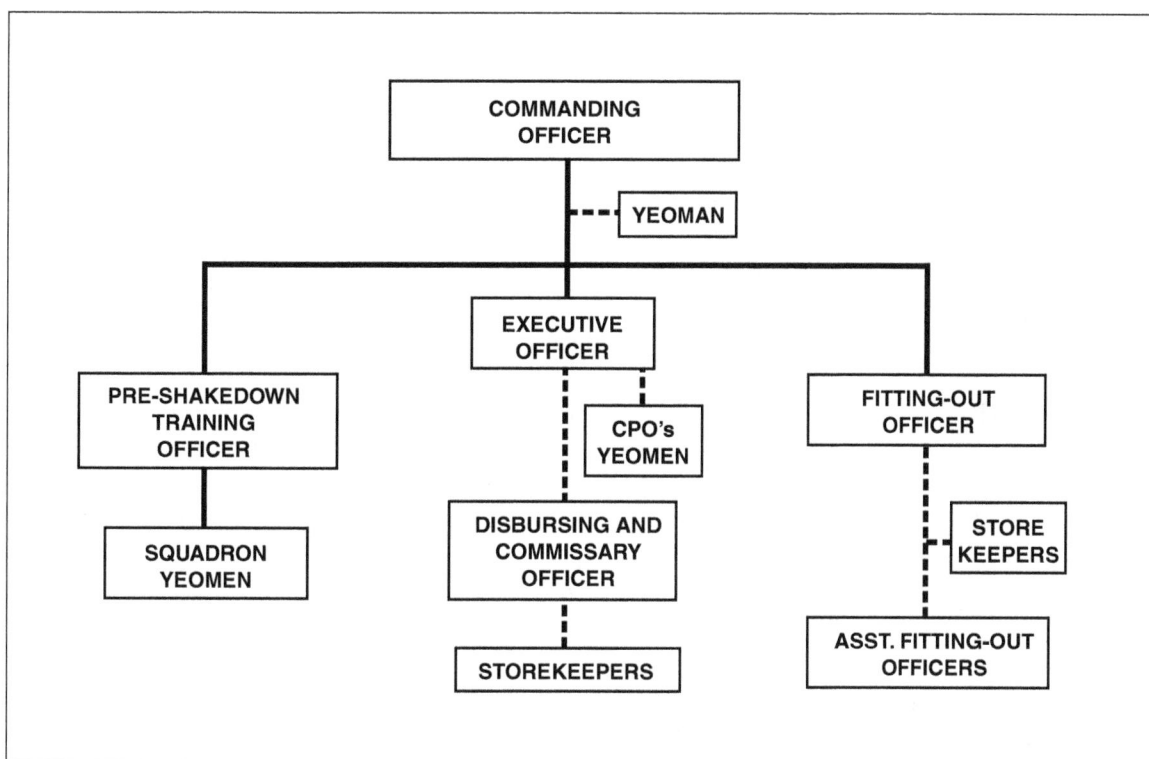

*Figure 26: **Internal Administrative Organization of Motor Torpedo Boat Commissioning Detail, Navy Yard, New York***

without the cognisance of the Commanding Officer of the Commissioning Detail. The Detail handled all its fitting-out with these officers, and thereby left all other squadron officers free for training and operational duties.

Operational training was considered an important adjunct of the Commissioning Detail, but the boats could not base at the Navy Yard while training. To solve this situation, the Commissioning Detail made arrangements for the boats to use Fyfe's Shipyard, Glenwood Landing, Long Island, New York for an operational training base, and when not in a work status at the Navy Yard the boats were supposed to base at Fyfe's.

During the whole commissioning period, the officers and men of the squadron were to be berthed and fed by the Commissioning Detail to the limit of the "Wheeling's" capacity. Pay records would still be handled by the Commissioning Detail under this plan of reorganization.

MATERIAL

Problems of material remained more or less constant despite the expansion of the Detail, but the reorganization did take into account the important factor of improvements to the boats. Often a modification to the boats was approved by BuShips, but just as often it was difficult for Elco to incorporate such modifications into production without some delay. The Commissioning Detail,

136

AN ADMINISTRATIVE HISTORY OF PT's IN WORLD WAR II
(Recreated October 25, 2010 by the members of the PT Boat Forum message board)

therefore, undertook to arrange for the Navy Yard to effect all new alterations until such time as the builder was able to incorporate them in the assembly line. This meant that all boats leaving New York were fitted-out with the latest available equipment.

The Commissioning Detail was also supposed to be on the alert for potential supply bottlenecks which would delay delivery of the boats, and to eliminate the basic cause before the bottlenecks had a chance to form.

REPORTS

Upon the departure of a squadron, the Commanding Officer of the Commissioning Detail was to submit to the Commandant of the Navy Yard a report on those items of equipment on the allowance list which were not delivered with an explanation for non-delivery, and also an explanation of when delivery would be effected. The Commanding Officer of the Commissioning Detail was also to prepare reports as called for by VCNO, BuShips and Training Commands.

PRINCIPAL DUTIES OF THE COMMANDING OFFICER

The principal duties of the Detail's Commanding Officer were to coordinate activities with the Navy Yard, VCNO, BuShips, SupShips Bayonne, CotClant, MTBSTC, Inspector of Navy Material, and the Port Director's Office. In addition he was to maintain a PT availability control chart, promulgate movement orders, supervise yard work, squadron work requests, and squadron requisitions in excess, and to control office, warehouse, and lighter space used by the Commissioning Detail and the Squadrons. If requested, he was to assist in the selection of officer personnel for MTBSTC. In addition to all this, he was required to submit weekly progress reports.

PRINCIPAL DUTIES OF THE EXECUTIVE OFFICER

The Executive Officer was to act as Senior Watch Officer, Personnel Officer and Operations Officer. Berthing and messing were to be under his supervision. He was to submit weekly reports as required by the Commanding Officer.

PRINCIPAL DUTIES OF THE OUTFITTING OFFICER

The Outfitting Officer was to maintain all copies of PT allowance lists assembled in allowance control books, which he was to keep up to date. He was to personally coordinate all activities of the Commissioning Detail with the Supply Department of the Navy Yard. He was to provide all squadron commanders with up to date allowance lists upon the commissioning of their squadrons. Personal checks on the Hull and Navigation allowance lists to ensure that allowances met requirements were also part of his duties.

AN ADMINISTRATIVE HISTORY OF PT's IN WORLD WAR II
(Recreated October 25, 2010 by the members of the PT Boat Forum message board)

137

He was also to determine the source of shipment of all items, record them in control books, and take all necessary steps to ensure delivery. Stowages bins and cages were his responsibility, and he was to submit a weekly report of the activities of his department to the Commanding Officer.

The Assistant Outfitting Officer was to secure all details which had bearing on BuOrd, BuY&D and BuMed allowance lists and insure that such allowances were adequate. He was to determine the source of all items listed and to take steps to eliminate any delays other than production delays.

The Second Assistant Outfitting Officer was responsible for all details bearing on BuShips and BuS&A allowance lists. He was to assist the Outfitting Officer and the Assistant Outfitting Officer in handling details of stowage on lighters and in warehouses outside the yard. In addition, he was to assist in assembling all large shipments and was to determine by sight the location of all items of these shipments.

The Third Assistant Outfitting Officer was to handle all requisitions needed to fill allowances. He was to follow up on all requisitions in excess with the Supply Department and the Naval Procurement office, and with the contractor, if necessary, in order to expedite delivery. He was to follow up on all open purchases and on all Bureau contracts which supplied items of spares generally shipped with the squadrons. Finally, he was to keep a running check on the Supply Department's delivery of spares as compared to the allowance lists, and to maintain control of all shakedown spares.

PRINCIPAL DUTIES OF DISBURSING AND COMMISSARY OFFICER

The Disbursing and Commissary Officer was to carry all squadron pay accounts until the Squadron Disbursing Officer was able to assume them. He was to mess all personnel of the squadrons fitting out. He was also to supervise the auxiliary mess at Fyfe's Ship Yard, and to provide needed rations for PT's operating from the Navy Yard.

CONTROL OF AVAILABILITY

In general, each PT was to be available to the Yard, ordered to temporary duty, or moored as follows; the first two weeks after delivery to be spent in fitting-out; the next two or three weeks ordered to MTBTSC on temporary duty (pre-shakedown); the next two or three weeks moored at Fyfe's for installation of additional equipment recently approved or made available; three or four days prior to shakedown departure in the Yard for final repairs and preparations; shakedown for three weeks; in the Yard for one week of post-shakedown; and then moored at Fyfe's until shipped.

A control chart of availability was kept to prevent interference with Yard work, to keep PT's in the Yard at a minimum, to make PT's available for all possible additional training, and to provide assistance to MTBSTC, which was short of boats for training purposes at the time.

PRE-SHAKEDOWN TRAINING

It was planned to instruct Squadron Commanders, Boat Captains and other officers and crews in shakedown procedure so that further instruction would not be necessary when the boats arrived at MTBSTC. The schedule called for blinker, semaphore, code, procedure, gunnery, physical education, boat handling and line handling classes, and any other classes deemed necessary by CotClant or MTBSTC.

In addition, practical instruction courses in the plants of equipment manufacturers outside the Yard were to be organized. These classes were primarily in those appliances and parts which had been giving operating personnel difficulty.

EFFECT OF REORGANIZATION

The Commissioning Detail operated on this reorganized system for the rest of the war, and the concepts of the reorganization were broad enough and elastic enough to engender constant successful prosecution of the basic task.

TRAINING AT THE COMMISSIONING DETAIL[9]

Training at the Commissioning Detail presented unique problems in that the activity was not in any sense a training activity, but rather an outfitting organization. Provisions for training had been loosely integrated in the plan outlined above, but definite policy was hard to define, for it was handmade to suit the need.

The Director of Training, Third Naval District, was in charge of training for MTB Squadrons. The Commissioning Detail obtained training facilities for its men through this office by two means, the first informal (and largely used), and the second via the regular chain of command. Once again it was a case of tailoring the method to suit the need.

Under the first plan, if the commissioning Detail had a group of men for who training was desired, a simple and logical action became the rule. The Executive Officer of the Commissioning Detail simply called up the District Training Office, told the Officer in Charge his needs, and when possible, that office immediately made assignment of available training. If no training was immediately available, often "bootleg" arrangements could be made to place men from the Commissioning Detail in classes already under way.

---

9. Much of the information on training has come from conversations with Lt. J. J. Romoda, USNR, at the District Training Office, Third Naval District. Lt. Romoda was liaison officer of the Training Office for the MTB Commissioning Detail.

AN ADMINISTRATIVE HISTORY OF PT's IN WORLD WAR II
(Recreated October 25, 2010 by the members of the PT Boat Forum message board)

139

By the same method, the commissioning Detail submitted its training needs on paper to the Fleet Administrative Office at the Navy Yard. This office in turn would forward them to the Third Naval District, and appropriate action would be initiated. As the Commissioning Detail grew, the swing toward this latter system began. The net change in results obtained was negligible, and by the summer of 1944, all requests were handled on paper.

For training which the Training Office at the Third Naval District could not provide, the Commissioning Detail applied directly to BuPers for authorization to send the men to the schools desired.

LOCAL TRAINING FACILITIES AVAILABLE

The Third Naval District was generally able to satisfy the Commissioning Detail with allocations for local training. Local training at the time was largely confined to training in the plants of industries which made equipment for the boats. This included the Bendix-Scintilla Corporation, Magneto Division, Sidney, New York, the Elco "Naval Academy" at Bayonne, New Jersey, and Joseph Van Blerck and Sons, Exhaust Stacks and Mufflers, Roosevelt, Long Island. This list was augmented by the Holley Service School, Holley Carburetor Corporation, Detroit, Michigan and Naval Training School (Fuel Cells), Akron, Ohio. Although the Packard Engines School was in operation at this time, no men were sent to this activity from the Commissioning Detail because of the length of the course (eight weeks).

The system of training men in industry was considered successful from every point of view. The rates selected for training were able to see equipment in production, to talk to the men who were designing and assembling the equipment, and to take their individual problems to the source. Personnel supplied by industry released navy men for further duty and insured competent teachers. To duplicate at the Navy Yard the facilities offered by the above mentioned industries would have cost the Navy approximately $100,000 and would have utilized 8600 square feet of floor area at a time when space was at a premium.

In addition to these industrial schools, men from the Commissioning Detail attended Fluxgate compress, radar operations, radar material and 40mm gunnery schools operated within the Navy yard plus a gunnery and signal school operated by personnel in the Commissioning Detail. [10]

ADMINISTRATIVE RESPONSIBILITY

When the Commissioning Detail was established it was directly responsible to the Commandant of the Navy Yard, and this relationship continued until 1944. In March of 1944 all Commissioning Details for surface ships were

---

10. MTB Commissioning Details IX28/P11-1 Serial 187, 17 march 1944.

consolidated,[11] and early April, a new command, Central Commissioning Detail East Coast was established.[12]

The MTB Commissioning Detail was responsible to the Commandant of the new command[13] until its disestablishment in April of 1945.[14] The Commanding Officer of the MTB Commissioning Detail then reported the Commandant, Third Naval District. This final chain of command was in effect at the cessation of hostilities.

CONCLUSION

The history of this Commissioning Detail points out administrative shortcomings held in common with other Commissioning Details, and these are capably sunned up in the final report of the Commandant, Central Commissioning Details, East Coast, as follows:

"At every turn throughout the life of Commissioning Details the work of these agencies was hampered by the lack of detailed directives from superior authority. The Navy Regulations in no way contemplate the existence of such agencies and all of the functions performed by the Commissioning Details were, as a matter of regulation and custom, the responsibility of other well-established naval agencies. The purpose for the establishment of Commissioning Details was to make up for the deficiency in training of personnel and the inability of other agencies actually charged with the responsibility to cope with the situation.

" . . . . by implication and frequent but direct conversation, it was assumed that Commissioning Details were, in fact, field representatives of the Chief of Naval Operations during the commissioning periods, inasmuch as vessels during that period reported to CNO as to type commander."[15]

POSSIBLE REMEDIAL ACTION

These problems were, of course, present at the MTB Commission Detail, and one of the most provocative subjects was the integration of training with outfitting at the Commissioning Detail. The general effect was negative, for it placed an added load upon an activity primarily concerned with operation work, in that the main object of the detail was to outfit the boats. True, training loads decreased as MTBSTC expanded, but no burden of the training should have been put upon the shoulders of Commissioning Detail personnel. If training could have been accomplished entirely at Melville, or failing that, through the

---

11. CNO's A4-1 Serial 0181323, 29 March 1944.

12. BuPars 9046 Pers-3a-DBK-6, 3 April 1944.

13. MTB Commissioning Detail's IX28/P16-3/00 Serial 176 (c), 15 <ay 1944; Com3's DHq-9b-ee over 52974, P16-3, Serial 03047, 18 April 1944; BuPers Pers 3125-DES (NC) (650) (P) 10 April 1944.

14. CenComDetEC's ON 73-3ND/A3 JAS:eqf, Serial 57, 27 August 1945.

15. History of Central Commissioning Detail, East Coast: Articles 19 and 23.

AN ADMINISTRATIVE HISTORY OF PT's IN WORLD WAR II
(Recreated October 25, 2010 by the members of the PT Boat Forum message board)

141

Figure 27: ELCO MTBRon 40 Commissioning Ceremony

efforts of the squadrons, delivery of the boats could have been effected much more swiftly and efficiently.

The other main problem an MTB Commissioning Detail is a type problem. These boats were entirely divorced from the type of combatant ship that a Navy Yard is accustomed to handle, and as structural orphans, they were different problem for the Navy yard. The work on these boats broke down into man-hours, was negligible compared to the work performed on major combatant craft, and consequently, the majority of workers at the Yard were those skilled in work on larger ships.

The solution to this problem would be the establishment of the Commissioning Detail at a small, independent yard, equipped to handle wooden boats of less than 100' overall length. The boats would have better artisans, barracks facilities could be provided for the men much nearer to the boats (an important morale factor), and the squadrons would not be confronted with the troublesome industrial manager system in short, the ideal situation would be a small yard with an autonomous PT Commissioning Detail; a training base could be established in the immediate vicinity for shakedown work; and the whole base would be away from the navy Yard organization which is much unwieldy for PT's.[16]

MOTOR TORPEDO BOAT COMMISSIONING DETAIL

NEW ORLEANS, LA.

The increasing tempo of PT production eventually brought the time-tested boat designer and builder into the picture, and his assembly-line methods were put to good use. In the spring of '42, Mr. A.J. Higgins' City Park Plant went into production of his first squadron, and the need for a commissioning detail was immediate and definite. To these ends, a Motor Torpedo Boat Commissioning Detail was established at the Naval Station, Algiers, LA. Lt. R.J. DRESSLING USN reported to Com 8 ND as the prospective O-in-C on 3 August 1945 with the experience of establishing the New York PT Commissioning Detail as qualification for the position.

An activity of this nature should be compact if it is to carry out its function at all expeditiously. Unfortunately, the existing facilities were such that the Detail was forced to carry on its activities in a rather horizontal manner. From the time of its establishment until the time of its disestablishment, the activity was spread out all over the Navy holdings. Much valuable time and equipment were wasted in hauling material and personnel from point to point, and this difficulty was never fully overcome.

BASIC FUNCTIONS OF THE COMMISSIONING DETAIL

As seen form the stand point of VCNO, who has jurisdiction over the vessels until they are ultimately assigned to a fleet, the Commissioning Detail was: to cooperate with ShipShips during the pre-commissioning period in connection with details and installations for PT's and to Form a liaison group which, in cooperation with various Bureaus, would perform the following functions:

(1) Fitting-out of boats after they are received from contractor.

(2) Compilation of complete squadron gear and allowance lists.

(3) Detailed follow-up of Outfit Supply Activity.

(4) Receipt and distribution of all Bureau-furnished material.

(This included the operation of the warehouse in Algiers.)

(5.) Procurement of all squadron publications and charts.

---

16. Conversations with R.J. Dressling.

AN ADMINISTRATIVE HISTORY OF PT's IN WORLD WAR II
(Recreated October 25, 2010 by the members of the PT Boat Forum message board)

143

(6.) Initiation and follow-up of all new special item requested by the outfitting squadrons.

(7) Act as agent of BuShips in execution of experiments or of special contracts entered into by the Bureau.

(8) Assume responsibility for proper shipping of approximately 90% of spare parts sent to squadron bases.

(9) Act as agent between a squadron and any other interested party the departure of the squadron, if requested.

An additional duty was assigned the Detail when Com 8 authorized it to accept delivery of the boats for the Commandant and turn them over to the PCO's.

The original complement consisted of Lt. R.J. Dressling, USN at O-in-C with one (1) Lt., four (4) Lt.'s (jg), one (1) machinist, and nine (9) enlisted men. This was later increased to the size as illustrated by the following chart. During its entire period of activity, the Detail was always under-manned, but performed its duties and extra-curricular activities in a most heartening manner.

ORIGINAL PHYSICAL ORGANIZATION

Administrative facilities were to change several times; but at its inception, the Commissioning Detail had use of Building #4, Naval Station, New Orleans (Algiers), La. This afforded office and stowage space for both the Detail and the squadron commissioning. Later, Building #149 was available for a warehouse, and Barracks #8 housed the base force and transient personnel. All hands ate general meals at the Naval Station and had the use of all existing facilities on the base.

Completed boats were brought down the Industrial Canal from Lake Pontchartrain and into the river to the Naval Station. Here they proceeded to get ripped apart by the passing traffic's wake and naturally strong currents. The trip itself was extremely hazardous to the boats because of the great quantities of debris which were constantly clogging the river. The boats had to go into a repair status before they were even commissioned.

All supplies were handled by the Naval Station supply department, who ordered from Mechanicsburg Supply Depot, This system remained in practice even after the Detail's office was transferred to Lake Pontchartrain.

FACILITIES ON LAKE PONTCHARTRAIN

On 25 March 1942, Com 8 had leased facilities at the Yacht Basin for joint use by the Navy and Coast Guard small boats. In order to save the boats from any more damage, it was decided to leave them in the Lake and move the Detail out there to the Yacht Basin. By December 1942, the Commissioning Detail had

144

AN ADMINISTRATIVE HISTORY OF PT's IN WORLD WAR II
(Recreated October 25, 2010 by the members of the PT Boat Forum message board)

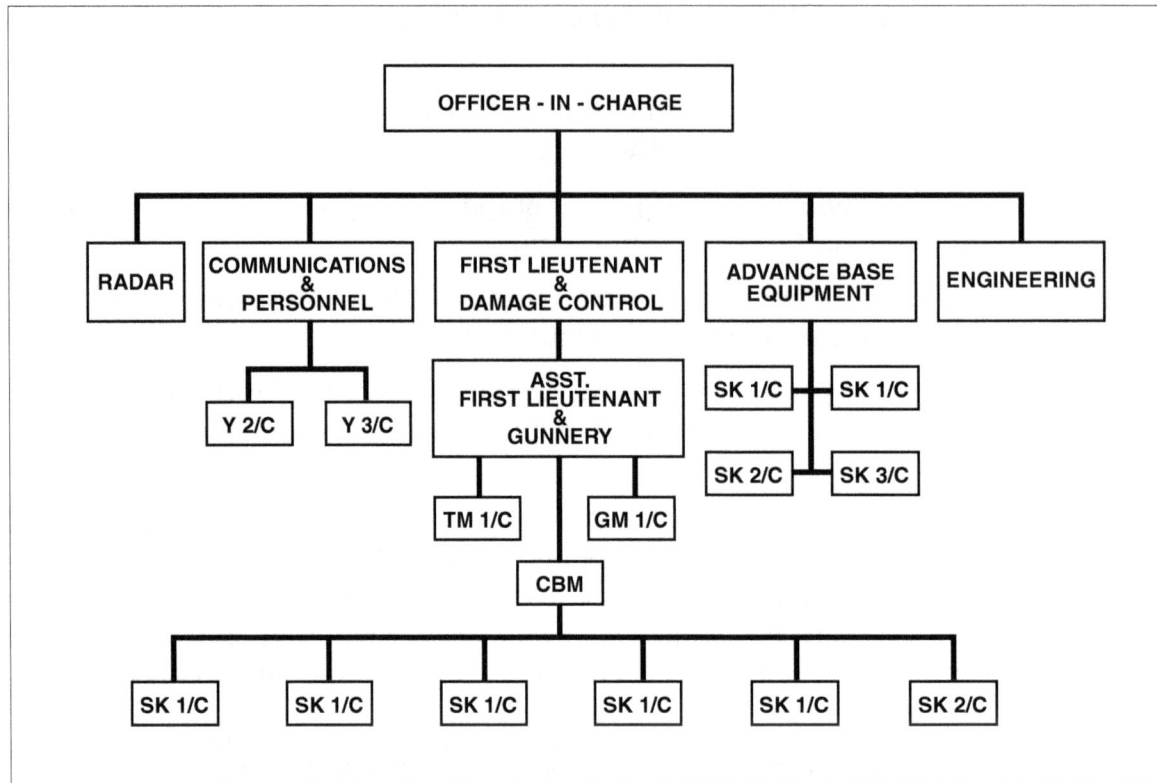

Figure 28: Internal Organization of Motor Torpedo Boat Commissioning Detail

eased itself into the Municipal Locker Building to such a degree that the Coast Guard ceased to use the building and immediate docking facilities.

Boats came up the lake from Higgins' plant and the Commissioning Detail accepted them for Com 8.

There were very few men in these early days of PT's who knew much about the boats, and work of the Detail was doubled due to the presence of a qualified staff of PT men.

Lake Pontchartrain offered very suitable conditions for testing the boats and training the crews while awaiting completion of the squadrons. The water was not deep enough to torpedo firing, but the lake was large enough for gunnery practice and extensive maneuvers. On the average, a squadron would be at the Commissioning Detail for three months. Delivers were averaging six boats a month and as a division was completed, it would move on to Miami for shakedown. Base force personnel were kept busy preparing the boats for the run to Miami and making last minute changes and repairs. Pre-shakedown could be conducted, to a limited extent on the lake, and the boat crews were not entirely green by the time they left to Miami.

One of the major short-comings of the Commissioning Detail was a lack of well organized training program for new squadrons. The boats were in

AN ADMINISTRATIVE HISTORY OF PT's IN WORLD WAR II
(Recreated October 25, 2010 by the members of the PT Boat Forum message board)

145

perfect position to conduct training schedules; but due to the absence of any well-defined plan, the PCO's had to organize their own training and testing programs.

Docking facilities were available for as many as eighteen boats, and there were 110-volt outlets on the docks for the boats.

Squadron personnel was scattered between Algiers and the Yacht Basin, and had to be transported back and forth in trucks supplied by the Naval Station. Nearly all squadron personnel reported to their new squadrons at the same times, and those awaiting boats spent most of their time in Algiers. Men assigned to the boats were out on subsistence, as there were missing facilities at the West End Station.

There was a great deal of lost motion in that arrangement; and, finally, on 6 October 1943 Com 8 authorized the leasing of the Southern Yacht Club Building from the Southern Yacht Club on the lake. This was located near the Municipal Locker Building and was obtained for the express purpose of housing and messing naval personnel of the MTB Commissioning Detail. The acquisition of this building consolidated the personnel of both the Commissioning Detail and the squadrons commissioning, but the supply problems were still very much in evidence.

The building was known as the West End Branch, Receiving Station, U.S. Naval Station, NOLA, and under the command of the O-in-C, MTB Commissioning Detail. This proved too much of a burden for him, however, and the activity soon went under the command of an officer supplied by the Naval Station. The Commissioning Detail had the use of the Yacht Club building until 31 July, 1945, when it was returned to the original owners, as agreed. [17]

SUMMARY

The Commissioning Detail was slow and a little vague in starting, but in spite of many handicaps, did an estimable job. There were a few bad moments experienced over some reports from the Shakedown Detail in Miami, but this could be expected because of the nature of the work of both the activities. From Miami, it appeared that the Commissioning Detail was reluctant to approve and effect changes recommended by the Shakedown Detail. The cause for apparent unwillingness to cooperate should be laid to the channels through which suggested changes must go before they can be incorporated in the program. Jointly, the two details, Miami and New Orleans, effected important improvements on the boats, successfully working through BuShips.

---

17. Com 8 ND ltr. Ser 19861 of 16 June 1945 which disestablished the West End Branch, Receiving Station as of 16 July 1945.

There was a short period in November 1943 when there was no American PT's commissioning but the Russian boats under construction continued to keep the Detail busy.

While the Detail labored under certain restrictions, i.e., it was under-manned and facilities were disjointed, it functioned successfully and thoroughly. The successive O-in-C's Lt. R.J. Dressling, USN, Lt. L.S. Rodgers, USN and Lt. G.H. Peresich, USNR, discharged their duties to such a degree of success as to receive letters of commendation from their immediate superiors.

Like the Detail in New York, the New Orleans activity was not directed to provide a training program for the new squadrons. However, with the existing facilities, a valuable training program could and should have been inaugurated for squadrons awaiting completion.

Lake Pontchartrain offered a most suitable training area, and boat crews could have undergone much more intensive training than they did. Miami Shakedown Detail commented several times on the poor crews coming out of New Orleans on the new boats, but no drastic measures were taken to correct these failings.

Aside from this apparent failure to utilize the favorable facilities for a training program, the Detail was a success in everyone's eyes.

The PT Ferrying Command, which was established late in the PT program, worked in conjunction with the Commissioning Detail and will be discussed under a separate heading.

COMMISSIONING DETAILS, USN, GULF AREA

Ship construction of all types mushroomed in the Gulf Area, and commissioning activities kept pace with this expansion. In order to have some semblance of unity among the various activities, CNO authorized the establishment of Central Pre-commissioning Details in New York, New Orleans, and San Francisco; with New Orleans responsible for the entire Gulf Area and part of Florida south of Jacksonville.[18]

The basic functions for each organization were:

(a) To prepare vessels for commissioned service in all respects as regards material and in conformity with Naval standards, working with Supervisors of Shipbuilding in an advisory capacity. Direct relationship with shipbuilders was to be avoided in order to prevent confusion. PCO's and their staffs were to deal only with Pre-Commissioning Detail CO or his staff.

(b) To cooperate with COCTLant and the CO's of the respective Receiving Stations in assembling prospective crews.

18. CNO's conf. ltr. Ser. 0736923 of 7 January 1944.

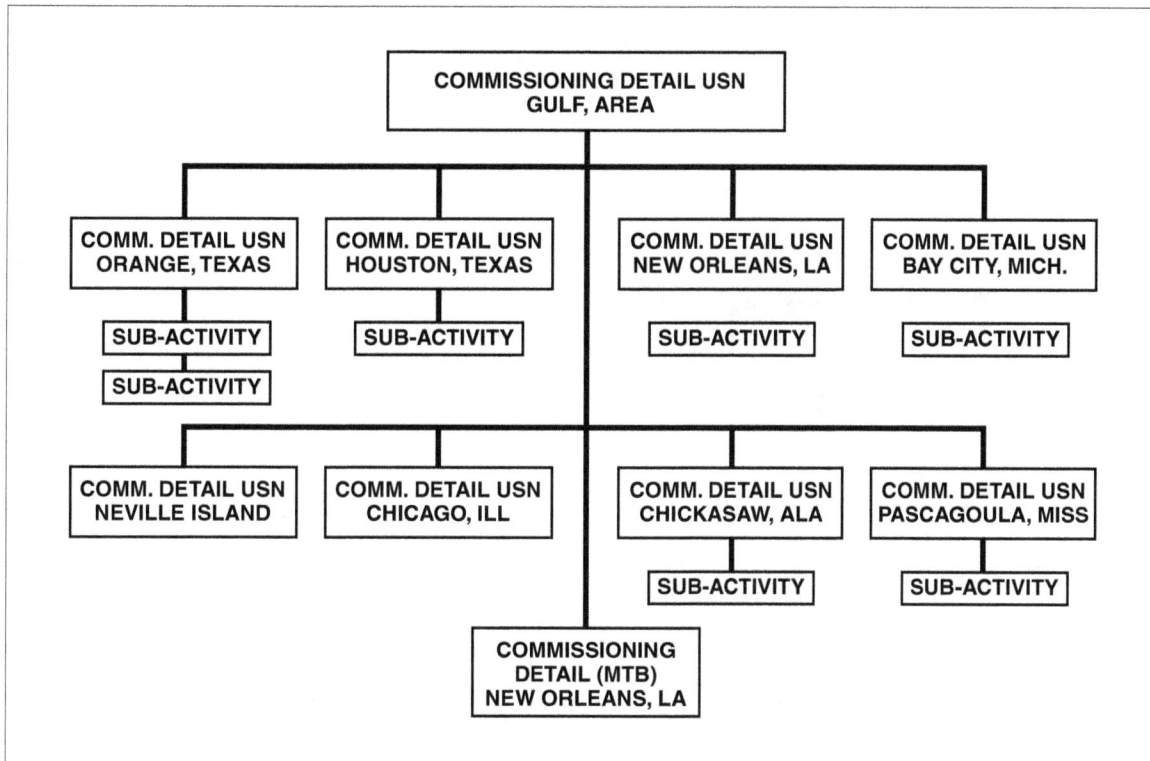

Figure 29: Administrative Organization of Commissioning Details Gulf Area and Relationship of Commissioning Detail (MTB) New Orleans, La.

(c) To cooperate with respective fitting-out yards and agencies in matters pertaining to assembly and outfitting material.

(d) To initiate necessary action towards the standardization of equipment. This action will be based on continuous experience in preparing successive vessels of the several types for commissioning.

On January 24, 1944, Com 8 in a letter to CNO stated "now is the time to go further than the coordination of auxiliary commissioning....by coordination of all commissioning activities in the 8 ND."[19]

As a result of the recommendation, CNO's directive of 26 January 1944 established the administrative organization known as the Commissioning Details, USN, Gulf Area.[20] Motor Torpedo Boat Commissioning Detail was one of the nine details to be consolidated under Com 8 ND. Comdr. L.W. Smyth, USN was appointed CO of the Commissioning Details, USN, Gulf Area, and was directly responsible to the Ass't Commandant (Logistics). In this capacity he was considered as CO of an independent command. He discharged duties assigned to Com 8, and in that status he performed duties of a member of the Commandant's Staff. Ultimate control of commissioning details rested in the hands of VCNO.

19. Com 8ND's conf. ltr. Ser. 0232 of 24 January 1944.
20. CNO's conf. ltr. Ser. 049323 of 26 January 1944.

Figure 30: Higgins PT Squadron 23 being commissioned at New Orleans Yacht Club Basin, New Orleans, La

Under the new administrative arrangement, all personnel of the various details and all additional personnel assigned to such duty reported to Com 8 for duty in Commissioning Details, USN, Gulf Area. This enabled the Commandant to shift personnel from one activity to another as the needs arose.

Further consolidation of commissioning activities in the New Orleans area was accomplished in May 1944 by a district order which merged Auxiliaries, Patrol and Minecraft Commissioning Details.[21] The PT Commissioning Detail was not included in the consolidation, however, because of its distance from the Naval Station in Algiers.

The original functions of the commissioning details were so broad in scope that virtually anything could be attempted which would improve and expedite new construction and insure that newly commissioned vessels would be, in all respects, ready for sea.

Officers and men were selected because of their sea background. In practice, the work of these details extended well beyond the original purpose of commissioning vessels.

---

21. 8ND District Order 8-44 dated 17 May 1944.

AN ADMINISTRATIVE HISTORY OF PT's IN WORLD WAR II
(Recreated October 25, 2010 by the members of the PT Boat Forum message board)

149

As contracts were completed, commissioning details were disestablished. By mid-year of 1945 so few of these details remained in operation that Com 8 elected to disestablish the organization known as Commissioning Details, USN, Gulf Area, and in its place stepped Commissioning Detail, 8 ND. This activity remained in operation until 15 December 1945, when it too, was disestablished. The PT Commissioning Detail remained under the jurisdiction of the abbreviated edition of Commissioning Detail, USN, 8 ND until it (PT Commissioning Detail) was disestablished on 1 October 1945.

PT FERRYING COMMAND

In late February 1945, Ron Forty-three (43) was transferred to the Russian navy and had to decommission in New Orleans. [22] Thirty-six (36) other boats, some under construction at that time, were also designated for transfer to the Russians. A total of forty-eight (48) boats were thus assigned to the Soviets, and had to be delivered to Seattle where the Russians accepted delivery.

To accomplish delivery of these boats, CNO established a Ferrying Command in New Orleans. [23] This activity was to fall "under the cognizance of Com 8 ND who was to organize the personnel in groups or in units as necessary to carry out their mission, and who will issue appropriate orders." [24]

LT. George C. Miller, USNR was appointed CO of the Ferrying Command, and by 16 March 1945, the activity was operating as authorized. A complement of one hundred and thirty-seven (137) enlisted men and twenty-four (24) officers, four of whom were base force personnel, was ultimately obtained.

The Command was responsible for forwarding all supplies for the Russia-bound boats to the West Coast where they were accepted by Russian representatives. Boats were loaded onto LST's, four (4) to a ship, and shipped to Seattle, Wash. Ferry crews were, for the most part, in a stand-by position; and would run the boats under their own power in the event the LST was sunk. The lashings were arranged for immediate release of the boats: if the LST sank, the boats would float free upon hitting the water.

This theory is ideal, but the practice is questionable. [25]

---

22. CNO Sec. disp. 211210 of Feb.'45 to CinClant. CNO Sec. ltr. Op-23D-MM Ser. 0077823 of 21 Feb. '45.
23. CNO Sec. ltr. Op-23D-MEM Ser. 0087223 of 28 Feb. '45.
24. Ibid
25. One of the most interesting PT stories concerns the sinking of a tanker loaded with six (6) PT's. Six 80' PT's of Ron Ten were loaded on board the S.S. STANVAC-MANILA for shipment to Noumea, New Caledonia. Four of the boats were located aft of the mid-ship section and two of them were forward. They were secured with the standard lashings and gripes as were then used. Each boat carried 1500 gallons of gas, which later proved to be the decisive factor in saving the boats and personnel. (Boats of Ron One which had been loaded on board U.S.S. RAMAPO for shipment to Manila from Pearl Harbor just a few days prior to 7 Dec. 1941 had been drained of fuel and their tanks filled with CO2. The turrets, which indirectly depended upon the auxiliary generator, were inoperative because of this lack of fuel. In order to use these guns, the crews were forced to break the hydraulic leads and operate the turrets by hand. Since then, it became the practice to carry fuel in the tanks while the boats were in cradles for overseas shipment.) PT's 165, 167, 171, 172, 173 and 174 of Ron Ten were

in cradles on board the S.S. STANVAC MANILA headed for Noumea when one or more torpedoes hit the vessel on the port quarter at 0407, 24 May 1943. The sea was moderate from the West and the wind approximately 16 knots from the Northwest. About two minutes after the torpedoes struck, the engine room flooded out. All boats let go their lashings and gripes and stood by waiting to float free. They began floating in their cradles, and the freshing wind and sea caused them to pound and shift positions. Two boats, PT's 165 and 173, stove large holes in their bottoms and all attempts to save them proved fruitless. They sank the moment they were free of the tanker. PT's 171 and 174 were able to get underway and back out of the floating debris and the sinking tanker, but not without staving great holes in their hulls. The remaining two boats. PT's 167 and 172, literally shot out of their cradles and through the air as the MANILA slid under the water. Both boats hit the foremast on clearing the ship, and PT 167 stripped her topsides on the mast while PT 172 broke her stem on the yardarm.

The fact that the boats could get underway upon floating free from the sinking tanker resulted in the saving of both personnel and boats. The lashings and gripes released quickly and freely for the most part, but the strongbacks and frames of the cradles damaged the boats considerably. Two sank and three were badly damaged as a result of pounding and shifting about in their cradles as the tanker slowly settled.

(From the Com MTBRon Ten's Sec. ltr. To SecNav FC8-10/L11-1 Ser. 62 of 25 June 1943)

The ferry crews would remain with the boats until delivery was accomplished and would then return to New Orleans for ferrying later boats of the program. Necessarily, close liaison was maintained with the Naval Transportation Service and with Commanders of Sea Frontiers concerned.

As stated by CNO, the duties of the Ferrying Command were to assist responsible authorities in outfitting, assembly of authorized spare parts and equipment, maintenance of equipment, monitoring of boats and equipment in transit, and to ferry PT's in such portions of transit as required where ship-born passage was not practicable. [26]

The command commenced operations on Lake Pontchartrain at the Commissioning Detail activity and remained here until 28 July 1945. Speed tests, trials, and outfitting were handled by the Ferrying Command, and the boats were in a sea-going condition by the time they were loaded onto the LST's for shipment. They were shipped with enough equipment aboard to make their own way to port if they were forced to hit the water.

To a limited extent, the activity performed the duties of a commissioning detail and conducted a small phase of pre-shakedown.

When the West End Branch, Receiving Station disestablished, the Command moved to the Florida Avenue Warehouse on the Industrial Canal. Here it remained until its own disestablishment on 17 December 1945.

The PT Ferrying Command was the only one of its kind and had nothing to go by for comparison and information. While it was originally planned to handle forty-eight boats, the activity actually ferried forty-two.

A few of these were delivered up the East Coast under their own power, while the majority of the boats, thirty-six, were shipped on LST's to Seattle. From what few reports exist on the Ferrying Command, it is gathered that the officers

26. Ibid

AN ADMINISTRATIVE HISTORY OF PT's IN WORLD WAR II
(Recreated October 25, 2010 by the members of the PT Boat Forum message board)

151

and men did a very satisfactory job. A report from the Russians could no doubt throw a little more light on the matter.

Lt. K.D. Clifford, USNR relieved Lt. Miller as CO in July, and he disestablished the Command upon completion of the final delivery.

Practically no records existed as a source of information on the Ferrying Command, and most of the material was comprised from talks with Lt. K.D. Clifford and from a copy of the letter from CNO authorizing the establishment of the command.

CHAPTER EIGHT

U. S. NAVAL STATION, TABOGA

SELECTION OF A SITE IN THE CANAL ZONE

Once the liberty port of the old sea dog Henry Morgan, Taboga Island was again to become the focal point of a modern navy.

The Navy planned to base a squadron of PT's at Panama to augment the defenses of the Canal Zone, and the task fell to Squadron TWO – seventy-seven foot Elco's. In June of 1942, the squadron arrived at the Canal and based at Balboa. The boats remained based here until September 1942, when they were relieved by Squadron FIVE – the first squadron of eighty foot Elco's.

Figure 31: U.S. Naval Station, Taboga

AN ADMINISTRATIVE HISTORY OF PT's IN WORLD WAR II
(Recreated October 25, 2010 by the members of the PT Boat Forum message board)

153

CNO had earlier decided that all Pacific-bound PT's would shakedown on their way to Panama, and a training and loading base should be established in that area. At that time, there were no facilities for basing PT's in the Canal Zone, and a base would have to be constructed for that purpose. The rough passage from Florida would necessitate repairs once the boats reached the Pacific side of the Canal. Since the tender "JAMESTOWN" was not then ready to take over the duty of tending the first squadrons to arrive in the Zone, a PT Repair Base was the natural alternative.

Representatives from the Bureau of Yards and Docks surveyed Fonseca, Galapago, Salinas, and a few other small islands and decided to construct the authorized base on Taboga. At this time, early '42, the island was a well known winter resort where gambling and other interesting sports contributed to the entertainment of the tourists. Property owners were most reluctant to part with their land investments because of their tourist trade value, and our Ambassador had a fairly stiff battle on his hands before he succeeded in obtaining base rights. Constant pressure from CNO kept our authorities busy until they reached an agreement with the Panamanian Government, who included the following specifications in the transaction. The site was to be vacated after the war, and all permanent improvements were to become the property of the Panamanian Government. [1] The proposed facilities were to include the following: pier, torpedo storehouse, work shop, motor overhaul shop, generator storehouse, 200,000 gallon gasoline storage (actually 160,000 gal.), water storage, plant for power, radio building, magazine for warheads, depth charges, small arms, and living and messing facilities for three hundred and seventy-six (376) men and forty-five (45) officers. The code name for this bit of steep rocky terrain was "Palisade". [2]

COMINCH serial 0983 of June 1942, required the loading on ships at Panama of PT's and crews assigned Pacific Ocean areas for transportation to their destinations. It was estimated that the boats would begin arriving the first of August of that year in the Canal Zone at the rate of one squadron per month. Boats would require voyage repairs, including engine overhaul and hauling out of the water before loading for shipment. A marine railway was to provide the means of hauling the boats out of the water for repairs, and a drydock was being assembled to augment this repair program. By June, requests for major overhaul items had been filed, and the base was scheduled to go into commission on 1 August 1942. Lt. Cdr. H. S. Cooper assumed command of the base on this date, and Rear Adm. Van Hook conducted an inspection of the base as part of the commissioning ceremonies. All this time, Ron TWO was at Balboa and remained there until September. Their duties included running a Ready Boat from Balboa to Taboga every day.

---

1. COM 15 dispatch to CNO – 021621 of May '42.

2. COM 15 dispatch to BuY&D – 012306 of April '42.

154

AN ADMINISTRATIVE HISTORY OF PT's IN WORLD WAR II
(Recreated October 25, 2010 by the members of the PT Boat Forum message board)

BASE FACILITIES AND ACTIVITIES

The official designation of the base was "Naval Station", and its mission was divided into two categories:

(1)   Major overhaul of MTB's and equipment; and operational training of personnel awaiting transportation to combat areas.

(2)   Major overhaul of ARB's attached to ComPaSeaFron.

There are no channels or approaches to the island and Taboga boasts a good, open harbor with 60' of water at low tide over a muddy bottom. For mooring purposes, sixteen MTB moorings using 4,500 lb. anchors were located around the harbor. Docking facilities were comprised of thirteen finger-piers, each 70' long and having from 9' – 19' depth alongside at mean low tide. The big drawback to these piers was the winds, which made their use hazardous. When the base first went into commission, the boats had to fuel at Balboa, but a high and low octane gasoline fueling pier was ultimately constructed. There was no crane at the base capable of handling a load over twenty tons, and all the loading and unloading of boats was done in Balboa.

Two marine railways capable of handling seventy-five tons, and a drydock capable of handling up to one hundred tons provided the equipment for underwater repairs. The repair shops were as follows:

> Packard and Hall-Scott Major Engine Overhaul Shop
> Base Maintenance
> Machine Shop
> Automotive School
> Hull Repair and Carpenter Shop
> Blacksmith Shop
> Torpedo Shop[3]

A sufficient water supply cannot be obtained on the island, and must be shipped in from the mainland by barge. For emergency, there are four evaporators in a standby condition. A limited amount of native food, consisting of pineapples, corn and native fruit in season, augments the main food supply which is shipped from NSD, Balboa. That section of the island not under Navy control falls under the jurisdiction of the Local Alcalde (mayor) and Corregidor (sheriff). Postal service is carried on daily by station small craft from F.P.O., Balboa.

The annual lease of the Station's site, covering 34.4 acres, amounts to the surprisingly small sum of $437.50. This also includes the "Casino", a large concrete and stone building sheltering 5300 sq. ft. of floor areas. The "Casino", minus its roulette wheels and "Blue Mooms", is a part of the Station's

3. Logistics Report, U. S. Naval Station, Taboga, Balboa, C. Z. period ending 31 March 1945.

AN ADMINISTRATIVE HISTORY OF PT's IN WORLD WAR II
(Recreated October 25, 2010 by the members of the PT Boat Forum message board)

155

recreational facilities, which include: Basketball, tennis courts, movies, pistol range, and swimming and fishing.

While the Station can accommodate one hundred and twenty-five (125) officers and seven hundred (700) enlisted men for messing, unfortunately the recreational facilities can handle the same number of officers but only three hundred (300) enlisted men. Liberty parties to the mainland help to ease the strain on these crowded conditions.

The temperature range for both the wet and dry seasons varies between 78 and 79 degrees, and the health conditions are quite favorable. Morale of the base force is high for an overseas station, but it should be remembered that the base is only nine miles from Balboa and can hardly be considered as rugged overseas duty.

By the nature of the base, only one radio station is required to serve the various commands associated with the Island. In addition to the CO, NavSta., Taboga, C. Z. the CO's of MTB Ron's PaSeaFron and MTB Ron's Transient Squadrons are served by this one radio station. Two circuits are operated on a twenty-four hour watch, and three circuits are available for special operations. No electronic navigational aids are operated by the base, and the Island is connected to Balboa by submarine telephone cables.

SEAPLANE FACILITIES

With the whole ocean serving as a landing strip, the Station can, naturally, service seaplanes, but the aviation facilities are considered as being of an emergency nature, at best. There are no direct fueling facilities for the planes, and any fueling has to done from drums delivered to the planes in small boats. Landings and takeoffs can be accomplished in most any direction, as the water is clear all around the outer harbor.

TRAINING PROGRAM

When the early squadrons arrived at Taboga they had no operational training program at their disposal. The CO's conducted operations of their own design and choosing and were quite independent of base supervision along these lines. This situation changed with the changes in command of the Naval Station, and an operational training program was eventually established.

This program and its mission are clearly defined in a letter which is included in this discussion.[4]

SUMMARY

Taboga served several functions, changing with the course of the war. At its inception, the proposed Naval Station was to serve as base for a squadron

4. CO, U. S. Naval Station, Taboga's conf. ltr. Op-23D Serial 357 of 7 July 1945.

of PT's acting as an arm of defense in the Canal Zone. Along with its use in a defensive measure, Taboga served as a base for major overhaul of PT's and equipment, and operational training of personnel awaiting transportation to combat areas. Further than this, ARB's attached to ComPaSeaFron had all major overhaul work done at the base.

The operational training program was non-existent at the time of the base commissioning and was developed largely under the command of Lt. Cdr. V. L. Wanselow, USN. Drills were run day and night and both the base and the boats were kept on their toes by these frequent drills.

Climactic and sea conditions were ideal for all phases of advanced shakedown. Torpedo firing, barge hunting, gunnery practice, anti-plane tactics, and navigational cruises were conducted almost uninterrupted. The many small island offered wonderful conditions for training in barge hunting and radar tracking.

As a Naval Station coming under Com 15, Taboga received logistical support from Balboa. The Atlantic Fleet Pool supplied the necessary enlisted men even though the station was in the Pacific. The function of the base was not so expansive that it could not be well executed and the station's routine was conducted with very few hitches.

On orders from CNO, U. S. Naval Station, Taboga was disestablished 28 September, 1945.[5]

---

5. COM 15 Conf. dis. 051810 Dec. 1945 to CNO

AN ADMINISTRATIVE HISTORY OF PT's IN WORLD WAR II
(Recreated October 25, 2010 by the members of the PT Boat Forum message board)

157

OPERATIONAL TRAINING

MOTOR TORPEDO BOAT SQUADRONS, PANAMA SEA FRONTIER

FORWARD

Motor Torpedo Boats temporarily stationed at U. S. Naval Station, Navy 40, while awaiting transportation westward are under the command of Commander Panama Sea Frontier who has cognizance of their operational training and has directed ComMTBRonPaSeaFron to carry out the details of this program.

Upon arrival the boats are checked for condition of readiness and the necessary work and overhauling schedule. When the required work has been completed, Staff Officers, in company with the Officer-in-Charge, inspect the personnel and the boats, laying particular emphasis on the cleanliness and operational condition of the boats.

Schedules for operations, classes, physical exercise, and medical or dental treatment are drawn up on the basis of a survey of shakedown reports, observations during the trip to this area, the number of boats to be in commission, and anticipated time in this area. Whenever possible, several functions are combined in a single operational exercise in order to provide maximum diversity of training in a minimum of time. A particular effort is made to promote the operational training of the Executive Officers of the boats in order to reduce the discrepancies between their abilities and those of their Boat Captains, many of whom are highly experienced.

The Officer–in-Charge and Staff personnel act as observers and offer suggestions and comments at a critique after each exercise.

/s/ J. B. Peltier,

J. B. PELTIER,
Commander Motor Torpedo Boats
Panama Sea Frontier

158

AN ADMINISTRATIVE HISTORY OF PT's IN WORLD WAR II
(Recreated October 25, 2010 by the members of the PT Boat Forum message board)

TRAINING PROGRAM AVAILABLE

1.   General Information for Operational Exercises.

(a) All exercise will be conducted with all hands at General Quarters in order to simulate war conditions as closely as possible. Kapok life jackets will be worn by all hands firing guns.

(b) A brief before each exercise will be held in the Operations Office.

(c) All communication will be according to U. S. Naval Station Navy 40, Communications Plan E.

(d) All exercises will be started at the specified time and completed at or before completion time as stated in operations order.

(e) It is the OIC'S responsibility to make certain any firing area is clear before commencing exercise.

(f) Operational Orders will be issued by ComMTBRons, PaSeaFron.

(g) OIC will be responsible for all navigation, safety regulations, and keeping clear of restricted areas as set forth in ComPaSeaFron dispatches.

2.   Operational Exercises.

(a) Gunnery.

(1) MG fire at Valladolid Rock of all calibers. Firing will be made to westward. Boats will make runs in any direction and as close to the Rock as desired. Point of aim should be the water-line of Rock or one of the caves. Firing may be during day or night.

(2) MG firing at a towed sled for all calibers. Fire to the eastward of a line running south for a distance of twelve thousand (12,000) yards from 79° 28' W and 08° 45' N, the original firing point. Firing may be during day or night.

(3) MG firing at a towed sleeve in areas as designated by Training Operations Order. Sleeve will be towed by either JM-1 or J2F. Boats will be in column while firing. Usual safety precautions for sleeve firing will be observed.

(4) Rocket firing at Valladolid Rock, same as for MG firing.

(5) Small arms firing on Morro Island available at all times. Schedule arranged through the Gunnery Officer.

(b) Torpedo Firing.

(1) A PC or SC will act as target for tracking and firing of Exercise Torpedoes. Target will run either on or about course 099° T or 270°

AN ADMINISTRATIVE HISTORY OF PT's IN WORLD WAR II
(Recreated October 25, 2010 by the members of the PT Boat Forum message board)

159

T, so as to ass about three (3) miles south of Taboga Island. Boats will fire either singly or by divisions and either one fish at a time or a spread. Each boat will follow its own fish and stand by it until it is recovered by a Station motor launch. Care must be taken to stay clear of Merchant Shipping. Boats will track by Radar and/or visually as directed by OCT.

(c) Night Search and Attack.

(1) As made available by ComMTBRons, three (3) DDs will proceed north through Sub Sanctuary to Taboga anchorage. PT's will search and simulate torpedo attack. Attack plan to be decided by OTC. Smoke may be used as desired.

(d) Fighter Plane Attack.

(1) Boats will proceed to area east of Taboga Island where they will be attacked by Army fighters, usually eight to twelve. Planes will simulate dive-bombing, strafing and suicide tactics. Boats will exercise in anti-plane maneuvers. Gun crews will practice tracking. Smoke may be used during second half of exercise. A small flag will be attached to the top of the radio antenna during exercises. Planes will be equipped with gun cameras when available.

(e) Night Observation Bomber Exercises.

(1) Eight officers will be transported to a Bomber air field where they will board B-24's. Planes will rendezvous with PT's, where the planes will make runs over the boats, one plane at 1000 ft. and one at 2000 ft. PT boats will run at 1800 RPM's, 600 RPM's, Idle on one engine, and lay-to as directed by Training Operation Order. During last part of exercise boats will attempt to evade planes by any means desired by OTC. Smoke may be used. Planes will drop large flares as available. Observations will be discussed at a critique by Army Pilots and Boat Officers.

(f) Joint Plane-PT Attack.

(1) When transmitting ships desire, PT's and Army fighters will make coordinated attacks east of Taboga Island. Smoke may be used. Although this exercise takes place usually during daylight, it affords tracking opportunities with capital ships as targets.

(g) Anti-Barge Exercise.

(1) Station ML's and ARBs, each with a squadron officer aboard, will attempt to enter Taboga Harbor. Barges will start from the west end of Taboga Island. PT boats will set up patrols around Harbor entrances. A PT search light held on a Barge for 30 seconds will put the barge out of the exercise.

(2) Using either other PT's or available Crash Boats as barges, a barge search and attack will take place in the Archipelago De Las Perlas. Current restrictions of the Submarine Sanctuary will be observed.

(h) Navigation Cruise.

(1) A cruise will be made among the Perlas Islands and up the Rio Tuira to La Palma. Boats will travel alone or in pairs at night, conducting emergency drills during the exercise. During daylight, boats will conduct division maneuvers.

(i) Compass Calibrations.

(1) Boats will swing ship in areas to the north of Taboga Island directed by the compass officer, who will be obtained from 15th Naval District.

(j) Radio Calibrations.

(1) TCS radios will be calibrated when boats are underway by contacting and checking with the base radio, which will be set up by a frequency meter.

(k) Radar Calibration.

(1) Ranges and bearings will be checked on various islands in the area.

(l) Speed Runs.

(1) Boats will make speed runs over the measured mile course north of Taboga Island. Average of runs in opposite directions will be required. Timing and speed curves will be made by boat personnel.

3. Non-operational Exercises.

(a) Gunnery Trainer.

(1) A Mark I gunnery trainer is in operation in the area and a schedule for its use can be arranged.

(b) Communications.

(1) A CW testing machine for group practice is set up for CW from five to two hundred and fifty words a minute.

(c) Training Film.

(1) Complete recognition slides and models are available for classes. The training film library is adequate, including the Packard visual aids program under the direction of a BuShips trained instructor.

(d) Lectures.

(1) Lectures in First Aid, PT camouflage and jungle warfare and living are provided.

AN ADMINISTRATIVE HISTORY OF PT's IN WORLD WAR II
(Recreated October 25, 2010 by the members of the PT Boat Forum message board)

161

(e) Athletics.

(1) A program of basketball, tennis, volleyball, swimming and hiking in jungles is encouraged to keep the men in top physical condition.

162

AN ADMINISTRATIVE HISTORY OF PT's IN WORLD WAR II
(Recreated October 25, 2010 by the members of the PT Boat Forum message board)

CHAPTER NINE

PT TENDERS

EVOLUTION OF THE TENDER

REPLACEMENT PHOTO - PROVIDE BY GARY PAULSEN

Figure 32: AVP-type AGP Tending a squadron of PT's

AN ADMINISTRATIVE HISTORY OF PT's IN WORLD WAR II
(Recreated October 25, 2010 by the members of the PT Boat Forum message board)

163

Parallel to our grouping in the dark while attempting to develop a suitable PT were our efforts in developing a suitable PT tender. From the outset, the Navy was not sure what it wanted and expected of a PT and by the same token did not know what to include in the design of a PT tender. It was like attempting to design a hutch for a pregnant rabbit – you could only guess at the ultimate demands made on the hutch.

The outstanding feature of the PT tender program is the fact that there was never a keel laid for an AGP. Several hulls ultimately wound up in the capacity of an AGP, but there were no originally designated AGP hulls. The whole program was born out of necessity and availability. A total of three (3) yachts, four (4) AVP's, ten (10) LST's and two (2) C-1 type hulls constituted the AGP program. As the needs increased, the available ships were pressed into service as PT tenders. Some were converted in the forward area, while others had the advantage of a ship yard for conversion. Their evolution has been interesting but erratic.

The first squadrons began shaking down along the Atlantic Coast in early 1941, and from the beginning, the CO's of Ron's ONE and TWO realized and appreciated the need for adequate repair bases. Constant and expert attention was required to maintain the boats in an operating condition, and the few scattered PT bases were not adequate. The obvious answer was to develop a tender, similar to those serving DD's. These tenders could accompany the squadrons when they operated outside the range of shore repair facilities.

Lt. W. C. Specht, USN and Lt. E. S. Caldwell, USN, CO's of MTB Ron's ONE & TWO, were constantly campaigning for the development of a PT tender which could keep pace with a squadron and fuel and effect major repairs for the squadron over long periods of time. As a partial means of alleviating the supply and repair problem, barges were stocked and stationed in some of the anchorages used by the boats while cruising the Atlantic Coast. This proved satisfactory only when the boats operated in the vicinity of a port where one of these repair barges was located.

CNO, unenthusiastically, requested BuShips, in November 1940, to purchase two or three vessels suitable for conversion to PT tenders. It was not practical to build a tender at that time because no one knew exactly what should be included in designing such a ship. In addition, the necessary money was not available at that time to lay the keel for a PT tender. For lack of anything better, BuShips purchased two yachts in December 1940, and attempted to convert them to PT tenders. At the outset, the Bureau was not sure just what should be included in the conversion program. Because of this uncertainty, the two vessels underwent several half-hearted repair programs and never approached the status of an efficient tender.

Criticism should not be directed solely at BuShips; the requirements and specifications of a PT tender simply were not known at that time, and a certain amount of guessing and groping was to be expected in attempting to evolve a satisfactory tender. Our present-day tenders, consisting of LST's, AVP's and C-1 hulls converted to tenders, are the results of three years of complaints and suggestions contributed by boat officers, squadron commanders and AGP personnel. The Bureau learned as it progressed, and the caliber of tenders improved, but never to a point where they were considered wholly adequate by the boat officers.

The main features of conversion consisted of increasing the air defenses of the vessels, installing degaussing equipment, increasing the fuel storage capacity, installing ammunition and warhead storage compartments, and major overhaul repair shops. All this could not be performed on the ships because of their basic designs. Some could not stand heavy gun mount installations, one leaked badly, and none of them offered the required storage space. In spite of these handicaps, the NIAGARA, JAMESTOWN, and HILO steamed into the operating areas in the early stages of the war and mothered the boats along on practically a shoe string. A few features of those early tenders are presented in the following discussion, and will illustrate the uncertainties and problems in the opening PT Tender program.

NIAGARA – AGP 1

The first yacht acquired for conversion to a tender was the HI-ESMARO, a 253'-3" by 34'-10" vessel built in 1929 at the Bath Ship Yards. Its original draft

Figure 33: AGP-I U.S.S. Niagara

AN ADMINISTRATIVE HISTORY OF PT's IN WORLD WAR II
(Recreated October 25, 2010 by the members of the PT Boat Forum message board)

165

was 16'-6" and displaced 1929 tons, but subsequent installations caused a variation in her draft and weakened her hull at the same time. The HI-ESMARO went into a repair status soon after her acquisition, and on 21 January 1941 was commissioned the USS NIAGARA, PG 52. Hardly resplendent in her new converted status, the NIAGARA wallowed down to Miami, Fla. to join Ron TWO for a shakedown cruise. The cruise was, in effect, a shakedown for both the squadron and the tender, and was to run from Key West to Cienfuegos, Cuba.

On the first leg of the trip, the NIAGARA sprung some bad leaks around her fuel tanks and the sea came flowing in to stop her dead in the water. The ship managed to get underway after some effective trouble-shooting, and finally reached Charleston where she was dry-docked. Upon release from the ship yards, PG 52 reported to the Naval Torpedo Station, Newport, R.I. for further work with the new group of Ron TWO boats which were replacing the 70's. By May, Elco was delivering the 77' boats contracted for in September of the previous year, and the old boats were being delivered to the British on a lend-lease basis. The NIAGARA became a floating classroom for the officers and men of Ron TWO while they were awaiting delivery of the new boats. A "Familiarization" school was held onboard, and after all hands attended program, they went to school at the torpedo overhaul shop and the Packard overhaul shop.

Figure 34: The U.S.S. Niagara under air attack

The ship spent all that spring and summer at Newport as a classroom and tender for the men and boats of Ron TWO. She later underwent more repairs, and in the process her longitudinal strength and stability were decidedly impaired due to overloading. On the 20th of September 1941, the NIAGARA was assigned to the homeport of San Diego. The ship proceeded to Pearl Harbor that fall, and went into another period of overhaul. CNO ordered the NIAGARA to report to INCAF as tender for Ron THREE when six boats could be loaded and shipped out to the Islands. On November 27, 1941 Lt. D. B. Coleman, USN relieved Lt. Cdr. E. W. Herron, USN as commanding officer of the NIAGARA. The ship continued operations in Pearl Harbor, and it was finally decided that she was unfit as a tender in the Hawaiian area.

Admiral Horne recommended, on 23 February 1942, that the ship proceed to Panama to facilitate the upkeep of Ron TWO who was down there on shakedown. She ultimately ended up in New York again for extensive repairs during the summer of '42.

Because the NIAGARA was seemingly unfit for a PT tender, it was recommended that she be assigned as a patrol craft. Someone in BuShips, however, still held hopes for making a go out of the hull which had been made seaworthy, and the repairs were completed and the ship routed to Pearl Harbor again. By this time, January 1943, a new class designation had been established, and the NIAGARA was then known as AGP 1. From Pearl Harbor, the ship proceeded to an operating area and tendered Ron EIGHT and various divisions.

On May 24th, 1943, she was steaming just south of San Cristobal in company with MTB Div. 23 and PT 110 when Japanese planes came over and bomber her, causing no damage. A few hours later, some more planes came over at 12,000 ft and stopped her in her wake with hits on her bow. The PT's picked up the survivors when the order came to abandon ship, and to make sure the ship would leave no trace of herself, Lt. Cdr. C. B. Coleman, CO of the NIAGARA, ordered one of the boats to sink her with torpedoes. PT 147 fired two torpedoes at the sinking vessel, one ran erratic (a final tribute to the torpedo overhaul shop on board the NIAGARA) and the other hit her amidships. The ship immediately burst into flame and sank in forty-five (45) seconds.

So ended the first ugly duckling of the AGP Class. From the outset, it should have been clear to BuShips that the ship was never going to make the grade as a tender.

The many attempts at conversion were unsuccessful, one of the reasons being that not enough money was authorized at one time to do a satisfactory job. Yet the successive allotments, had they been lumped together, would have fitted out the vessel much sooner and in a more finished condition than it ever obtained. The urgent demand for a tender in any condition was mainly responsible for the old ship ever reaching a combat zone.

While the NIAGARA was running out its short life, two more converted yachts were undergoing the stages of trial and error in attempting to produce a satisfactory PT tender from converted yachts; namely, the JAMESTOWN and the HILO.

JAMESTOWN AGP 3

Soon after the NIAGARA was put into harness as a PT tender, Operations realized that more ships of this type would be needed to take care of the increasing number of boats. BuShips representatives scouted around and came up with another yacht which they felt was suitable for a tender. (Subsequent performance indicated that they could have looked farther and made a better choice). The Gov't purchased the 294' yacht ALDER for the nominal sum of $275,000 on the 6th of December 1940. At its purchase it was designated as a PG, and was to be converted to such when the proper appropriations were allotted. The vessel was diesel powered and had a cruising range of 11,000 miles at 15 knots.

BuShips representatives inspected the ship and estimated that conversion costs would amount to $800,000.

It was further discovered that the JAMESTOWN could not stand the weight of all the armament required on a ship of that type without costly major repairs

Figure 35: AGP-3, U.S.S. JAMESTOWN

and shorings. The present decking could not hold the 4"/50 cal. Guns that were required on a ship of that class.

It was ultimately decided that the proposed conversion would not take place. While the Auxiliary Vessels Board was deciding what repairs would be made in the hopes of evolving a satisfactory tender, Rear Admiral Brainard recommended that the vessel undergo minor repairs and be used to train the U. S. Naval Academy midshipmen on their summer cruises. This minor conversion job would only cost the Navy $25,000, and after the conversion the ship could accommodate one hundred (100) midshipmen. The changes were made, and the old ship was seen steaming up and down Chesapeake Bay with a crew of midshipmen blinking lights and running up flag hoists in the summer of '41.

Comdr. A. P. Lawton, USNR, assumed command of the JAMESTOWN when she went into commission of the 26th of May '41. The vessel needed extensive repairs, from the bilges to the deck houses, and was never given the complete treatment at any one time. Consequently, there were three periods of repairs undergone before she finally sailed for the South Pacific. Shops and store space were never fully provided for in any of the conversion periods, and constant reference was made regarding the needed repairs. Torpedo overhaul shops were a prime necessity aboard the tender, yet these facilities were far from adequate for overhauling a torpedo thoroughly. Berthing spaces for the boats' crews were likewise inadequate.

In spite of these shortcomings, the JAMESTOWN traveled to the South Pacific and went through the Guadalcanal campaign with Squadron TWO and THREE. As other tenders arrived in the area, the duties as a tender decreased for the JAMESTOWN and she became a utility vessel.

Some of the most constructive criticism on PT tenders came in the form of a letter from Lt. W. C. Specht, USN written to CNO on 3 July 1941. Ron ONE had been working with the NIAGARA for the past few months down in Miami and up at Newport, and had come to see the shortcomings of the vessel as a tender. Lt. Specht had compiled some pregnant ideas on what a tender should offer a squadron, and the NIAGARA was far from satisfactory in living up to those ideas. He therefore drew up some basic characteristics of a tender and submitted them to CNO. The recommendations were as follows:

(A) Undertake immediate construction, to be completed at the earliest possible date, three (3) MTB tenders to have the general characteristics and facilities as follows:

    (1) Speed of 25-30 knots.

    (2) Stowage capacity for 100,000 gallons of 100-octane gasoline.

    (3) Berthing and messing facilities for 25 officers and 200 enlisted men in addition to own complement.

    (4) Torpedo overhaul shops and equipment adequate for overhaul of four (4) torpedo afterbodies at one time.

(5) Reload warhead and torpedo stowage.

(6) Machine shop overhaul and repair facilities for MTB engines.

(7) Lifting boom with capacity for lifting 75 tons.

(8) Additional office, storeroom, and magazine space for use of MTB Rons.

(9) Stowage space for twelve (12) spare MTB engines.

(B) Make conversions to USS NIAGARA and USS JAMESTOWN as have already been recommended for the USS NIAGARA. These two vessels to serve as tenders for MTB Ron assigned to the Atlantic and Pacific U. S. Coastal Areas and permit the employment of the three PT tenders constructed as such in more distant outlying areas.

(C) Undertake immediately the construction of ten (10) squadrons of PTs (120) vessels, for exclusive use of our Navy, these boats to be distributed to the previously mentioned areas and to be tendered by PT tenders as much as is practical.

HILO – AGP 2

The third and final converted yacht of the PT tender program was the ex-MOANA, purchased on the 28th of November 1941. She was 268' by 38'-2", and the needed alterations were basically the same as those on the other

Figure 36: AGP-2, U.S.S. HILO

two yachts. Resplendent in her new degaussing belt, the HILO went into commission 11 June 1942 as PG 58 after the necessary conversions and installations had been effected. In the fall of that year she went to Pearl Harbor and awaited further orders to the operating areas. From Pearl Harbor she proceeded to Funafuti and on to New Guinea where she suffered the usual troubles of converted yachts.

LST TYPE

Compared to the converted yachts, the LST's seamed the answer to the problem of developing a suitable PT tender. Late December 1942, COMINCH requested that two (2) LST's be converted to AGP's (as they were later designated) on or about 1 April 1943.[1] At that time, three (3) LST's were destined for Battle Damage Repair ships and COMINCH further requested that one of these be converted to a PT tender to be ready 1 February 1943.

At the outset, the conversion was to consist of the following:

A. Berthing, mess and sanitary facilities for a total of forty-one (41) officers, twenty-one (21) CPO's, and two hundred and twenty-five (225) enlisted men.

Figure 37: LST type AGP (AGP-14, U.S.S. ALECTO)

AN ADMINISTRATIVE HISTORY OF PT's IN WORLD WAR II
(Recreated October 25, 2010 by the members of the PT Boat Forum message board)

171

1. COMINCH's conf. ltr. To VCNO Serial 03141 dated 18 December 1942.

(B) Armament:

    (1) One (1) 3"/50 cal. dual purpose gun.

    (2) Eight (8) 40mm guns in two quadruple mounts.

    (3) Eight (8) 20mm guns with eight magazines and ready service stowage.

(C) Stowing and handling facilities for two (2) 36' MLs.

(D) Radio and radar equipment for type.

(E) Life rafts and floater mats for abandoning ship.

(F) Four (4) boat booms.

(G) Two (2) 5-ton booms.

(H) Shop and equipment for maintenance of one 12-boat squadron of PT's to include carpenter, shipfitter, engine overhaul and torpedo overhaul shops.

(I) Laundry facilities.

(1) CDMINCH's conf. ltr. to VCNO Serial 03141 dated 18 December 1942.

(J) One (1) heavy lifting boom of about 50-ton capacity.

(K) Two (2) 4,000 gallon capacity evaporators.

(L) Stowage for fresh and dry provisions and general stores (including shop supplies) for 45 days.

(M) Stowage facilities for 48 torpedoes.

(N) Stowage space for 6 spare PT engines.

(O) Magazine stowage facilities for standard allowances of ammunition for one 12-boat PT squadron less ammunition normally carried aboard boats of a squadron.

(P) Gasoline stowage of approximately 60,000 gallons capacity with facilities for fueling PT's underway.

(Q) Two torpedo air compressors of 20 cubic feet capacity each.

(R) Sickbay and facilities for medical officer.

The first of the LST's, the PORTUNUS, was converted according to specifications, but the specifications were not complete. Before she could relieve the HILO in New Guinea, several changes had to be effected on the spot. The same general design persisted until the AGP 14 appeared on the scene as the new, improved version of the LST type.

There had been a tendency to over-stock the ships with equipment and heavy machinery which was seldom used. The boilers below deck made living almost unbearable. There were not enough "reefers" topside to carry the desired amount of fresh food. Communications facilities were inadequate, and spare parts were scarce. The AGP 14 was the answer to these deficiencies and was considered as the model for succeeding tenders. Spare parts became more plentiful and tenders carried more spares and fewer workshops.

LST's were becoming available as tenders, and with the improvements incorporated they offered about as good a tender as was obtainable. One of the better features of the LST type was the "A" frame which could lift a boat out of the water for underwater repairs, and this did away with having to tow a dry dock into advanced areas. With their ramp bows the ships could sometimes work in conjunction with a base by simply running up to the beach and opening the bow. Thus the machine shop and other facilities were available to the beach.

Unfortunately, few of the later designed LST type tenders reached the forward areas and did not have an opportunity to prove themselves.

AVP TYPE

The class designation AGP was recommended by VCNO on 13 January 1943 and approved that same day – thus the PG 52, 55, and 58 came to be known as AGP's 1, 2, and 3.[2] That same day the PT tender program received another class of ships. Four of the small seaplane tenders, AVP's, declared surplus by BuAer, were designated for conversion to type flagships and tenders for Motor Torpedo Boat Squadrons. Their top-heaviness had made these ships unsatisfactory as seaplane tenders, and it was hoped that they could be put to good use with some of their top hamper removed.

VCNO designated that the following characteristics be incorporated in the conversion:

(a) Provide berthing, messing and sanitary facilities for personnel of one (1) PT squadron, in addition to ship's complement.

(b) Provide tender and shop facilities for one (1) 12-boat PT squadron to include torpedo overhaul, engine overhaul, carpenter and shipfitter's shops. It is considered that the order of importance of shops and equipment are: Carpenter, torpedo, engine overhaul and shipfitter.

(c) Retain present gasoline stowage and provide facilities for fueling PT's at sea.

(d) Stowage for forty-eight (48) torpedoes.

2. VCNO's ltr. to SecNav Ser. 338 dated 13 January 1943.

REPLACEMENT PHOTO - FROM "AT CLOSE QUARTERS".

Figure 38: Fueling from AV-9 at sea

(e) Boat stowage for two (2) 36' ML's and one (1) 26' motor whaleboat.

(f) Sickbay and facilities for medical officer.

(g) Stowage for six (6) spare PT engines.

(h) Laundry facilities adequate for the ship's complement and personnel of a PT squadron.

(i) Magazine stowage for standard ammunition allowance of one (1) 12-boat squadron, less ammunition actually carried on boats.

(j) Radio, radar and underwater sound equipment for type (AGP).

(k) Armament:

(1) Two (2) 5"/38 guns with director.

(2) Eight (8) 40mm guns in four (4) twin mounts.

(3) Eight (8) 20mm guns pending installation of Mark 50 director and six (6) 20mm thereafter.

(4) Two (2) depth charge racks of seven (7) 300-lb capacity each.

174

AN ADMINISTRATIVE HISTORY OF PT's IN WORLD WAR II
(Recreated October 25, 2010 by the members of the PT Boat Forum message board)

Figure 39: AVP type APG (AGP-8, U.S.S. WACHAPREAGUE)

(l) Provide living and administrative facilities for type commander.

(m) Provide facilities for fueling PT boats at sea.

(n) Provide facilities for towing PT boats. [3]

It is interesting to note that at this time ComSoWesPacFor considered as a deficiency a tender's inability to lift the stern of a PT boat clear of the water.

The ships of this class were 310' by 41' and had an economical cruising speed of 13.8 knots with a top speed of 18.2 knots. The messing and berthing quarters were very comfortable, but shop and stowage space were insufficient. The greatest limiting factor was the lack of any means of drydocking PT's. The proposed method of lifting a boat's stern out of the water to change wheels, struts, and rudders was a bit impractical if not impossible, and the AVP type tender needed a drydock to assist in tending a squadron.

The first of the AGP 6 – 9 Class was the OYSTER BAY, AGP 6, which went into commission 17 November 1943. She was subsequently followed by her three (3) sister ships, the MOBJACK, WACHAPREAGUE and WILLOUGHBY. With their AA armament they were able to proceed independently with the PT's, and often became advanced echelons on minor operations.

The greatest drawbacks to this type of tender were, as has been pointed out, lack of proper stowage and shop space, lack of drydocking facilities, and top-heavy construction. With these shortcomings, however, the ships still filled an important place in the PT program of advanced operations.

3. VCNO's conf. ltr. to BuShips & Ord ser. 033423 dated 2 February 1943.

AN ADMINISTRATIVE HISTORY OF PT's IN WORLD WAR II
(Recreated October 25, 2010 by the members of the PT Boat Forum message board)

177

was entirely new to them. It is not possible to say which type hull makes the most satisfactory AGP, since all the various types were not available.

Changes in PT design incurred varying demands upon the tenders, and the supply of spare parts changed the type of shop facilities needed. The improved LST type and C-1 types proved to be the better tenders, but whether or not they are the last word in AGP's is problematical.

Most PT officers, upon being questioned about PT tenders, had very colorful statements to make. The cause of their complaints seemed to lie in the personnel of the ships rather than the ships themselves. The general opinion was that the tenders lost sight of their objective. I.e. tending PT's., and appeared more concerned with tending themselves. Be that as it may, the boats were tended and the tenders executed their duties.

The short lifespan of the AGP class was erratic and the future of them can only be guessed at.

APPENDICES

APPENDIX A

PT BUILDING PROGRAM
(By Companies)

Company	Boat Numbers
Elco:	PT's 10-19, 20-68, 103-196, 314-361, 372-383, 486-563, 565-622, 731-760. PT's 623 and 624, 761-790 (Construction halted/contract cancelled). BPT's 1-20.
Higgins:	PT's 5 and 6, 70, 71-94, 197-254, 265-313, 450-485, 564, 625-660, 791-796.
Annapolis:	PT's 400-429, 661-730 (Vospers). BPT's 21-28, 49-68. (Vospers).
Herreshoff:	PT's 430-449 (Vospers). BPT's 29-36 (Vospers).
Jacobs:	PT's 384-399 (Vospers). BPT's 37-42.
Harbor:	PT's 362-367 (Elco 80' type). BPT's 43-48.
Huckins:	PT's 69, 95-102, 255-264.
Canadian and Scott-Paine):	PT 9, PT's 368-371.
Fisher:	PT's 3 and 4.
Miami:	PT's 1 and 2.
Philadelphia Navy Yard:	PT's 7 and 8.

AN ADMINISTRATIVE HISTORY OF PT's IN WORLD WAR II
(Recreated October 25, 2010 by the members of the PT Boat Forum message board)

179

Figure 42: MTB Ron one on board for overseas shipment

PT BUILDING PROGRAM
(By Boat Numbers)

No.	Manufacturing Company
1 and 2	Miami
3 and 4	Fisher
5 and 6	Higgins
7 and 8	Philadelphia Navy Yard
9	British Power Boat Co. (Purchased by Elco)
10-68	Elco
69	Huckins experimental boat.
70	Higgins (Higgins "Dream Boat")
71-94	Higgins
95-102	Huckins
103-196	Elco
197-254	Higgins
255-264	Huckins
265-313	Higgins
314-361	Elco
362-367	Harbor (Elco model (In Kit Form) built on West Coast)
368-371	Canadian Power Boat Company (Scott-Paine's, originally Dutch)
372-383	Elco
384-399	Jacobs (Vosper boats for Lend-Lease)

No.	Manufacturing Company
400-429	Annapolis (Vosper boats for Lend-Lease)
430-449	Herreshoff (Vosper boats for Lend-Lease)
450-485	Higgins
486-563	Elco
564	Higgins (Experimental "Hellcat", 70' boat)
565-622	Elco
623-624	Elco (Contract cancelled)
625-660	Higgins (For Lend-Lease to USSR)
661-730	Annapolis (Vosper boats for Lend-Lease)
731-760	Elco (Shipped to USSR knocked down)
761-796	Higgins
797-808	Higgins (Contract Cancelled)

British PT's (BPT's)

(By Boat Numbers)

No.	Manufacturing Co.	No.	Manufacturing Co.
1-20	Elco	37-42	Jacobs
21-28	Annapolis	43-48	Harbor
29-36	Herreshoff	49-68	Annapolis

Figure 43: 70' Vosper PT

AN ADMINISTRATIVE HISTORY OF PT's IN WORLD WAR II
(Recreated October 25, 2010 by the members of the PT Boat Forum message board)

181

APPENDIX B

PERSONNEL DISTRIBUTION

PT's were represented in Washington by a desk in the Fleet Maintenance section of CNO, which promulgated changes and improvements on the boats; by a type desk in BuShips which published a bi-monthly news letter for PT's and which initiated improvements, and by a type desk in the officer distribution section of BuPers.

The assignment of enlisted men to the PT program was handled by the Enlisted Men's Distribution Division of BuPers. Plans and Operations send recommendations to the Enlisted Man's Distribution Division, and this section in turn sent allowances to "A" schools and to other units for PT's. The men selected were sent to Melville for training, and upon completion of their schooling, MTBSTC would inform the Enlisted Men's Distribution Division of the number men trained.

The Enlisted Men's Distribution Division would then make assignments to either the Pacific or Atlantic Fleets or to new construction. For men assigned to the operating areas, final assignment to squadrons was made by the type commander in the area. Men sent to new construction were sent to definite squadrons and awaited commissioning of their organization at the Commissioning Detail at New York or New Orleans.

Officers assignments were handled exclusively by the PT desk in the Officer Distribution Section, although Melville was allowed to select prospective Commanding Officers and Prospective Executive Officers for relief of squadrons in the field.

The accompanying chart, shown on the next page, illustrates typical PT enlisted distribution before the elimination of the COMTBRONSOPAC command.

182

AN ADMINISTRATIVE HISTORY OF PT's IN WORLD WAR II
(Recreated October 25, 2010 by the members of the PT Boat Forum message board)

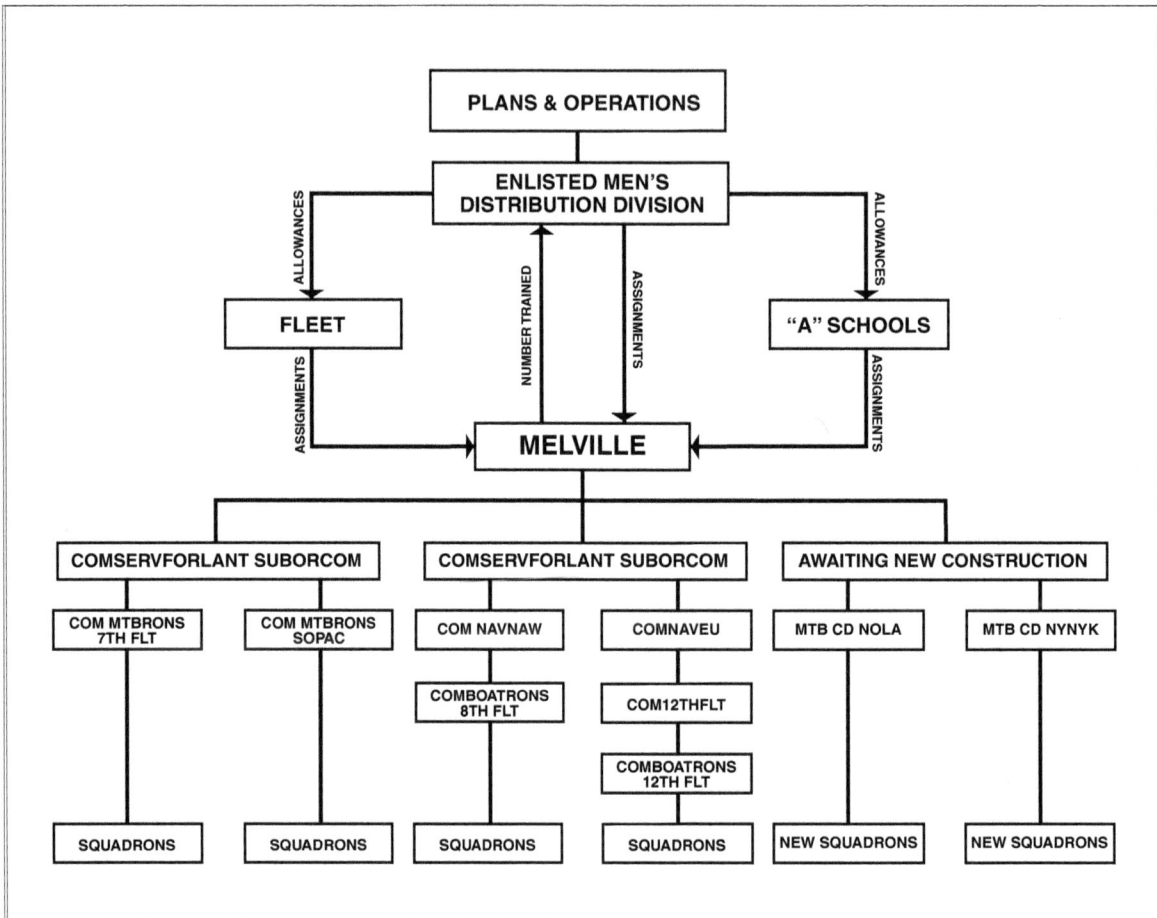

Figure 44: Typical PT Enlisted Distribution

AN ADMINISTRATIVE HISTORY OF PT's IN WORLD WAR II
(Recreated October 25, 2010 by the members of the PT Boat Forum message board)

183

APPENDIX C

PT OPERATIONAL LOSSES

PT	Event	Location	Date
22	Badly damaged in storm	North Pacific	11 Jun, 1943
28	Wrecked in storm	Dora Harbor, Alaska	12 Jan, 1943
31	Destroyed to prevent capture	Subic Bay, P.I.	19 Jan, 1942
32	Destroyed to prevent capture	Sulu Sea	13 Mar, 1942
33	Destroyed to prevent capture	Off Pt. Santiago, P.I.	15 Dec, 1941
34	Destroyed by enemy aircraft	Off Cauti Island, P.I.	09 Apr, 1942
35	Destroyed to prevent capture	At Cebu, P.I.	12 Apr, 1942
37	Destroyed by enemy warship	Off Guadalcanal I., Solo.	01 Feb, 1943
41	Destroyed to prevent capture	Lake Lanao, Mindanao, P.I.	15 Ap., 1942
43	Destroyed by enemy warship	Off Guadalcanal I. Solomons	10 Jan, 1943
44	Destroyed by enemy warship	Off Guadalcanal I. Solomons	12 Dec, 1942
63	Destroyed by fire while in port fuel.	Off New Ireland (Emirau)	18 Jun, 1944
67	Destroyed by fire while in port fuel.	OFF Tufi New Guinea	17 Mar, 1943
68	Destroyed to prevent capture/grnd'd.	New Guinea	01 Oct, 1943
73	Destroyed to prevent capture/grnd'd.	Philippines	15 Jan, 1945
77	Destroyed by U.S. Ship, Faulty I.D.	Off Talin Pt., Luson, P.I.	01 Feb, 1945
79	Destroyed by U.S. Ship, Faulty I.D.	Off Talin Pt., Luson, P.I.	01 Feb, 1945
107	Destroyed by fire while in port fuel.	Off New Ireland (Emirau)	18 Jun, 1944
109	Destroyed by enemy warship	Blackett Straits, Solomons	02 Aug, 1943
110	Lost in Collision	Off New Guinea	26 Jan, 1944
111	Destroyed by enemy warship	Off Guadalcanal I. Solomons	01 Feb, 1943

112	Destroyed by enemy warship	Off Guadalcanal I. Solomons	10 Jan 1943
113	Destroyed as a result of grnd'd	Off Buna, New Guinea	08 Aug, 1943
117	Destroyed by enemy aircraft	Rendova Harbor, Solomons	01 Aug, 1943
118	Destroyed to prevent capture/grnd'd	Vella Lavella, Solomons	7 Sept., 1943
119	Destroyed by fire while in port fuel.	Off Tufi, New Guinea	17 Mar., 1943
121	Destroyed by allied aircraft	North of New Britain	27 Mar., 1944
123	Destroyed by enemy aircraft	Off Guadalcanal, Solomons	1 Feb., 1943
133	Destroyed by enemy shore batteries	Off New Guinea	15 July, 1944
135	Destroyed to prevent capture/grnd'd	New Britain	12 Apr., 1944
136	Destroyed to prevent capture/grnd'd	Vitiaz Strait, New Guinea	17 Sep., 1943
145	Destroyed to prevent capture/grnd'd	New Guinea	4 Jan., 1944
147	Destroyed to prevent capture/grnd'd	New Guinea	19 Nov., 1943
153	Destroyed to prevent capture/grnd'd	Solomons	4 Jul., 1943
158	Destroyed to prevent capture/grnd'd	Off Wunda Pt., Solomons	4 Jul., 1943
164	Destroyed by enemy aircraft	In Rendova Harbor, Solomons	1 Aug., 1943
165	Lost in transit – tanker torpedoed	23°45' S 166°30' E	23 May, 1943
166	Destroyed by U.S. aircraft	Off New Georgia, Solomons	20 July, 1943
172	Destroyed to prevent capture/grnd'd	Off Vella Lavella, Solomons	7 Sep., 1943
173	Lost in transit – tanker torpedoed	23°45' S 166°30' E	23 May, 1943
193	Destroyed to prevent capture/grnd'd	Fourfoor I. New Guinea	25 Jun., 1944
200	Lost in collision	Off Newport R.I.	22 Feb., 1944
202	Destroyed by enemy mine	Off Pt. Aygulf, France	16 Aug., 1944
218	Destroyed by enemy mine	Off Pt. Aygulf, France	16 Aug., 1944
219	Damaged beyond repair in storm	Off Attu, Aleutians	Sep., 1943
239	Destroyed by fire while in port fuel.	Solomons	14 Dec., 1943
247	Destroyed by enemy shore batteries	Off Bougainville, I. , Solomons	5 May, 1944
251	Destroyed by enemy shore batteries	Off Bougainville, I. , Solomons	26 Feb., 1944
279	Lost in collision	Off Bougainville, I. , Solomons	11 Feb., 1944

AN ADMINISTRATIVE HISTORY OF PT's IN WORLD WAR II
(Recreated October 25, 2010 by the members of the PT Boat Forum message board)

185

283	Destroyed by U.S. warship w/spotting	Off Bougainville, I. , Solomons	17 Mar., 1944
300	Destroyed by enemy suicide plane	Off Mindora I. Philippines	18 Dec.,1944
301	Badly damaged by explosion in port	Off New Guinea	7 Nov., 1944
311	Destroyed by enemy mine	Ligurian Sea (Med.)	18 Nov 1944
320	Destroyed by enemy aircraft	Off Leyte, Philippines	5 Nov 1944
321	Destroyed to prevent capture/grnd'd	San Isidora Bay, Philippines	11 Nov., 1944
322	Destroyed to prevent capture/grnd'd	Off New Guinea	23 Nov., 1943
323	Destroyed by enemy suicide aircraft	Leyete Gulf, Philippines	10 Dec., 1944
337	Destroyed by enemy shore batteries	Hansa Bay, New Guinea	7 Mar., 1944
338	Badly damaged by grounding	Mindoro, P.I.	28 Jan., 1945
339	Destroyed to prevent capture/grnd'd	Off Biak, New Guinea	27 May, 1944
346	Destroyed by U.S. aircraft	Off New Britain	29 Apr., 1944
347	Destroyed by U.S. aircraft	Off New Britain	29 Apr., 1944
353	Destroyed by Allied aircraft	North of New Britain	27 Mar., 1944
363	Destroyed by enemy shore batteries	Kaoe Bay Halmahera N.E.I	25 Nov., 1944
368	Destroyed to prevent capture/grnd'd	Off Halmahera, N.E.I.	11 Oct., 1944
371	Destroyed to prevent capture/grnd'd	Halmahera, N.E.I.	19 Sep., 1944
493	Destroyed by enemy warship	In Surigao Strait P.I.	25 Oct., 1944
509	Destroyed by enemy warship	English Channel	9 Aug 1944
555	Destroyed by enemy mine	Off Cape Couronne, (Med.)	23 Aug., 1944

grnd'd = grounded

DESTROYED AS DIRECT RESULT OF ENEMY ACTION:

By Surface Ships . . . . .PT's 37, 43, 44, 109, 111, 112, 493, 509

By Aircraft. . . . . .PT's 34, 117, 123, 166, 300, 320, 323

By Shore Batteries. . . . . . . .PT's 133, 247, 251, 337, 363

Lost in Transit – Transporting

Ship Sunk. . . . . .PT's 165, 173

By Mines . . . . .PT's 202, 218, 311, 555

186

AN ADMINISTRATIVE HISTORY OF PT's IN WORLD WAR II
(Recreated October 25, 2010 by the members of the PT Boat Forum message board)

OPERATIONAL LOSSES:

Destroyed to prevent capture . . .PT's 31, 32, 33, 35, 41, 68, 73, 118, 135, 136, 145, 147, 153, 158, 172, 193, 321,322, 339, 368, 371

Destroyed by Allied or
U.S. aircraft . . . . .PT's 121, 164, 346, 347, 353

Destroyed by U.S. surface
vessels. . . . . .PT's 77, 79, 283

Destroyed as a result of
grounding or storms,
not in enemy waters . . . . . . .PT's 22, 28, 113, 219, 338

Destroyed by fire or
explosion while in port. . . . . .PT's 63, 67, 107, 119, 239, 301

Lost in collision . . . . .PT's 110, 200, 279

APPENDIX D

HIGGINS CORRESPONDENCE

CONCERNING PT ADMINISTRATION

(See Next Page)

OFFICE MEMORANDUM

June 24, 1943

From: A. J. Higgins Sr.

To: A. J. Higgins, Jr.   Subject: Attached copy of report
       F. O. Higgins   by Admiral Berry of
       Ted Sprague   alleged deficiencies in
       E. C. Higgins   M.T.B. construction.
       Dave Young

And to all our people having anything to do with, or having a
knowledge of our construction and design or having made any
contribution to the construction of our Motor Torpedo Boats.

I guess all of you are aware that we do not maintain a lobby in Washington, with entre'
to the White House; with close friendships with civilians or ex-civilians in the Bureau of
Ships; or friendly with the Elco Company; and certainly we are not maintaining anybody
there friendly to us. We do not have any representation close to the "Thorne".

All we have been trying to do, is to work as Americans, to give our Government the best.

Now the Navy is a funny organization. There is a lot of politics involved with them. When
they fight, they know how to fight, but they are only fighting a part of the time and it is an
old adage that a person on a boat, with not enough to do, has all the attributes of a gang of
women in a sewing society, or the old ":Washerwoman's Club of Gossips", such as found in
every yacht club pen. It looks as if the officers and the crews of the Motor Torpedo Boats
quality to go to the head of the class as to above referred to characteristics.

We have tried to see how good a boat we cold build, and how cheaply we could build it,
and we haven't paid a damned bit of attention to the specifications, that is, the limitations
of the specifications, as we have never put any limitations on ourselves. We have never
worried whether Elco was getting $254,000 for a 70' boat, or by our actions forced down
to take $176,000 for an 81' boat, when we were building a 78' boat for $116,000. If we
thought a ventilator system, or a heating system might be needed, and wasn't called for in
the specifications, we put it on and never asked for an extra. If we thought a spray strip
on the bottom adjacent the chins, would make the boat drier when she was running at the
lower speeds, and prevent the drive of the of the spume across the deck from a quartering
wind, we put it on, - but when we put it on we did not guarantee it couldn't be knocked off
if some wet-behind-the-ears, young "snot nose" didn't know anything about navigation and
ran the boat with this adjunct on the bottom up to a mud flat, let alone onto a coral reef.
All of us have done plenty to try and teach these young boys seamanship, and to give them
a knowledge of the care and attention necessary in the handling of small boats. We have
led them by the hand – we have wet nursed them. Thank God, the majority of them were
not too completely helpless, but, unfortunately, a big percentage of them were so dumb, or
so lazy, or so prejudiced, or so full of themselves in their newly-found place in the Navy
that they were so helpless that they had to take their boats back at the Government's
(taxpayers') expense to our plant to have our workmen clean up their own mess. Many of
them did every god-damned thing except ask our workmen to **"redacted words"**, but close
to this, they did ask us to clean out the toilets that were clogged up, because they were so
dumb, careless, or lazy that the toilets were clogged up with strings, rags, paper, cigarette
butts, these items finding their way there because there wasn't proper respect for the
authority of their Commander, who apparently did not know how to authorize, or impress
his authority upon the alleged officers, and the personnel (and in connection with the
personnel, they will be no more enterprising that the officers), all of whom did not have

AN ADMINISTRATIVE HISTORY OF PT's IN WORLD WAR II
(Recreated October 25, 2010 by the members of the PT Boat Forum message board)

189

the common sense or the ingenuity, or the initiative to rectify the trouble; to clean out their own filth, or trash.

Well, - when "mama's little darlings", "helpless little snot noses", and "wet behind the ears "redacted words" can make trivial reports to where it goes up high enough to where an admiral will make a horse's ass out of himself by making a report, a copy of which has just been submitted to me by and through the Supervisor of Shipbuilding (copy attached) it is time that we take stock of the kind of personnel the Navy is selecting to serve on motor torpedo boats, - a service that is suppose to be for heroes and not "redacted words".

To each of you, to who this letter is addressed, will be attached a copy of Admiral Berry's letter of June 18th, 1943. To each one of his memorandums of deficiencies or criticisms, I want each one who gets this to make an answer.

Particularly do I want A. J. Higgins Jr., Frank D. Higgins, E.. C. Higgins, and Ted Sprague, to incorporate in their reply, and each to make an answer separately, and list in some replies the many things that we put on these M.T.B.s, that are not called for in the specifications, and for none of which do we ask one 10¢ piece as an extra.

I want all of your reports to be dictated to a stenographer, particularly a man stenographer so that you may express yourselves freely – and send me these reports in quadruplicate, because I want to send 3 copies of everybody's letter, including my own summarization and consolidation of these reports which I will make as an answer to the Admiral's letter, to the Supervisor of Shipbuilding.

A. J. Higgins

COPY

COTClant/S8/L2-1
((70-hrs)
Serial: 20581

UNITED STATES ATLANTIC FLEET
FLEET OPERATIONAL TRAINING COMMAND
Naval Operating Base
Norfolk, Virginia

18 June 1943

From: The Commander, Fleet Operational Training Command,
        United States Atlantic Fleet.
To: The Vice Chief of Naval Operations.
Via: The Commander in Chief, United States Atlantic Fleet.

Subject: Motor Torpedo Boat Squadron 17 (PT 225-234) Arrival in
        Miami, Florida – Material condition of.

Enclosure: (A) CO, SCTraCen Miami, Fla., ltr. NC130/A4-1 dated
        5 June 1943.

    1.   Enclosure (A) itemizes the material defects found during arrival inspection of MTBRon 17 at SCTraCen Miami, Florida.

    2.   Many of the defects noted were minor and required only a short time to correct, but necessarily caused some delay in shakedown training. Defects such as Hull (13) and (14); communications (10); Seamanship and Navigation (10); and Engineering (1), (2), (3) and (16) of enclosure (A) were major and seriously interfered with the shakedown training schedule.

    3.   It is believed that had there been a larger percentage of experienced personnel in these crews many of the subject defects could have been remedied prior to leaving builder's yard.

    4.   I am of the sincere opinion that defects in such number and quantity on small boats of this character are wholly uncalled for. It shows a flagrant carelessness in carrying out specifications and provisions of the contract. Quantity production is admittedly most desirable but such quantity must be in accordance with the specifications and Navy Standard quality requirements. Quality certainly can not be dispensed with to the extend indicated in the enclosure.

    5.   It is recommended that necessary corrective measures be taken at the earliest practical date to insure the product of the Higgins Industries, New Orleans Louisiana, will comply with the specifications.

                /s/ D. B. BEARY

Copy to:
    COTClant Rep. 8th ND   CominCh (Readiness Section)
    Co. SCTraCen Miami, Fla.   BuOrd
    BuShips   MTB Pro Com Detail New Orleans La
    BuPers   ComEight

AN ADMINISTRATIVE HISTORY OF PT's IN WORLD WAR II
(Recreated October 25, 2010 by the members of the PT Boat Forum message board)

191

COPY

January 8, 1944

Lt. Commander C. W. Leveau,
Assistant Supervisor of Shipbuilding,
U. S. Navy
22 Virginia Court,
New Orleans, La.

Dear Commander: -

During the first part of the this week, there was a discussion regarding the increasing of the speed of PT boats by me of hydroplane steps, or additional bottom conformations. I find that I wrote you early this week a rather disjointed, hurriedly written letter on this subject, my letter dated, January 4th.

This being Saturday afternoon, and in dispair of writing to any of your superior officers who would give any attention, for my own satisfaction, I take this means of making a record, if for nothing else than my own satisfaction and to refer to in the years to come:-

I, personally, if not my companies as now organized, had quite considerable to do with the construction or the purveyance of materials for the construction of small boats during World War I.

Then, as now, the holies in the Navy could not see, countenance or stomach small boats, but, by God, at that time there was another iconoclast, the Assistant Secretary of the Navy, a young and enthusiastic man who knew considerable about small boats; true that he knew more about sailing boats than he did power boats, but who in the hell in that day and time knew much about power boats? I am referring to Franklin Delano Roosevelt. There was also a Pharoa in the Navy who was a naval attaché in London. His name was Furer. He had seen what the British were doing with 80 foot boats and apparently he questioned whether battle ships alone were the whole answer to naval supremacy or a naval need for combat and defense vessels.

In that time came forward a man, A. Loring Swaysey. Somewhere from them came a design for a 110 ft. boat, to be built of wood. In my opinion, then and now, the design was not all that it should have been, but these boats built largely out of green lumber, in the emergencies of those times, and as poorly constructed as they were, did a good service for which they never received any recognition and by reason of such fact they merited the title "Cinderellas of the Sea".

1-8-44

- 2 -

One of the inherited hysterias of that war was the Prohibition law, resulting in its violation, said violations being countenanced, acclaimed, and chortled by everyone. The opportunity of designing boats of all classes was a Roman holiday for us, for even our worst efforts were appreciated. The only competition we had for designs was to design something more seaworthy and faster than previous craft, a boat of shallow draft characteristics, and our only competitors in design was the Government, and what could have been easier? We did not even have to make drawings of the boats. We were paid for them in advance. We controlled all the elements. We could test our boats and spend somebody else's money correcting our own mistakes, a few of which we admit happened.

When war approached did our Government ask us to give them the benefit of those experiences; this practical knowledge; this technical knowledge. No, they did not, and have not since, and are not doing so now.

Sometimes I wonder whose war this is?

Who is jockeying for positions; who is striving for some credit; who is striving for profit; who is striving for some complement? By God, I am not. I just want to contribute something to win the war, and anybody may have the credit for this.

Now, I have never had the ear of anybody in any of the Navy's bureaus, and nobody in the Navy has asked me for my advice, - but, on the other hand, many of the officers and men in the navy and the fighting forces write me and it is a coincidence that just in the last three days a lot of information has come to me about the use of Motor Torpedo Boats, both of our own design and construction, as well as the ones built by the Elco Company; information about what these boats have done, not alone in the South Pacific area, but in the Mediterranean, and in the Aleutians. Men returning to the States for hospitalization, or otherwise, at their own expense come by New Orleans to visit me. Many of them write me. So, even thought I am not consulted, or considered, and know nothing of the intentions of the Navy bureaus, I am through the enthusiasm of the service forces quite familiar with the conditions of operations and what has been done, and what has been suffered.

Another reason I am prompted to write you this letter is; that if you have it in your power, or within your province, to guard against the haphazard installation of steps on the 70' motor torpedo boat which we delivered to the Navy at Miami, which boat we gave the nickname of "Hellcat". I have heard that the Navy is planning on putting some form of step angles on the bottom of this boat, but this should not be done without their consultation with us, as the principal characteristic of that boat is the concave sections of uniform radius from stem to stern on either side of the keel. A haphazard installation of steps, eighter (sic) of flat sections, or steps of conforming radius will make this boat "tricky" at the higher speeds.

AN ADMINISTRATIVE HISTORY OF PT's IN WORLD WAR II
(Recreated October 25, 2010 by the members of the PT Boat Forum message board)

193

1-8-44

- 3 -

Without knowing what the Navy wants, it is hard for us to go into discussions and set up a hypothetical case, or cases, of this or of that. We have heard from many men just back from the South Pacific that what they want is all the fire power they can get. Many of these same men say that they are satisfied if their boats can carry another cannon and more ammunition and make only 30 knots. These and other men tell us that no matter how beautifully tuned up the engines may be that heat; humidity; the fouling of the bottom of the boats; the abrasions on the bottom; the drag on the electrical lines due to moisture; the inadequacy of servicing at the base all cause mechanical deficiencies that reduce speed.

A while back, when the Japanese had their Destroyers running about freely in the Pacific, the boys back from that section told us that what they needed was more PT boats with less weight on them – they even wanted to carry only two torpedoes to enable them to get the last bit of speed; every last bit of maneuverability; to get in there and shoot their wad and get the hell out. They wanted the smallest possible boat and the fastest boat they could get. So, - that was one kind of boat.

Now, other of the boys coming back from around New Guinea and New Britain told us that they were even installing 37 mm and 1.1 guns that they got from the Navy, and had been stealing Jap guns and ammunition and all the other cannon that they could beg borrow, or steal on the decks of the Motor Torpedo Boats; that there were no Jap destroyers in that area to fight; that they weren't worried about having torpedoes – had no need for them – but that they needed guns with which to blast the Jap barges which run in shallow water and which barges make about 9 knots speed.

Maybe what the Nay will have to decide upon will be to have two types of motor torpedo boats, one a very fast and highly maneuverable boat, and in order to get every last bit of speed out of them to cut down the weight of the torpedoes and tubes. Maybe the day will come when the Japanese Fleet will come out in force, at which time the PT's which have the small cannon on them, and are slow, will not be worth a goddam, - but it would be a happy occasion for a lot of small, fast torpedo boats to have a field day. This would mean that the navy would have to have a big investment and a lot of organization tied up in these small, fast boats, but maybe in the meantime, and what they certainly do need now is a type of boat in which speed is not so highly desirable, in that they do not have Jap destroyers to run away from. These slower boats could carry all the weight of cannon they want at the expense of reducing speed to a determined minimum.

In other words, the Navy should make up their minds whether they want Motor Torpedo Boats or Motor Powered Gun Boats. Maybe they need two classes of vessel. You can't eat your cake and keep it too, and when you make a compromise you can't have the best of both elements.

1-8-44

- 4 -

All this business about the Elco people trying to overcome the b----- s----- about how fast their boats are, and when it was proven that they were no faster than our heavy, rugged boat, they decided to change to hydroplane type of steps the bottom, this is something we had proposed to the Navy in 1939 or 1940, but when we proposed it to them, we warned them against too quick an acceptance of the idea of a step hydroplane boat.

In comparative tests of our 78' boat with the Elco boat it was found that the boats, running side by side from Miami to Fort Lauderdale and back, our boat consumed some forty gallons of gasoline less per hour. Now that means a hell of a lot – it means increased cruising range, - for these boats are not rushing round madly at all times, at full speed, because if they did, these "prima donna", high speed Packard engines would not hold up or hold together. A lot of this trouble they are having is because of the enthusiastic young men on them, out where their lives are at stake, and when they want to strike strong blows, are already operating the engines beyond a proper, full horsepower output.

If the Navy wants something sensible, why the hell don't they listen to people like us who have had years of experience. They don't have to accept what we tell them. If they want to maintain their dignity, let them order us, from their great wisdom, to build the goddam 70' boat (prohibited to be referred to as the "Hellcat") with flattened instead of concave sections. She will still be a good boat at slow, intermediate, or full speeds; with fuel economy. She won't be quite as soft in riding action in a seaway as she is now with a rock to the keel and chine lines and the concavitures, but at that she will be more seaworthy and have a better riding action than the flatter bottomed Elco boats.

Somewhere along the line I have heard that the people in the Bureaus in Washington have determined, or surmised or drawn a conclusion, or otherwise made up their minds that the 70' boat cannot carry a full military load such as has been prescribed for our 78' footer, or for the Elco boat. Well, whoever has drawn this conclusion has not referred to the past record, for our 70' boat will carry the same load that our 78' boat, or the Elco boat will carry, and she will be faster. Our 70 footer has more battle deck space than has the Elco boat. There are many other advantages; - a smaller boat; a boat that can be transported on the decks of steamers and which can be handled by the derrick equipment on most steamers: a boat that has more maneuverability; a boat that has a lower silhouette; a boat that can punch and dodge and get away; is far more facile than is the Elco boat, and faster than our 78 footer. The 70-footer can be built more rapidly; they are cheaper (if we should be crazy enough to think about cost, when there doesn't seem to be much concern on the part of anybody else as to cost).

AN ADMINISTRATIVE HISTORY OF PT's IN WORLD WAR II
(*Recreated October 25, 2010 by the members of the PT Boat Forum message board*)

195

1-8-44

- 5 -

I had better draw this letter to a conclusion. I am getting disgusted, and I might get worse, and step on somebody's feelings, - but I cannot close without this dirty crack and comment; that I have devoted my life to the design of small boats; that boats of my design hold practically all worthwhile records, many of the records not published; that form a small one, we are now a big organization, and that we have as much, in fact more talent than we once had; that the oil companies and concerns who know how to earn and how to spend a dollar, come to us, but our own Navy does not; that I am forced many times to abide by the decisions of young men, many of them who could not get a position with me as a draftsman, let alone a designer, yet many of their senior officers who might know a lot about battleships and cruisers acknowledge to me that they don't know much about small boats; yet they are all in position to tell me what to do, and do not ask me for advice.

I could keep on ad nauseum.

Sincerely,

Andrew J. Higgins, President,
Higgins Industries Inc.

ajh/ewp

www.ingramcontent.com/pod-product-compliance
Lightning Source LLC
Chambersburg PA
CBHW050619110426

42813CB00010B/2609